Creating Entrepreneurial Community Colleges

Creating Entrepreneurial Community Colleges

A Design Thinking Approach

CARRIE B. KISKER

HARVARD EDUCATION PRESS
Cambridge, Massachusetts

Paperback ISBN 978-1-68253-575-2
Library Edition ISBN 978-1-68253-576-9

Library of Congress Cataloging-in-Publication Data is on file.

Published by Harvard Education Press,
an imprint of the Harvard Education Publishing Group

Harvard Education Press
8 Story Street
Cambridge, MA 02138

Cover Design: Wilcox Design
Cover Photo: 10'000 Hours/DigitalVision via Getty Images

The typefaces used in this book are Classica Pro and Open Sans.

CONTENTS

INTRODUCTION

In late 2015, following the Arizona legislature's decision to curtail all state allocations to the state's two largest community college districts in Phoenix and Tucson—writing them out of the state constitution altogether—a group convened by then chancellor Rufus Glasper at the Maricopa Community Colleges posed three simple questions: (1) How many workers with a college certificate or associate degree will be needed in the county's six fastest-growing industry sectors over the next decade? (2) How might Maricopa best meet those workforce needs? and (3) What will this cost and how will the district pay for it without any state support?

To explore these questions, we (I was a consultant hired to lead the project) embarked upon a collaborative exercise with Arizona State University's Decision Theater, an organization and physical space that helps visualize and test solutions to complex problems. The first of the three questions was relatively easy to answer based on data from environmental scans and economic modeling reports. The following two questions were more complex; they involved numerous stakeholders—students, faculty, administrators, governing board members, policy makers, the business community—but more importantly, answering them necessitated a wholly different approach to community college operations, one that relied less on adapting existing programs to meet external pressures, and more on identifying future opportunities and experimenting with the (perhaps substantial) internal changes necessary to take advantage of them.

As our group and several stakeholder audiences surfaced numerous possible solutions to address how Maricopa might best meet identified workforce needs and how to pay for it, I came to two major realizations. First, if Maricopa is to provide the education and training necessary to meet employment demand, it can no longer rely solely on the community college's three historic revenue sources: state subsidies; local support, primarily through property taxes; and tuition. In Maricopa's case, state subsidies were already gone. In theory, the district could attempt to raise property taxes, but a statewide voter referendum limiting expenditures of taxpayer dollars—as well as an overall aversion to higher taxes in Barry Goldwater's home state—made this option less probable. As well, a governing board ideologically predisposed to maximizing efficiencies before raising revenues made it clear that tuition hikes were off the table. Yet little if any fat remained to be trimmed from the budget; Maricopa, like many other community college districts across the country, would require a more entrepreneurial approach to financing and operations if it was to mitigate state disinvestment and preserve its ability to meet the economic and workforce needs of the community.

My second major realization was that although Maricopa and other colleges may be quite experienced in adapting to external pressures—adding a program here, taking on a new type of student there—historically they have not been particularly well equipped to *innovate*, or to engage in the type of creative, intentional change that may disrupt established ways of doing business. In some states, legislative directives that public colleges should not compete with private industry stymie entrepreneurial impulses. Decades-old budgeting and planning processes tied to full-time-equivalent (FTE) students and available allocations from state and local governments act as barriers to more strategic revenue generation and cost- or need-based budgeting proposals. Tenure and collective bargaining agreements support expansion of the colleges' à la carte model of providing something for everyone but inhibit contraction. And fears of more closely aligning a public institution with corporate interests constrain new ideas about industry partnerships and profit-generating initiatives. Clearly, Maricopa needed to become more entrepreneurial in order to survive, but lacked a process by which it could identify and evaluate entrepreneurial options and experiment with the internal (strategic, budgetary, organizational) changes necessary to optimize outcomes for stakeholders and reduce dependence on state allocations in ways that do not conflict with the institution's mission and values.

• • •

Maricopa does not face this dilemma alone. Across the country, states have systematically disinvested in public higher education in general and community colleges in particular.[1] Between 2001 and 2011, state and local allocations per FTE community college student decreased by 23 percent; by 2017, states were appropriating roughly $2,000 less per student than they had been in 2001.[2] This trend toward disinvestment—coupled with heightened pressure for workforce credentials and greater educational attainment—has put pressure on colleges to seek out new, more entrepreneurial approaches to raising money and cutting costs, yet this shift has the potential to upend long-established organizational and financial models and raises fears that the colleges will prioritize profits over students, leading to an erosion of academic values.[3] Therefore, college leaders need a framework for exploring entrepreneurship in an empathic manner, one that ensures that new ventures amplify—rather than sacrifice—the institution's mission and the human needs of its stakeholders.

Design thinking—a fundamentally human-centered process in which a diverse group of professionals seeks a deep understanding of stakeholder needs and then tests the desirability and feasibility of new ideas through hands-on experimentation and prototyping[4]—provides such a framework. The process is exceptionally well suited to the challenge of community college entrepreneurship as it is grounded in empathy for college stakeholders and prioritizes the institution's mission and values throughout all stages of the innovation process, thus heading off one of the major critiques of entrepreneurial activities: that revenue-generating behaviors are antithetical to higher education's commitment to serve the public good.[5] In this book I argue that positioning a college or university's entrepreneurial actions as *market-oriented*, as many scholars and commentators critical of such activities often do, creates the false dichotomy that a college either serves students or serves the market. Because design thinking begins by empathizing with stakeholder needs and iteratively prototypes and tests new programs or ideas with those same stakeholders, the process can guide colleges in pursuing a *mission-oriented* approach to fiscal sustainability.

OVERVIEW OF CREATING ENTREPRENEURIAL COMMUNITY COLLEGES

Creating Entrepreneurial Community Colleges is organized in three parts. Part I provides context for the central arguments presented in this book and outlines how design thinking can be a useful framework for community colleges to identify and evaluate entrepreneurial opportunities. Specifically, chapter 1 examines the current state of entrepreneurship in American community colleges, describing fiscal uncertainty and other drivers of innovation, offering definitions and examples, and detailing the major theoretical lenses through which entrepreneurial actions have been understood and critiqued. Chapter 2 examines community college entrepreneurship in a historical context—illustrating how it has been limited by an ever-prevalent *add everything, change nothing* ethos within the colleges. The chapter then explores why this next wave of entrepreneurship might be different and argues that an empathic, mission-oriented approach to organizational change is necessary if community colleges are to transcend their history of incremental adjustments and effectively finance and carry out their education, training, and community-uplift missions in the future. Chapter 3 describes design thinking as an approach to innovation and outlines a process whereby college leaders can identify and evaluate options for entrepreneurship and experiment with the internal changes necessary to optimize outcomes for stakeholders.

Part II, "Stories from the Field," illustrates community college entrepreneurship in action at four community colleges and districts across America: the Maricopa Community Colleges (Arizona), North Iowa Area

Community College, Tarrant County College (Texas), and Valencia College (Florida). Throughout 2018 and 2019, I visited these exceptionally forward-thinking institutions, conducting in-depth qualitative interviews with more than fifty current and former leaders, faculty, and staff.[6] All interviews were audio recorded, transcribed, and coded for adherence or divergence to the central tenets of design thinking as well as the four questions in Jeanne Liedtka, Randy Salzman, and Daisy Azer's 2017 book, *Design Thinking for the Greater Good: Innovation in the Social Sector*, which is used as both an organizational framework and a conceptual framework for this book (and is described in detail in chapter 3). Part II thus comprises four chapters, each dedicated to one of the four questions outlined in Liedtka et al.'s approach: What *Is*, What *If*, What *Wows*, and What *Works*. Stories appearing in these chapters illustrate how these four community colleges have approached entrepreneurship in ways that correspond with the design thinking framework (or do not), as well as their challenges, failures, course corrections, and achievements. Chapter 7, "Understanding What *Works*," also explores the role of institutional leaders in cultivating an entrepreneurial culture, as well as the crucial role of external partnerships in community college entrepreneurship and innovation.

Part III transitions from stories of entrepreneurship at the four colleges highlighted in this book to how community colleges everywhere can begin to innovate in mission-oriented ways. In particular, chapter 8 considers the ways in which colleges might modify organizational structures and financial practices to better support and sustain innovative ideas, explores how institutional size and location affect opportunities for entrepreneurship, and investigates the extent to which entrepreneurial actions have reduced the colleges' reliance on state or other sources of governmental funding. This concluding chapter then looks to the future, offering ideas for how colleges might design the next wave of mission-oriented entrepreneurship on their campuses and how the community college sector as a whole can function as one giant learning laboratory in which the creation, testing, and refining of new ideas can be shared across institutional boundaries and tailored to fit each organization's historical, demographic, political, and cultural contexts.

I hope that readers find the design thinking process to be a useful framework for guiding efforts to engage in mission-oriented change, and that the stories contained within these pages provide inspirational examples of how community colleges can identify opportunities to better serve students and communities and experiment with the sometimes-substantial internal changes necessary to take advantage of them. It is important to emphasize that one need not work for an exceptionally well-heeled community college, or one with a long history of entrepreneurial behavior, to embark on this journey. A culture of innovation can gestate just as quickly in small, rural colleges as it can in large urban institutions, and as this book illustrates, an entrepreneurial mind-set can be cultivated and implemented just as easily by biology or agriculture faculty as those in business departments or administrative suites.

ABOUT THE COMMUNITY COLLEGES HIGHLIGHTED IN THIS BOOK

Stories of entrepreneurial efforts at the four colleges and districts I visited are sprinkled throughout this book, especially in chapters 4 through 7. The following provides a bit of context and background information about these institutions, which share a commitment to entrepreneurship and innovative thinking but differ greatly in size, geographic location, and historical and curricular emphases.

Valencia College, Florida

Valencia College, located in the greater Orlando area, is one of the largest community colleges in Florida, enrolling over 62,000 students per year across its seven campuses, Advanced Manufacturing Training Center, and School of Public Safety. The college's extraordinary growth since its inception in 1967 mirrors that of its surrounding area; driving between Valencia campuses feels like an expedition past newly built apartment and office complexes and ever-expanding infrastructure projects. Since 2000

Valencia has focused on scaling academic and workforce development programs through partnerships with area businesses, educational institutions, and community organizations. These include a guaranteed transfer pathway to the University of Central Florida, the Walt Disney World Center for Hospitality and Culinary Arts, a criminal justice institute, and numerous corporate training partnerships, including with Lockheed Martin, Sysco, and Universal Studios. In 2011, Valencia began offering bachelor's degrees in certain applied areas, including nursing, cardiopulmonary sciences, computing technology and software development, radiologic and imaging sciences, business and organizational leadership, and electrical and computing engineering technology.

Among students enrolled in Valencia's credit programs, more than three-quarters are younger than twenty-five, although adults make up the majority of students in continuing workforce education and adult vocational programs. More than half of Valencia's students are from races and ethnicities historically underserved in institutions of higher education and roughly 65 percent attend part-time.[7] Valencia also has a robust international student population, numbering nearly 1,700 in fall 2017.[8] Since 2000 Valencia College has been led by Sanford (Sandy) Shugart, a charismatic, soft-spoken man whose long career in education and writings on leadership are evident in the near-reverent way his employees speak of him and in the thoughtful manner in which he describes the intentions behind various Valencia initiatives.

North Iowa Area Community College

North Iowa Area Community College—NIACC, for short—sits on a small rise on the periphery of Mason City, Iowa. Surrounded by cornfields and pastures, five hundred acres of which are owned and operated by the college, and with several enormous windmills in the distance, NIACC's agricultural roots are obvious, although one step into the college's new science and math wing or robotics laboratory makes clear that the college is also thinking deeply about how it can best prepare students for the increasingly technical and highly skilled jobs of the future. NIACC is the oldest community college in Iowa: its three hundred faculty and staff and roughly five thousand credit and noncredit students celebrated its one-hundred-year anniversary in 2018.[9]

NIACC students reflect the surrounding population; the vast majority are white, although historically underserved populations nearly doubled between 2005 and 2014 to 11 percent. More than three-quarters of NIACC students are twenty-two or younger, and over half attend part-time. Like many rural community colleges, NIACC has a robust intercollegiate athletics program as well as on-campus housing, used primarily for athletes, international students recruited to the campus, and those who live on the outskirts of the college's 3,700 square-mile service area.[10]

NIACC is the only community college in the state to operate a John Pappajohn Entrepreneurial Center, which works to spur economic growth by providing programs, services, and resources for aspiring and existing business owners in the surrounding communities. (The other five Pappajohn Centers are located at the University of Iowa, Iowa State, the University of Northern Iowa, and Drake University.) NIACC's Pappajohn Center provides a vital connection between the college and community, and its director, Tim Putnam, works closely with NIACC faculty and administrators to help students learn about and incorporate an entrepreneurial mind-set into their everyday lives. NIACC is led by Steven Schulz. A native Iowan and former K–12 superintendent, Schulz's emphasis on partnerships and creating a collaborative work environment has transformed NIACC into one of the most entrepreneurial colleges in the Midwest. Schulz sits on the board of the National Association for Community College Entrepreneurship (NACCE), a member-serving-member organization dedicated to promoting entrepreneurship through community colleges.

Maricopa Community Colleges, Arizona

One of the largest community college districts in the country, Maricopa's ten colleges and two skill centers are located throughout the greater Phoenix area and serve nearly 200,000 credit and noncredit students each year. Roughly half of all Maricopa students are from races and ethnicities historically underserved in higher education; the vast majority of these are Latinx. Fifty-three percent of students are the first in their families to attend college; 71 percent attend part-time. The average age is twenty-five.[11]

Under the leadership of Rufus Glasper (chancellor from 2003 to 2016), Maria Harper-Marinick (chancellor from 2016 to 2020), and interim chancellor Steven Gonzales, Maricopa has developed numerous entrepreneurial ventures, including Maricopa Corporate College (MCOR), which holds training workshops, boot camps, and employee development and recruitment programs, as well as the Center for Entrepreneurial Innovation, a full-service business incubator located at the district's GateWay campus. Maricopa has a long history of entrepreneurial innovation, however, dating to the inception of Rio Salado College, one of the first "colleges without walls." In 2016 Maricopa and its sister colleges across Arizona campaigned successfully to make entrepreneurial dollars exempt from legislative expenditure limitations, which in theory (if not yet in practice) will allow the district to utilize revenue from entrepreneurial partnerships and programs to mitigate state disinvestment.[12]

Tarrant County College, Texas

From 1965 to 1999, Tarrant County College (TCC) was known as Tarrant Junior College, and its history as the premier transfer institution in the Fort Worth area has shaped much of its institutional culture. Home to six campuses—including TCC Connect, an online campus established in 2015—TCC enrolls nearly 1 in every 22 Tarrant County residents each year, or roughly 51,000 students. Over half of these are from historically underserved races and ethnicities; 72 percent attend part-time; and 71 percent are twenty-four or younger.[13]

TCC's chancellor, Eugene (Gene) Giovannini, was recruited to the institution in 2016 after serving as the founding president of Maricopa Corporate College, in part to introduce the same kind of entrepreneurial thinking at TCC that he had brought to the Maricopa system. A fast-speaking, gregarious man with a thick New York accent, Giovannini gives the impression that his mind is several chess moves ahead of what is currently occurring, and his enthusiasm for TCC's future as an institution that utilizes entrepreneurship as a method to deliver on its mission is contagious. Under his leadership, TCC has expanded its corporate solutions and economic development work through customized training at the TCC Opportunity Center, embarked upon an aggressive online education business model with TCC Connect, and is in the process of an organizational and cultural orientation to three basic goals: to operate as one college, to be student-ready, and to serve and partner with the community, including businesses and the workforce. Giovannini is past chair of the board for NACCE.

PART I

Design Thinking as a Framework for Entrepreneurship in Community Colleges

1 Entrepreneurship in American Community Colleges

Without innovation and an entrepreneurial mind-set, our community colleges are in danger of being exterminated.[1]

In speaking with community college leaders, I hear two common refrains, often from the same person. The first is there has never been a more exciting time to work in community colleges. And the second? That there has never been a more frightening and frustrating time to work in community colleges. In 2020, with technology rapidly changing the ways we work and live (a trend exacerbated by the global pandemic), with an economy demanding millions of highly skilled workers in vocations requiring less than a bachelor's degree, and with policy makers and grantors asking the higher education sector to increase the percentage of Americans with a postsecondary credential, community colleges are set to become the linchpins of regional economic development and higher education attainment efforts. As TCC chancellor Gene Giovannini put it, "You know what, country? You can't do without us . . . We have never been more viable. This is a perfect time to be in our sector."

Yet community colleges are also on the brink of financial collapse. As Giovannini shared, "Every morning I get my *Inside Higher Ed* and read about the latest college to close or merge . . . Yesterday it was a college in New Rochelle, in New York. Used to be a great school; not gonna make it." Even colleges that aren't shuttering programs or outsourcing their back-end operations are looking to cut costs or reexamine ways of doing business as state and local governments systematically disinvest in institutions of higher education. Indeed, community college leaders who are not already seeking entrepreneurial strategies for mitigating financial uncertainty will soon have to explore such opportunities if their institutions are to effectively carry out their education and training missions. Yet this shift has the potential to upend decades of strategic, budgetary, and operational plans that incrementally expand or contract according to available allocations from state and local governments and raises fears that the colleges will prioritize profits over students, leading to an erosion of academic values.[2] Therefore, college leaders need a framework for exploring entrepreneurship in an empathic manner, one that ensures that new ventures amplify—rather than sacrifice—the institution's mission and the human needs of its stakeholders.

Design thinking—a concept borrowed from the business literature but recently extended to social-sector organizations and independent K–12 schooling—provides such a framework. Design thinking is a creative, iterative, possibility-driven approach to problem solving.[3] It is a fundamentally human-centered process in which a diverse group of professionals seeks a deep understanding of stakeholder needs, then tests the desirability, viability, and feasibility of new ideas through hands-on experimentation and prototyping.[4] As a process for leading innovation, design thinking is exceptionally well suited to the challenge of community college entrepreneurship. Yet what sets it apart from other change models and makes it particularly useful in the community college setting is its emphasis on empathy for college stakeholders—students, faculty, staff, and community members—and its foregrounding of the institution's mission and values throughout all stages of the design process.

Design thinking can also help community colleges head off one of the major critiques of entrepreneurial activities: that revenue-generating behaviors are antithetical to higher education's commitment to serve the public good.[5] Indeed, positioning a college or university's entrepreneurial actions as *market-oriented*, as many scholars and commentators critical of such activities often do, creates the false dichotomy that a college either serves students or serves the market. Because design thinking begins by empathizing with stakeholder needs and iteratively prototypes and tests new programs or ideas with those same stakeholders, the process can help college leaders bypass this zero-sum quagmire. In other words, design thinking will help colleges engage in *mission-oriented* behaviors that may utilize the market as a vehicle for ensuring fiscal sustainability. By all accounts—and as the following section explores in detail—this may be the defining task of the next decade.

FISCAL UNCERTAINTY AND OTHER DRIVERS OF COMMUNITY COLLEGE ENTREPRENEURSHIP

> *It's like your budget at home; if you've got to stretch a dollar you've got to think of some new ways to do it.*[6]

Fifteen years ago, Texas community colleges received nearly 70 percent of their funding from the state. Today, this source accounts for only 17 or 18 percent of revenues. Furthermore, Giovannini pointed out, Texas used to pay two-thirds of all faculty and staff benefits; now policy makers argue that they should only pay an amount proportionate to state allocations (roughly 17 percent), which to many college leaders feels like a double whammy to the bottom line.[7] Iowa community colleges are feeling similar pain. NIACC president Steven Schulz noted that "when our model was created, it was supposed to be supported one-third by tuition, one-third by the state, and one-third by the local property taxpayers. Today, almost 60 percent is tuition, 30 percent the state, and 4 percent local property taxes." As a result, "we have the top five most expensive community colleges in the country because we don't fund it down."

Iowa and Texas are not alone; nearly every state in the nation has experienced a disinvestment in community colleges over the last several decades, a pattern that has intensified since the Great Recession in 2008. Between 2001 and 2011, state and local allocations per FTE community college student decreased by nearly one-quarter. And while state and local revenues to community colleges have risen slightly in the years since, in 2017 states were still appropriating roughly $2,000 less per student than they had been in 2001.[8] These national averages mask incredible variation across states, with some faring far worse than others. According to the State Higher Education Executive Officer's Association, twenty-two states experienced additional declines in per-student appropriations in fiscal year 2018; only nine have returned to pre-2008 funding levels; in eleven states, current funding is below the low point of the Great Recession.[9]

To add insult to injury, few analysts expect public funding for community colleges to rebound meaningfully in the coming years, at least on a per-FTE basis. Richard Romano and James Palmer, authors of *Financing Community Colleges*, explain:

> Among the factors that will impinge on the ability of many state and local governments to fund higher education, in the near term, are the overhand of underfunded public pension funds and the rising cost of Medicaid. In fact, current efforts to shore up pension funds can distort data on state higher education appropriations because, in some states, payments to pension funds are included in appropriations figures. For instance . . . Illinois increased its per-student appropriations to higher education by almost 50 percent from 2009 to 2014. This was much larger than the increase in any other state. However, almost all of the increase was accounted for by payments to the state's pension fund for retired college and university personnel . . . Once the pension appropriations were taken out of the calculation, the funding to support college operating budgets actually declined.[10]

Furthermore, despite policy makers' protestations about the rising cost of college, the availability of tuition as an alternate revenue source makes it easy for state legislators to forgo funding increases to community colleges and other institutions of higher education. This puts college leaders in a double bind, as they understand that they can only raise tuition so much without disenfranchising economically vulnerable populations (which, for community colleges, is most of their student bodies). And while Pell and other state and institutional grants help defray tuition prices, Temple

University professor Sara Goldrick-Rab explains that financial aid falls far short of expectations: the average net price of attending a community college (after all grants are subtracted from the total cost of attending college) is about $8,000 for students from families earning an average of $20,000 per year, a full 40 percent of family income for those in the bottom quartile.[11]

Reductions in public funding for community colleges have thus become an existential problem, both literally—many colleges are in danger of financial collapse—and figuratively, as many more contemplate directing available funds toward certain purposes (e.g., workforce preparation) at the expense of others (open access, transfer education), effectively severing the functioning of the college from its historic mission to serve all comers, regardless of race, religion, socioeconomic status, educational preparedness, or professional or vocational goals. It is no surprise, then, that many community college leaders have turned to entrepreneurial strategies—especially those linked to alternative revenue streams and/or cost-sharing partnerships—as a way of mitigating fiscal uncertainty and ensuring their institution's ability to carry out its education and training purposes.

• • •

As the preceding pages suggest, public disinvestment is the primary driver of entrepreneurial behavior by institutions of higher education. This belief is supported by the theoretical constructs of neoliberalism and academic capitalism (discussed more fully later in this chapter, but which essentially position educational entrepreneurship as a response to public policies that favor the market and public-private partnerships as the ideal catalysts for growth), as well as general consensus among community college leaders that a scarcity of resources has forced their hand. Take Valencia College, for example. When asked why his institution began thinking entrepreneurially, President Sandy Shugart said, "We've been treated badly by the state and continue to be treated worse than anyone else in the state by a large measure. We have the lowest funding per full-time student, the lowest amount of space per full-time student, the least funding per graduate, the least—I mean, you name the measure." Executive Vice President and Provost Kathleen Plinske added, somewhat jokingly, "The state funding is so low that there's actually semi-serious discussions about just succeeding!" For Loren Bender, Valencia's vice president of business operations and finance, the problem is not just low levels of state appropriations, it's the fact that the allocations are inconsistent from year to year, which—along with a tuition rate that is set by the state and has been flatlined for the past five years—makes planning very difficult. Joe Battista, executive vice president for professional and continuing education, agreed: "It's not a good business model because we have no control over [tuition] . . . it's just not sustainable."

Maria Harper-Marinick, chancellor of the Maricopa Community Colleges from 2016 to early 2020, came to a similar conclusion. After witnessing the Arizona legislature reduce allocations for several years, eventually eliminating funding for the state's two urban community college districts in Phoenix and Tuscon, she knew it was time "to find different ways to generate revenue." Former chief strategy officer Sasan Poureetezadi put it this way:

> When we got defunded, this idea that we've got to look at other things differently . . . There were some concepts of public-private partnerships that we probably never would have thought about before, and now that's considered okay, whereas in the past it might have been frowned on . . . There was more propensity to say let's look outward. We don't have the resources to do it alone, and let's look at some creative and different ways of doing it as long as it's ethical and above board.

In short, in education as in most industries, a scarcity of resources "is the primary fuel for innovation."[12] Yet it is not the only driver of entrepreneurial behavior in community colleges. Political and philanthropic pressure for greater educational attainment—twenty-four states are now working to achieve the Lumina Foundation's goal that 60 percent of America's working-age population hold a postsecondary credential by 2025—encourages college leaders to develop new short-term certificate programs and consider how existing programs can be restructured to improve persistence and completion.

Similarly, a renewed emphasis on the community college's commitment to serving the needs of its community and the costs of doing so provide an impetus for entrepreneurial thinking. As *service to community* becomes more broadly understood to include educating workers for local businesses and industries and acting in ways to help drive the economy, many colleges are building new or rapidly scaling existing technical programs, many focused on middle-skills jobs such as industrial maintenance or wind turbine technicians. State legislatures are frequently supportive of these efforts (indeed, most of the increased allocations to Iowa community colleges over the past five years have been in workforce training dollars), but there's a catch-22 in that career-technical programs, especially middle-skill programs, cost colleges substantially more to offer than courses in the arts and sciences. Schulz shared:

> When the economy is asking you to invest in these high-end and expensive programs with not much of an ROI [return on investment], how do you do that? Because in Iowa, the dirty little secret is the reason we are comprehensive community colleges is that we can pay for career-technical programming on the backs of arts and science enrollment . . . but that can't last forever without private investment in public programs.

For many colleges, alternative revenue streams or cost-sharing partnerships will be necessary to provide facilities and train students on the equipment they will be utilizing in their future careers, and to maintain and upgrade that technology.[13] (Connected to this issue is the challenge of recruiting and retaining faculty qualified to teach these courses, when starting salaries in some middle-skill professions are substantially higher than most community colleges can hope to pay.)

The costs of providing developmental education to educationally disadvantaged or returning adult students—as well as the growing expense of providing support services to facilitate the persistence and attainment of *all* students—also factor into community college leaders' decisions to act entrepreneurially. Developmental education is often considered the red-headed stepchild of community college missions (unwanted and begrudgingly cared for), and while precollege courses are not among the most expensive, the support offered to educationally underprepared and other students at risk of stopping or dropping out—supplemental instruction, learning communities, intrusive advising, tutoring, mentoring, and so on—*does* cost institutions a pretty penny. A report from The Century Foundation summed up the issue nicely: "A central problem is that two-year colleges are asked to educate those students with the greatest needs, using the least funds, and in increasingly separate and unequal institutions."[14] This, too, is an unsustainable business model.

A final notion spurring a sense of entrepreneurial urgency is that the way we prepare students for traditional careers is no longer sufficient to train them for the jobs of the future. Many of today's highest-demand occupations didn't exist five or ten years ago—think of the 34 percent of today's workforce that participates in the gig economy—and according to the EdVenture Group, 85 percent of jobs that will exist in 2030 have yet to be invented.[15] To be successful in the jobs of the future, whatever they may be, students must develop and practice the social and emotional skills of creativity, empathy, adaptability, resilience, and collaboration that will help them succeed in a rapidly changing, technologically driven world.[16] Yet as Bree Langemo, president of the Entrepreneurial Learning Initiative (ELI), writes, our current educational system pushes students into career paths at an early age, often developing only a single technical skill set, and in so doing "pigeonholes graduates into an area of expertise that may or may not create value in the future, while failing to provide them with the noncognitive skills that will help them adapt."[17]

Many community college leaders view developing an entrepreneurial culture as a way to combat inertia created by the structures and traditions of the academy and innovate how institutions prepare students for the jobs of the future. As Hillsborough Community College professors Andrew Gold and Mary Beth Kerly write:

> At the core of inertia, one will often find an organizational culture that is fearful of failure . . . But what if we leveraged an entrepreneurial

> mindset across the community college domain and redefined the meaning of failure? Imagine the transformational change that might occur within that college! Faculty, staff, and administrators would feel empowered to give things a go, to try and add value through innovative practices, knowing that whether the initiative was a success or a failure, accolades would be delivered. This would, in turn, lower the level of employee disengagement and better serve students.[18]

Gold and Kerly (and many other community college faculty and administrators) are clearly excited about the prospect of utilizing the tenets of entrepreneurship—including embracing failure and rewarding risk taking—as a way of creating transformational change in their institutions and meeting the needs of their communities. Some even see it as the only path forward. Schulz called it "core work." Giovannini agreed: "Yeah, [money from] the states is disappearing, so everyone has to be more nimble. More self-sufficient. And that was probably the thing that got some people in here and there. But I think what really sticks is that this is what is necessary to deliver on the mission today. Your organization needs to be entrepreneurial."

WHAT IS COMMUNITY COLLEGE ENTREPRENEURSHIP? DEFINITIONS AND EXAMPLES

> *We speak in terms of entrepreneurial and entrepreneurial mind-set, but when we really drill down, what does that mean? We don't have a common language yet.*[19]

Fifteen years ago, John Roueche and Barbara Jones wrote in *The Entrepreneurial Community College* that "resting on reputation and traditional ways of doing business will not deal sufficiently with the problems" community colleges face.[20] As the preceding section illustrates, this sentiment may be even truer today. But for all the talk about how community colleges must be entrepreneurial if they are to survive, few faculty, staff, administrators, or trustees have a clear sense of what that means on a day-to-day basis. Indeed, many—faculty in particular—have a negative or limited understanding of what it means to act entrepreneurially as (or in) a community college and conflate thinking in an entrepreneurial manner with being an entrepreneur. Thus, although they may support their business departments teaching students processes for developing new products and bringing them to market, many don't see a connection between that narrow view of entrepreneurship and what occurs in arts and science classrooms. Yet as author and philanthropist Ted Dintersmith has argued, "If we conceive of entrepreneurship as starting the next Facebook, we are missing the boat. But an entrepreneurial mind-set is necessary to succeed in the future of work."[21]

So what *is* entrepreneurship in the community college setting? In a monograph titled *The Entrepreneurial Domains of Higher Education*, Matthew Mars and Amy Metcalfe define entrepreneurship as "those activities that combine *risk, innovation,* and *opportunity*, particularly in times of uncertain resources."[22] Academicians Suzanne Flannigan, Thomas Greene, and Barbara Jones elaborate further, stating that entrepreneurship involves "taking and creating opportunities within an institutional context that leads toward the generation of monetary profit for the institution and its participants."[23] For Flannigan and her colleagues, this means thinking creatively about how a college can leverage its resources to generate revenue or reduce operating costs. However, some scholars have suggested that educational entrepreneurship may be more akin to *social entrepreneurship*, in which organizations prioritize the advancement of a social mission over the creation of economic wealth, as not all community college entrepreneurial activities have a net positive impact on the bottom line.[24]

These definitions may be useful in the academic sense, but they tend to leave me with more questions than answers. What do we mean by *risk*, *innovation*, and *opportunity*, and what kind of actions combine them? Is entrepreneurship limited only to those activities that lead to the generation of monetary profit, or can it be understood as something broader? Can one prioritize a social mission *and* the creation of economic wealth? And perhaps most importantly, how can these components of entrepreneurship be practiced in community colleges? Let's break the definitions down to their component parts and come up with our own, more intuitive understanding of community college entrepreneurship.

Risk

> *Perhaps the most important thing that college presidents and trustees can do is to develop and nurture a culture that rewards risk and innovation while allowing for failure.*[25]

Community college faculty and administrators take little risks every day: in interacting with students, in proposing new programs or pedagogical approaches, in hiring new instructors, and so forth. What differentiates these little risks from the bigger *risk* that Mars and Metcalfe are talking about? I believe the only difference is that with the little risks, our fear of failure is minimal, because what is being risked is not integrally tied to our own welfare or that of our institution. Furthermore, even if we fail, the results are likely predictable: a student doesn't respond well to your encouragement to work with a tutor; the department chair says there isn't enough professional development funding for you to learn that new approach this year; the new instructor resigns after a year because she found a better position. But with bigger risks, the fear of failure is greater, in part because there is ambiguity around what you are risking (Your reputation? That of your institution? All of the discretionary funds you have fought so hard for?) as well as the potential rewards for taking that risk (More money? A better-designed program? Improved ability to serve students?).

Over and over again, we are told to embrace risk, that risk is "essential for unlocking the full potential" of innovation.[26] Yet the more ambiguous the risk, and the more it has the potential to affect our welfare or that of our institution, the more fearful we become of taking it. In many colleges, this fear is amplified by an overriding sensibility that we are already asked to do so much with so little that we can't afford failure. The only way to combat this fear is to create a culture where experimenting with new ideas—even if they fail—is celebrated and rewarded, and where there is a process in place for mitigating risk, not by taking the safe or tried-and-true path, but by iteratively designing and testing new ideas to ensure that the rewards are objectively better than what was risked to get them (or not, in which case the idea needs to be tweaked or abandoned). Design thinking, discussed in detail in chapter 3, provides a useful framework for helping community college faculty and staff take measured entrepreneurial risks.

Innovation

> *Institutions of higher education continue, in the main, to be highly tradition bound. Consequently, ubiquitous innovation is not a cultural norm or an urgent imperative in contemporary postsecondary education.*[27]

In his *Little Black Book of Innovation*, Innosight partner Scott Anthony recalls a 2010 blog that listed twenty-five separate definitions for the word *innovation*. Twenty-five definitions! All for a word that most of us intuitively understand (but still struggle to explain). Anthony provides a simple definition. To him, innovation is "something different that has impact."[28] Two words are key to this pithy explanation: *different* and *impact*. An innovation must be different in the sense that it bestows new benefits on the innovation target—a customer, user, student, or community—but it does not need to be something that has never been done before. Steven Gonzales, interim chancellor of the Maricopa Community Colleges, reinforced this point: "Innovation to me can be something that perhaps we have tried before and maybe it's with a different spin and maybe it's using knowledge that came last time, and whether that worked or didn't work. Because most of the time it didn't work before." An innovation must also have impact: a measurable effect on a product, a process, or someone's life. Without impact, a creative idea is just that: an idea. Anthony writes: "When we set out to innovate, we should make sure that we don't fall into the trap of turning it into an academic exercise where we think, think, think, but never do. The doing is the thing."[29] Yet doing, as the quote at the top of this section attests, often feels antithetical to the ethos of the academy, which is far more aligned with inertia than innovation.

Opportunity

> *I can't do it just because we have to see if we can make more money. There has to be real purpose in what we are doing.*[30]

Taking measured risks to create something different that has impact is a reasonably intuitive definition for entrepreneurship. Where, then, does *opportunity* fit in? Perhaps more to the point, opportunity *for what*? For community colleges, entrepreneurial opportunity lies in any action that results in an improved ability to serve students and/or communities. Tapping into alternative revenue streams and engaging in cost-sharing partnerships certainly have potential to improve service to students and communities (insofar as they secure funding to carry out these functions), but opportunity also lies in improving internal process; developing new programs and services (or offering them in new markets or in different ways); engaging in strategic alliances with businesses or community groups; providing training for local companies or industries; managing small business development centers or incubators; outsourcing technology or ancillary services such as bookstores and cafeterias; utilizing college foundations to bring in tax-deductible donations to fund college initiatives; building maker spaces or other laboratories for creativity; and creating a shared culture of supporting and rewarding innovative thinking on campus (an entrepreneurial mind-set).

Community college entrepreneurship can thus be understood as *taking measured risks to create something different that has a positive impact on students or communities.* By this definition, the generation of monetary profit (or the mitigation of institutional costs) is not an end in itself; rather, it is a tool—albeit an indispensable one—to achieve a greater goal.

Entrepreneurial Mind-set

> *The most important thing for a community college and a community college leader is the adoption of an entrepreneurial mind-set that [can] permeate the culture, not only of the college, but a community.*[31]

Community colleges across America have experimented with various entrepreneurial activities for decades, and some have been quite successful in terms of bringing in a few extra dollars or improving programmatic offerings or partnerships. Yet as chapter 2 explores in more detail, many of these new ventures are located at the margins of institutions and have not fundamentally altered how students, faculty, staff, or external constituents interact with and benefit from the college. In Scott Anthony's parlance, these entrepreneurial efforts have had limited impact because they have not widely bestowed benefits on the innovation targets.

For entrepreneurial institutions such as the four colleges and districts highlighted in this book, limited and isolated success is not enough: they are aiming for a wholesale rethinking of what it means to practice entrepreneurship in a community college. As Sandy Shugart shared: "I think it took us a while to discover that invention, collaboration, design, entrepreneurship—that those are sort of overlapping circles on the Venn diagram. And they overlap a lot, not just a little bit. And people use those words almost interchangeably. And it's practiced largely as a spirit. A spirit of entrepreneurship. A spirit of collaboration. A spirit of invention." Constance Carrol, chancellor of the San Diego Community College District, expressed it similarly: "Entrepreneurialism is about transformation in spirit toward service of others."[32]

Put simply, the development of an entrepreneurial mind-set or spirit of innovation across campus is key to a community college's ability to effect transformative change. For this to occur, college leaders must create a culture that values, supports, and rewards "rethinking what our stakeholders need, what our students need, what our community needs. And [considering] how do we serve that, rather than how do we continue to do what we've always done?"[33] It means asking: "How can we have a growth mindset? How can we look at things from different perspectives? How can we try things at a small scale and see if those things succeed? And if they don't, then what do we need to tweak to make it better?"[34]

Helping faculty and staff feel safe engaging with these questions and thinking creatively about how to improve service to students and communities is integral to the entrepreneurial success and sustainability of any community college. But as Shugart reminded us, establishing an entrepreneurial culture also requires discipline. "There are well-known processes to do these things," he said. "Without the disciplines people end up skipping steps, and it costs them time and resources, and often undermines the project." This book offers design thinking as a framework for practicing entrepreneurship in community colleges, but there is substantial overlap between design thinking and other creative problem-solving processes (see chapter 3). While I am partial to design thinking, many of these frameworks can be used to guide the adoption of an entrepreneurial mind-set across campus.

FEARS, CHALLENGES, AND CONTROVERSIES SURROUNDING COMMUNITY COLLEGE ENTREPRENEURSHIP

> *If you don't like change, you'll like irrelevance even less.*[35]

While many acknowledge the potential of entrepreneurship to diversify and stabilize community college revenues and create opportunities for greater synergies between colleges and their communities, scholars and those who have spent their careers in publicly funded institutions often view it as a necessary evil at best, and at worst an existential threat to the colleges' missions and values. Quotes like the one offered at the beginning of this section, often repeated to cajole reluctant faculty and administrators to get onboard with an entrepreneurial agenda, do little to quiet these fears, many of which are grounded in theoretical frameworks like neoliberalism and academic capitalism that critique market-oriented behaviors in institutions of higher education. The sections that follow detail many of the fears, challenges, and controversies related to community college entrepreneurship.

Demand-Side Fears, Neoliberalism, and Academic Capitalism

> *The cultivation of intellect, long a central objective of university life, is threatened by political and economic pressures that are redefining and reshaping the functions of higher learning.*[36]

In exploring the theoretical traditions of entrepreneurship, Mars and Metcalfe distinguish between supply-side theoretical approaches in which individual entrepreneurs seek conditions to act entrepreneurially and demand-side perspectives where environmental (political or economic) conditions are created to encourage entrepreneurship or market-oriented behavior. They write, "[T]he demand-side condition is the most recognized contributor to academic entrepreneurship."[37] As such, many of the most common fears and controversies surrounding entrepreneurship are associated with demand-side theories such as neoliberalism and academic capitalism.

University of California, Riverside professor John Levin describes "the political and economic ideology referred to as neo-liberalism" as "one of the more influential forces shaping institutions over the past two decades."[38] As noted previously, neoliberalism is grounded in the belief that the private marketplace is the ideal catalyst for advancing economic growth. The tenets of this ideology include a commitment to competition as a way to increase efficiency and productivity, reduced state or governmental funding for social programs, and increased state support for individual actors or organizations as a way to compete in global economic markets focused on the advancement of knowledge and the rapid commercialization of technological innovations—what Levin and others call the "New Economy." Numerous scholars have discussed entrepreneurial behavior in colleges and universities as a response to neoliberal policies, but the neoliberal ideology extends far beyond the reaches of academe. The concept of academic capitalism, however, can be understood as neoliberalism applied specifically to institutions of higher education.

Higher education scholars Sheila Slaughter and Larry Leslie first introduced the concept of academic capitalism in 1997, arguing that reductions in unrestricted funds to universities in the United States, Australia, Canada, and the United Kingdom resulted in increased resource-seeking behavior among faculty and administrators in those institutions.[39] Seven years later, Slaughter and researcher Gary Rhoades published a more comprehensive theoretical framework of academic capitalism, which positioned entrepreneurial behavior in the academy as a shift from the *public good knowledge/learning regime* to an *academic capitalist knowledge/learning regime.*[40] Specifically, Slaughter and Rhoades argued that revenue-seeking behavior in institutions of higher education has resulted from a combination of reduced and uncertain funding bases and changing policy environments that promote or encourage such activities. They and other scholars contended that this shift fundamentally moves colleges and universities away from serving the public good (by providing a free flow of knowledge) and toward service of the "private, profit-driven sphere of the marketplace" where knowledge is construed as a private good that can be commodified and sold.[41]

Many critiques of educational entrepreneurship—especially those made by sociologists and higher education scholars—are associated with neoliberal and academic capitalist theories. Levin, for example, has argued that as "globalization shifts the nature of the economy and the labor market," community colleges have begun to emphasize training and skills development at the expense of liberal arts programs, transfer curricula, and citizenship development.[42] Critical pedagogy theorist Henry Giroux went a step further, contending that higher education has been corporatized to such an extent that when it comes to curricula and pedagogy, market forces have trumped the freedom of inquiry and curiosity.[43] Other scholars deride an increased reliance on public institutions to train workers for private enterprise; some worry that faculty will become so enamored with market-driven opportunities that they will distance themselves from the idea that they are public employees providing public goods (or that tenure-track faculty will be replaced by contingent instructors hired out of industry, who may not share the academic ethos); and still others point to a collapse of shared governance and the growing power of college administrators, who may be more likely to respond to political and market forces than to faculty, students, and the needs of a learning enterprise.[44]

Supply-Side Fears and Compromising Academic Values

> *In the pursuit of innovative approaches or simply survival tactics to respond to their various communities and stakeholders, as well as to maintain their reputational image, community colleges have*

> *lost the humanistically meaningful part of their mission while attaining economic and political goals.*[45]

Unlike demand-side theories, which describe educational entrepreneurship as a response to external forces, supply-side explanations view entrepreneurial behavior in community colleges and other institutions of higher education as stimulated by an individual or collective drive to innovate. As such, from a supply-side perspective, entrepreneurship and academic culture are not always antithetical to one another; indeed, they share the values of inquisitiveness, creativity, and often, commitment to serving the public good (especially if we view community college entrepreneurship as a form of social entrepreneurship). Yet supply-side explanations also raise alarm bells for faculty and others working in community colleges, as they allow for the potential that entrepreneurial individuals—especially if they are in positions of power—will compromise academic values in their quest to disrupt established patterns of doing business and tap into new revenue streams.

Fears related to the actions of an entrepreneurial individual or group typically take the form of the slippery slope argument. For example, in *Universities in the Marketplace*, Derek Bok shares a fictional "dream"—a thought experiment, really—in which he, as president of Harvard University, borrows $2 billion to "assemble the greatest faculty, the finest facilities, and the most talented student body the world had ever seen."[46] After enjoying some initial success and acclaim, he begins to engage in entrepreneurial behavior in order to meet his escalating loan payments. He starts by upgrading athletic facilities and selling luxury boxes—not such a controversial move, at least these days. He then moves on to selling "redundant" works of art from the university's renowned museum and begins to offer companies the exclusive rights to license scientific discoveries. Selling advertisements on course syllabi comes next, followed by a suggestion (from the financial planner, of course), to auction off a hundred spots in each entering class to the highest bidders. Bok, becoming more and more uncomfortable with each successive money-making scheme, ends his fictional dream by asking, "Was everything in the university for sale if the price was right?"[47]

While entrepreneurship in community colleges often looks very different than it does in universities, critics of such behavior often make a point similar to Bok's, wondering if it is possible to extract just a few revenue-generating activities from Pandora's box before re-securing the locks. Community colleges will always need more money, they say; how will we know when we have gone too far? At what point will entrepreneurial activity at my institution begin to compromise essential academic values or run counter to our commitment to serving the public good? Will entrepreneurship run amok fundamentally shift the nature of our college from one providing public benefits (upon which our public support is ostensibly contingent) to one serving primarily private interests?[48]

Many critics of entrepreneurship in community colleges cite a changing culture at their institutions as evidence that revenue-seeking behavior has already gone too far. In particular, they view an emerging business ethos in which administrators increasingly imitate corporate managers as evidence that economic development has already eroded other missions of the community college, including open access and community service. Academic values cannot be upheld, they argue, when students are viewed as consumers or commodities and faculty are treated more like employees than educational partners.[49] To many critics of educational entrepreneurship, something irreparable has already been lost in the community college's drive to diversify its revenue base; the only question is how much will be sacrificed in what may well be an unending pursuit of *more.*

Practical Challenges and Concerns

> *Sometimes we get a little frustrated because we have these ideas for things that we can do because of the facilities and equipment we have. But the problem is time. When you've got faculty that are teaching full loads and overloads . . . there's just so many hours in the day.*[50]

Although many of the fears and concerns related to community college entrepreneurship are grounded in theories of neoliberalism and academic capitalism, several others are more practical in nature, having more to do with *if* and *how* institutions can act entrepreneurially than whether they should. For example, the community college's historic commitment to a specific service area (often legislatively mandated and defined by county or neighborhood borders) complicates the development of entrepreneurial programs or services that extend beyond those boundaries. Similarly, college location carries inherent advantages and disadvantages for entrepreneurial efforts. Urban environments, for example, tend to offer more numerous opportunities to collaborate with nearby businesses or community organizations, but metropolitan colleges seeking to expand into new markets also face greater competition from corporate, nonprofit, and other entities than do their rural counterparts.

The size of a community college may also affect its ability to act entrepreneurially. In some ways, smaller colleges can (and must!) be nimbler, as small enrollment shifts can determine whether or not a particular program will run each term. Small colleges have more experience turning on a dime. On the other hand, larger institutions with more students and greater resources risk substantially smaller percentages of their operating budgets to experiment with new programs or services and thus may be more likely to take those chances. Larger colleges also have a greater number of faculty and staff with time to contribute to innovative thinking and programming; at smaller institutions, faculty and administrators may already wear several hats, and thus carving out time to lead major innovations can be difficult.

The ways in which colleges are governed may also encourage or limit entrepreneurial behavior. Trustees at some institutions may feel that faculty and administrators cannot move fast enough to chase down new revenue opportunities or serve new constituents; at other colleges, governing board members may be more hesitant to engage in such behaviors. In addition, colleges with a strong culture of shared governance, particularly those in union environments, may experience a slower pace of organizational change or greater resistance to modifying traditional ways of doing business. Finally, initiative fatigue among faculty at all types of institutions can dampen enthusiasm for entrepreneurial projects, especially if the impetus for that work is not directly connected to their day-to-day responsibilities.

These and other challenges to entrepreneurial efforts at community colleges—as well as the ways in which the four colleges described in this book are addressing them—are discussed more fully in chapters 6, 7, and 8.

One final layer of concern surrounding entrepreneurial behavior within community colleges centers around the *processes* by which entrepreneurial actions are undertaken. These apprehensions frequently echo my own sentiment that community college entrepreneurship—in and of itself—is neither good nor bad. What matters is that entrepreneurial opportunities are pursued in a way that prioritizes the needs of college stakeholders—chiefly students, faculty, administrators, trustees, and community members—and that they are evaluated by their ability to further the college's mission. Approached in this way, community college efforts to ensure fiscal stability through entrepreneurship can be viewed as *mission-oriented* rather than *market-oriented*. But shifting how colleges evaluate and act upon new opportunities is often easier said than done, which may explain why entrepreneurship has not yet had the impact on college finances and functioning that many expected. The chapters that follow explore historical reasons for the (thus far) limited impact of entrepreneurship in American community colleges and illustrate how design thinking can guide faculty and administrators in taking measured risks to create something different that has a positive impact on students or communities.

2 Transcending a History of Incremental Change

The current economic, social, and political climate presents such an unprecedented threat to the mission of community colleges that only radical changes will secure a future in which their quality and purpose are maintained. Incremental, short-term responses are futile in the face of this next reality.[1]

Over the past two decades, many community college leaders have worked tirelessly to identify alternative revenue streams, engage in cost-sharing partnerships, and seek new ways of serving their communities. Yet with very few exceptions, these entrepreneurial efforts have not substantially reduced the colleges' dependence on public financing, nor have they disrupted underlying organizational or financial practices that are based largely on enrollment rather than cost or programmatic outcomes. There are numerous explanations for the slow pace of change in colleges and universities—academic management has frequently been described as akin to herding cats—but a primary reason why community college entrepreneurship has not yet transformed established ways of doing business lies in the institution's long history of responding to external pressures to serve new constituents by simply adding on to their à la carte menu of programmatic offerings, utilizing the same budgeting and planning processes, and rarely if ever questioning whether a traditional approach to serving students or communities is the best one. The pages that follow explore this explanation for the (thus far) limited impact of entrepreneurship in American community colleges and then consider why the next wave of entrepreneurship may be different.

A CENTURY OF RESPONDING TO EXTERNAL PRESSURES BY ADDING ON

> *Community colleges thrived on the new responsibilities because they had no traditions to defend, no alumni to question their role, no autonomous professional staff to be moved aside, no statements of philosophy that would militate against their taking on responsibility for everything.*[2]

As Arthur Cohen, Florence Brawer, and I describe in *The American Community College*, one of the hallmarks of the institution is its responsiveness to societal needs. Beginning in the early 1900s, community colleges expanded to accommodate the growing number of high school graduates (in the process, relieving universities of the burden of providing general education instruction to all college goers). Over the next several decades, the community colleges added numerous vocational programs to train students for direct entry to the workforce, as well as industry advisory committees to improve the colleges' ability to develop curricula aligned with the needs of local businesses. Over time, community colleges also added continuing (often called adult or noncredit) education and community service functions, and by the 1960s, nearly every college offered developmental or remedial coursework. Thus was born the tripartite mission of community colleges: transfer preparation, occupational training, and community service. (Developmental education is often considered the hidden fourth mission, one that faculty and administrators wish was not necessary.)

Yet the colleges didn't stop there. By the dawn of the twenty-first century, community colleges were experimenting with baccalaureate programs in applied fields, offering courses to students in grades 11 and 12 through dual-credit and early college high school programs, providing contract training opportunities for local businesses, and incorporating every conceivable instructional or curricular form, including online education, short-term and open entry/exit courses, classes on army bases and in prisons, and opportunities for civic and democratic engagement.[3] In short, with each new societal demand, the community college expanded its *anyone, anywhere, anything, at any time* business model.[4] Former president of the College of Central Florida Charles Dassance put it this way: "The comprehensive mission of the community college reflects the impossible goal of being 'all things to all people.'"[5]

George Vaughan, president emeritus of Piedmont Virginia Community College, once conceptualized the community college mission as a balloon that, when faced with changing societal pressures, swelled to encompass the new function but did not alter or diminish the core elements of the mission contained within.[6] One explanation for the community college's incremental, additive response to changing societal demands—its desire and ability to continually expand the mission balloon—may be the fact that the institution developed outside the grade-level traditions of secondary schools and universities, and without coordination at the state or federal level. As such, the colleges had little external pressure to prioritize one mission over another. And indeed, Dassance penned, "It would be hard to find evidence of priority setting in regard to the comprehensive mission of the community college."[7]

Another reason is that it is simply easier to "take incremental steps to deal with the new reality" than to continually assess the relative worth of various programs and services and expand or trim accordingly.[8] This incremental approach to organizational change could very well continue ad infinitum if funding for the colleges remained constant, but what will happen when public support diminishes to a point where, to continue Vaughan's metaphor, the colleges no longer have enough air to inflate their balloon? Will college leaders be forced to retrench and mercilessly sacrifice one mission to save another? Will only those functions that have the potential to bring in revenue be prioritized and everything else (community service, transfer preparation, developmental education) be jettisoned? Will an ever-greater burden be placed on students in the form of higher tuition and fees, effectively closing the open door?

It may not be heretical to suggest that community colleges have already reached this point; certainly the college leaders interviewed for this book believe that incremental responses are no longer sufficient to deal with contemporary challenges. James Tschechtelin, former president of Baltimore City Community College, agrees: "The community college mission has been stretched beyond the breaking point in terms of sustaining access and quality and beyond the ability to serve both enrollment and student outcome goals."[9] Yet as I wrote in the introduction, because of their long history of responding to external pressures by adding on, community colleges are not particularly well equipped to innovate or engage in the type of creative, intentional change that may disrupt established ways of doing business without sacrificing their commitment to students and communities. Furthermore, many long-utilized organizational, financial, and planning processes act to inhibit change, making a shift to mission-oriented entrepreneurship even more challenging.

FINANCIAL AND PLANNING PROCESSES INHIBITING CHANGE

> *Pragmatically, incremental adjustments result in a fragmentation that hinders organizational effectiveness.*[10]

Numerous scholars have noted that throughout the community colleges' history, even as they incorporated new functions and curricular offerings, they have not substantially modified their underlying organizational, financial, or planning systems and practices.[11] To be sure, most colleges now undergo intensive long-term strategic planning processes, typically based on environmental scans that can help predict enrollment surges or declines, growing industry sectors, and so forth. Most colleges also specify major institutional goals in their mission statements and strategic plans, and work to ensure that funding (specifically, undesignated funding) is allocated in ways that support institutional priorities. But as with the curriculum, community college financial planning processes typically follow those that have been utilized for most of the colleges' history, and rarely (if ever) are they substantially altered or are historic missions or curricular emphases eliminated or defunded. If anything, long-established programs or services are simply rebranded to better align with new institutional priorities, thereby justifying the same or similar levels of funding as in the past. This can stand in the way of transformational change.

Community college budgeting processes, in particular, have changed little over the past century. As former Bellevue College interim president Laura Saunders explains, this is due in part to the fact that college leaders have relatively little control over how their funding can be allocated:

> Budgeting in community colleges takes place in an environment where resources are constrained and opportunities for growth can be limited. Often as much as 80% or more of the annual budget is already committed to existing staff, essential operations, and facilities overhead. New, undesignated funding is precious. Reallocation can be contentious. At the same time, "earmarked" or designated program funding may or may not related to the goals in the strategic plan.[12]

Because of these factors, most colleges utilize incremental or line-item budgeting. Just as public subsidies to community colleges follow a prior-year base but fluctuate with enrollment, incremental budgets within the colleges utilize the previous year's allocations as a starting point and increase or decrease in a relatively uniform manner across line items. As scholar James Palmer explains, this approach to budgeting puts a premium on historical continuity and has the added advantages of being scalable and easy to implement. And because budget reductions or increases are often assessed across the board, incremental budgeting can dampen conflict or competition among various college units.[13]

However, incremental budgets have long been criticized for their inefficiency and inflexibility. Nearly forty years ago, Ellen Chafee (now a senior fellow at the Association of Governing Boards of Universities and Colleges) warned that incremental budgeting processes would become increasingly inefficient as they perpetuate historical practices and are oblivious to how changing educational needs might require shifts in resource allocation.[14] More recently, scholars and presidents have argued that incremental approaches may "paper over the inefficiencies of poorly performing units when they receive the same marginal increases awarded to highly performing units" and that they commit funds to certain budget areas "without evidence that the base allocation or additional monies [are] needed to meet and accomplish institutional goals."[15]

In light of these drawbacks, many community colleges have experimented with alternative budgeting approaches, including *formula budgeting*, which attempts to tie budget decisions to actual programmatic or institutional costs; *zero-base budgeting*, in which each budget starts from scratch and managers must analyze which programs and services offered in the past are still needed and, if so, how much money is necessary to fund them; *planning, programming, and budgeting systems*, which base resource-allocation decisions on cost-benefit analyses that compare various ways of achieving certain institutional goals; and *responsibility center budgeting*, in which program or department heads are responsible for allocation decisions within their own areas of responsibility and then compete to maximize revenues for their units.[16]

With the exception of zero-base budgeting, which was attempted with some frequency in the 1960s and 70s but then largely abandoned as the associated annual examination of budget priorities proved difficult "if not impossible" in practice, community colleges have rarely utilized any of these alternative budgeting approaches exclusively.[17] And while some community colleges have adopted elements of zero-base, responsibility center, or formula budgeting, what Palmer calls "the enduring incremental approach" still lies at the heart of financial planning and resource allocation at most institutions.[18] As such, scholars David Murphy and Stephen Katsinas argue, "[T]he budgeting process itself may become a roadblock in the way of achieving strategic goals and objectives."[19]

Furthermore, regardless of the budgeting approach utilized, "none supersedes organizational politics and bargaining as drivers of budget development within colleges."[20] Turf battles and empire building may be minimized with an incremental approach, but they still get in the way of effective budgeting and planning, as faculty and administrators find ever more creative ways to hide money in obscure line items, maintain heavy rainy-day fund balances, and protect low-enrollment programs in order to preserve faculty appointments.[21]

The ways in which community colleges have historically responded to declines in state and local allocations also serve to reinforce the status quo. In most instances, college leaders choose to absorb funding declines without making programmatic cuts or taking any other steps that might directly limit enrollment, as fewer students mean even fewer dollars from the government.[22] The most popular strategies for closing budget gaps are across-the-board cuts, deferred maintenance, and furloughs.[23] Other frequent targets are professional development, extra faculty stipends or contracts, release time for faculty performing nonessential administrative functions, and scaling back community services. In short, community colleges tend to trim around the edges in times of fiscal contraction, but they rarely defund or eliminate academic programs, choosing to (potentially) lower the quality of the ingredients rather than pare down the menu.

Of course, at some point it is no longer possible to cut costs without sacrificing programs, and community college leaders must look to revenue-generating opportunities in order to preserve their institution's education, training, and community-uplift missions. By and large, college leaders are not taught how to do this: a 2006 American Association of Community Colleges survey indicated that respondents felt "taking an entrepreneurial stance in seeking ethical alternative funding sources" was among the responsibilities for which they felt least prepared.[24] Graduate programs for future college leaders often do not prioritize training in resource management (let alone how to financially plan for innovation), and thus most presidents learn about forecasting, planning, and budgeting on the job, further perpetuating historic, incremental processes. Moreover, as Robert Muñoz, vice president for community and industry education at TCC, pointed out, even when colleges have worked to increase revenues, "typically we've looked at breakeven: have you covered your costs. And that's not including the staffing costs." Asking faculty and administrators to think about generating revenue above and beyond the breakeven point requires a paradigm shift, one for which most feel utterly unprepared. It is much easier to—as the song goes—keep on keeping on than to embark upon a wholesale rethinking of the community college's missions, priorities, strengths, weaknesses, and opportunities and then redesign organizational and budgetary practices to support the new regime. Yet as chapter 8 explains, that may be what is required for the colleges to transcend their history of incremental change and begin serving students and communities in innovative ways.

WHY MIGHT THIS NEXT WAVE OF ENTREPRENEURSHIP BE DIFFERENT?

> *Now more than ever, community colleges are realizing that business as usual is untenable. Traditional structures and systems, established when these colleges first opened, today limit their capacity to be productive. Colleges are looking instead toward innovative methods to transform themselves into flexible, adaptive, responsive, and financially secure entrepreneurial organizations.*[25]

In 1989, Alvin Toffler wrote *The Third Wave*, which described how societies and cultures have transitioned through three separate waves of history—from the agrarian age, to the industrial age, and finally to the information age—with each new wave pushing the previous one aside.[26] Fifteen years later, scholars Mark Milliron, Gerardo de los Santos, and Boo Browning applied Toffler's notion to community college entrepreneurship, arguing that the colleges similarly change according to societal trends.[27] To Milliron and his colleagues, as well as to researchers Brent Cejda and Michael Jolley, who extended scholarship on this topic, the first wave of entrepreneurship refers to the expansion of the colleges' *anyone, anywhere, anything, at any time* business model. In the first wave, Cejda and Jolley explain, "entrepreneurship existed through the addition of programs."[28] The second wave refers to activities such as contract training and partnerships with local businesses that colleges develop to meet specific needs in their service areas. Most second-wave entrepreneurial activities are noncredit, Cejda and Jolley write, staffed with separate faculty and administrators, and exist outside of traditional college functioning. As this chapter explains, the vast majority of community college entrepreneurship to date can be considered second wave.

Indeed, according to Cejda and Jolley, very few community colleges exhibit elements of third-wave entrepreneurship, which is characterized by partnerships with business, governmental, and nonprofit groups that promote educational, community, and economic development for the long-term sustainability of a college's region and, in turn, the college itself. Third-wave community colleges—including the four described in this book—have moved "beyond isolated activities that bring additional resources to the institution" and instead are entering into "fuller partnerships that create win-win outcomes for the community college and for the broader constituencies the community college serves."[29] Moreover, third-wave colleges are actively developing institutional cultures that embrace or value entrepreneurial thinking and reward faculty and staff for creatively considering how they might transform programs and practices to better serve students and communities. In other words, establishing and supporting an entrepreneurial mind-set across campus is necessary for community colleges to paddle past the riptide of incremental change and ride the third wave of entrepreneurship.

Of course, as this chapter has described, accomplishing this is much more easily said than done. Over fifteen years have passed since Milliron and his colleagues wrote about the third wave of entrepreneurship; why might the next few decades be any different than the last? What has changed that could propel community colleges to the third wave en masse?

One answer is that more community college educators than ever before are actively learning about entrepreneurship and sharing best practices for developing entrepreneurial mind-sets and cultures at their institutions. Nearly one-third of all US community colleges are now members of the National Association for Community College Entrepreneurship (NACCE), which involves more than two thousand faculty, staff, administrators, and presidents in regional and national conferences and local centers of practice. In 2019, NACCE published *Community Colleges as Incubators of Innovation: Unleashing Entrepreneurial Opportunities for Communities and Students*, an edited book illustrating how various colleges have worked to develop entrepreneurial ecosystems that will "help individuals, communities and colleges prosper."[30] Without a doubt, this organization and the smaller centers of practice it supports will introduce more colleges to entrepreneurial ideas and help them shift entrepreneurship "from the perimeter to the core of education."[31]

But a simpler, and perhaps more powerful answer to the *why now* question is that community colleges may not have a choice. The *add everything, change nothing* response to societal demands is no longer sufficient to overcome the challenges described in chapter 1, nor are attempts to append a few small revenue-generating units to the margins of the institutions. As public subsidies decline, as the costs of providing instruction increase, and as the jobs of the future demand new approaches to education, training, and retraining, community colleges will have to embrace third-wave entrepreneurship if they are to survive. NIACC president Steven Schulz put it this way:

> It used to be enough for us to provide programs. People came to us and we spit them out the back end. And that met the need. Those were the days when there were lines at every workforce place that would hire the best and they didn't have to dig too deep into the pool to find the quality they needed to be successful . . . The role we play now is to try to find more creative ways to upskill people, rather than just saying, "Here are the programs, come to us." It's really: how do we get to them? How do we create those partnerships with employers so that we both benefit? It's not enough to just offer opportunities anymore.

For community colleges to ride the third wave of entrepreneurship, they must transcend their history of incremental changes to form and function. In actively exploring new ways to mitigate costs and generate revenue, college leaders must consider transforming operational processes—especially those related to budgeting and organizational structure—so that new or redesigned ventures are not simply tacked on at the periphery but are instead central to the ways in which the college plans and budgets for the future, serves students, trains workers, and partners or interacts with the community. TCC's strategic reorientation around its Three Goals and Eight Principles (discussed in detail in chapter 5) is one example of how a college can embark upon this process. Valencia College's incorporation of purpose-based budgeting (see chapter 8) provides another. The specific organizational and financial changes implemented at each college will likely be unique reflections of their curricular emphases, regional needs and opportunities, and student populations, but adopting a planning and budgeting system that emphasizes the true costs of educating and training students is likely necessary. Whether this is best accomplished by dividing organizational units into revenue and cost centers and charging revenue centers for the services provided by cost centers (libraries, human resources, facilities, equipment, student services, and so forth) or by training faculty and staff to incorporate these costs into program reviews and budget requests will be for each individual college to decide.

However, it is imperative that college leaders approach these financial and planning changes without losing sight of their institution's values or the needs of its stakeholders. As Muñoz shared, "I think colleges have to be more intentional about, if we're going to be more entrepreneurial, what is going to be the process?" Specifically, college leaders need a framework for establishing an entrepreneurial mind-set across campus, for carrying out the organizational and budgetary changes necessary for transformational change, and for empowering faculty and staff to identify innovative ways to educate students for the jobs of the future and ensure the long-term economic vitality of communities. Design thinking, a concept borrowed from the business literature but recently extended to social-sector organizations and independent K–12 schooling, provides just such a framework. The following chapter describes this empathic, stakeholder-driven approach to entrepreneurship and the chapters in part II illustrate how four community colleges have utilized the tenets of design thinking to drive mission-oriented change.

3 Design Thinking as a Framework for Mission-Oriented Change

The tools of conventional market research can be useful in pointing toward incremental improvements, but they will never lead to those rule-breaking, game-changing, paradigm-shifting breakthroughs that leave us scratching our heads and wondering why nobody ever thought of them before.[1]

Design thinking as a framework for innovation emerged at a time when many scholars, scientists, and futurists began connecting the increasingly fast pace of societal and technological change to a need to be nimble, fail fast, check one's assumptions, and draw upon heretofore untapped sources of knowledge. For example, in their 2016 book *Whiplash: How to Survive our Faster Future*, Joi Ito and Jeff Howe describe the future as running on an entirely new operating system (OS), one undergirded by wholly different assumptions than those of previous eras: no longer is strength automatically better than weakness, knowledge always preferred to ignorance, or individual talent more desirable than difference. Indeed, in the new OS, resiliency is more important than strength; an ability to navigate the unknown is far more essential than a knowledge of the terrain; and a diversity of thought and perspective is more powerful than any individual's ability. Yet, as Ito and Howe write, "[O]ur current cognitive toolset"—forged in previous assumptions about the world—"leaves us ill-equipped to comprehend the profound implications posed by rapid advances in everything from communications to warfare."[2] To survive in the future, they argue, leaders in education and industry alike must learn to navigate this new OS, to learn how to innovate not once, but over and over again.

The concept of design thinking came out of the Silicon Valley design firm IDEO, founded by David Kelley, and gained popularity with the 2009 publication of CEO Tim Brown's book *Change by Design*. In the introduction to his book, Brown positions design thinking as a framework to guide innovation and a tool to help organizations transform in ways that will position them for success in a future characterized, as Ito and Howe write, "not just by rapid change, but by *constant* change."[3] Brown argues: "What we need is an approach to innovation that is powerful, effective, and broadly accessible, that can be integrated into all aspects of business and society, and that individuals and teams can use to generate breakthrough ideas that are implemented and that therefore have an impact. Design thinking . . . offers just such an approach."[4]

Brown defines design thinking as "a way of describing a set of principles that can be applied by diverse people to a wide range of problems."[5] In other words, design thinking is just as applicable to the development of new programs and services—in industry, education, or other public or social-sector organizations—as it is to the creation of commercial products. Thomas Lockwood and Edgar Papke, authors of *Innovation by Design*, contend that design thinking may be even *more* important in the academy:

> One of the greatest benefits that design thinking can deliver, and one of its greatest challenges, is in the realm of education . . . Education is all too often a system based on time and performance, linearity and conformity, batching people in a mechanical process . . . As human beings, design thinking creates a powerful link to our basic needs and desires and makes it ideal as a path to the development of skills and knowledge necessary to engage in the creativity and innovation required to succeed in the future.[6]

Design thinking—whether applied to the transformation of colleges and universities or the development of a new product or service—is an empathic, iterative, and possibility-driven approach to problem solving.[7] It is a fundamentally human-centered framework that seeks to "solve problems and develop new products/ideas by helping designers better understand the people for whom they are designing."[8] For community colleges, design thinking offers an approach to innovation which ensures that new ideas amplify—rather than sacrifice—the institution's mission and the needs of its stakeholders.

THE DESIGN THINKING PROCESS

> *As organizations develop this organization-wide capability for innovation, they will enhance their ability to achieve their objectives by generating more innovative and effective outcomes and processes that create better value for the stakeholders they serve and that make the organizations more effective in meeting their missions.*[9]

The design thinking process has been characterized in various ways, but the most common description comes from Stanford University's Hasso Plattner Institute of Design (or d.School), cofounded by IDEO's Kelley. Known as the EDIPT model, this framework asks designers to first *empathize* with key stakeholders by seeking to understand their physical and emotional needs, how and why they do things, and what is meaningful to them. Next, designers work to *define* the problem that needs to be solved, make sense of the information gathered, and create an actionable problem statement or design brief. From there, a design team will *ideate*, or brainstorm a wide variety of possible solutions to the problem at hand. In the last two phases, both of which are highly iterative, designers select a handful of the most promising ideas to *prototype* and then *test* one or more ideas with end users—seeking to understand why a solution does or does not meet stakeholders' needs—and retool as appropriate.

FIGURE 3.1 Steps and considerations in the design thinking approach to mission-oriented change

What *Is*	What *If*	What *Wows*	What *Works*
Empathize with stakeholders Identify unmet needs Define the problem Draft the design brief Establish design criteria	Brainstorm Develop concepts Create napkin pitches Establish design teams The importance of creative space	Prototype and surface assumptions Mitigate risk by failing fast Gather feedback through rapid experiments Dealing with resistance	Run learning launches and design the on-ramp Role of college leaders Cultivating an entrepreneurial culture Establishing external partnerships

Source: Adapted from Jeanne Liedtka, Randy Salzman, and Daisy Azer, *Design Thinking for the Greater Good: Innovation in the Social Sector* (New York: Columbia University Press, 2017). Used with permission.

In their 2017 book, *Design Thinking for the Greater Good*, Jeanne Liedtka, Randy Salzman, and Daisy Azer reconceptualize the EDIPT model into four simple questions—What *Is*, What *If*, What *Wows*, and What *Works*—that can help designers identify and implement solutions to the wicked problems and competing interests that frequently characterize public and social-sector organizations (see figure 3.1). Although Liedtka et al.'s four-question approach to design thinking in many ways parallels the EDIPT model, its simplicity makes it an especially useful framework for community colleges, which have multiple missions, complicated shared governance structures, numerous (and often competing) stakeholders, employees who can be reluctant to take risks and who are often rewarded for compliance rather than performance, leaders who frequently have short tenures, and users—students, partners, citizens—whose expectations can rise as fast as resources to meet them decline. This book utilizes *Design Thinking for the Greater Good*'s four-questions as a macro-framework for understanding the design thinking process and—in the chapters that follow—as a structure for illustrating how community colleges can engage in mission-oriented entrepreneurial change.

WHAT *IS*

In *Design Thinking for the Greater Good*, Liedtka and her colleagues list seven steps that precede and make up the What *Is* process. Like all good derivative work, however, this book presents some of these steps out of order and combines others, mixing them up with insights and advice from numerous other influential design thinkers (see figure 3.1). I'm sure Liedtka et al. won't mind; as they say, "Once innovators get comfortable with design thinking's methods, tools, and mindsets, they mix and match the steps, emphasizing some and skipping others, and pick and choose among the variety of tools offered."[10] Where I do not stray from their approach, however, is in emphasizing that nearly half of the design thinking process "is spent laying the foundation for innovation, before we even get to idea generation."[11] In other words, speed through the What *Is* stage at your own risk. Per Lockwood and Papke: "Successful problem solving requires finding the right solution to the right problem. We fail more often because we solve the wrong problem than because we get the wrong solution to the right problem."[12] The components of the What *Is* process are key to ensuring that we identify and solve the right problems.

Empathize and Gather Information from Stakeholders

> *The skills of listening and seeking understanding are key to empathy, the first step in the design thinking process.*[13]

Design thinking is fundamentally human centered in that it privileges the basic human needs of stakeholders and seeks to develop products or services that will improve lives. For design thinkers, empathy is the critical component of human-centered design. Empathy, according to Lockwood and Papke, is "putting yourself in someone else's shoes and understanding how they feel, thereby having the ability to relate to and experience the emotion of another person."[14] As Brown writes, having empathy for others, namely one's stakeholders, ensures that human beings remain at the center of the story.

Empathy is achieved by actively listening to, seeking understanding of, and gathering information from stakeholders—in community colleges, these would include students, faculty, staff, trustees, community members, policy makers, representatives from nearby businesses or industries, local university personnel, and so forth. The designers themselves may also be stakeholders, especially in community colleges, where design teams often include faculty and administrators. In such cases, designers should be careful not to prioritize their perspectives over others' but be equally cautious not to disqualify their own understanding of a given idea or problem.

The process of empathizing with stakeholders in many ways mirrors ethnographic study, as it involves seeking an emotional understanding of what various populations feel, what touches them, motivates them, scares them, and so on.[15] Like ethnography, it involves gathering as much information as possible about the contextual aspects of a given situation; observing real behavior (i.e., how do stakeholders behave in the wild); asking probing questions—including *who* is included in a stakeholder group (its size and characteristics), *why* the stakeholder thinks there is a problem, *what* they propose as a solution or think they need, and *when* and for how long a solution will be needed—and following up on any surprises or unexpected responses.[16] Often, by asking open-ended questions, encouraging stakeholders to tell stories about their lives, and repeatedly asking *why* people think, feel, or believe something, designers can discover latent needs that students, community members, and other populations may not even realize for themselves. Treating faculty and other college personnel as important stakeholders also helps to surface possible points of contention down the road; understanding the emotions and motivations that frequently bind people to the status quo is critical to helping them embrace a different vision of the future.

Identify Unmet Needs and Define the Problem

> *Everything we do is need-based. I don't have CNC [computer numeric control] machines because someone decided, "Oh, let's do CNC!" We have it because businesses in the area were coming*

> *to us and saying, "We don't have enough skilled folks and we've got retirements that are coming up in five to ten years, and we need to find a way to get some people at least up to an entry-level skill so that we can hire them."*[17]

In the process of empathizing with stakeholders, community college design teams will often identify needs that are not being met (or are being met, but poorly, or with negative externalities). As the preceding quote from the director of corporate solutions and economic development at the TCC Opportunity Center illustrates, unmet needs might be simple and well defined—local businesses need more workers trained in precision machining—but more often than not they are poorly defined (the problem itself is unclear, or there may be multiple paths or numerous possible solutions) or they are *wicked* problems. As Michael Lewrick, Patrick Link, and Larry Leifer, authors of *The Design Thinking Playbook* write, wicked problems are characterized by a high degree of uncertainty, multiple paths to a deeper understanding of the problem, and different (sometimes competing) views of what a positive solution might be—plenty of these in community colleges.

All three types of problems are appropriate for the design thinking process, and regardless of type, a community college design team will want to seek a greater understanding of the problem before seeking possible solutions. This can be accomplished by writing down as many potential problem statements as possible, each based on information or perspectives gained from empathizing with stakeholders. To continue with the TCC example, potential problem statements might include:

- There are not enough workers trained in precision machining.
- Companies no longer provide their own CNC training to incumbent workers.
- CNC machines are expensive; community colleges cannot afford to buy and maintain them.
- Young people are no longer looking to manufacturing for jobs; precision machining is not "sexy."

Sharing and discussing possible problem statements is perhaps even more important than selecting a single problem statement on which to focus (although that is the eventual goal), as it ensures that all stakeholders' thoughts and feelings about the problem are accounted for and because the final problem statement will often incorporate numerous perspectives of the issue. During this process, community college design teams may experience aha! moments in which different pieces of the puzzle seem to come together in a new way or things just seem to *click*. Many times, these aha! moments lead to more nuanced and interconnected problem statements.

Draft the Design Brief and Establish Design Criteria

> *The design brief, in short, is the North Star of the project, providing a constant answer to the question, "Where are we headed?"*[18]

The final components of the What *Is* phase include crafting a design brief, establishing design criteria, and making plans for next steps. As Liedtka et al. write, a design brief is "a short write-up that clarifies the project's intent, underlines the questions a team wants to explore ... and postulates what success might look like (though not yet how to get there)."[19] Michael Lewrick and his colleagues put it more simply: "A design brief is the translation of a problem into a structured task."[20] Often, design briefs are crafted at the very beginning of the project and include plans for empathizing with stakeholders and gathering information about a problem. Yet just as frequently they are written after stakeholder input has been received and problem statements evaluated. Both approaches are viable.

Regardless of when it is written, the following questions should be considered in every design brief:

- What is the problem and why is it necessary for your organization to solve it?
- Who is the target population or populations? What other stakeholders will be affected?
- What are your goals?
- What resources can be brought to bear?

- Who might be a competitor?
- What are internal and external constraints?
- When does this need to be accomplished and for how long?
- How will we evaluate possible solutions?
- And, finally, what are the next steps?

In other words, the design brief specifies the parameters of the project. If these are too broad or vague, the project will result in paralysis; there are simply too many facets of the problem to consider. Yet design briefs that are too narrow in scope tend to result only in incremental change. To achieve the right balance of flexibility and specificity, design teams should carefully consider real and perceived project constraints and ask themselves which are important and immutable and which are not. In community colleges, lack of funding and available space are common limitations, as are long-standing college or departmental traditions, but they are rarely immutable and can be reframed as design challenges rather than barriers. Yet other constraints—faculty contracts, legislatively mandated policies, and so forth—may be more rigid; it is important to distinguish between the two.

The design brief should be considered a work in progress, something that can and should be modified over time, but it should also provide enough specificity to ensure clarity and transparency in the management of the project and to "ground its ideas in the lives of their intended beneficiaries."[21] Establishing design criteria—the yardstick by which possible solutions to the problem will be evaluated—is critical to achieving the latter. To identify design criteria, Liedtka et al. suggest posing the question: "If anything were possible, our ideal solution would . . . ?"[22] For community colleges, one of the answers to this question should always be a more specific version of "improve service to students or our community" in order to ensure that possible solutions remain tightly coupled with institutional mission. Other criteria might reference a need for solutions to generate revenue or remain cost neutral, be deployed within a certain time frame, be undertaken in a collaborative and collegial manner, and so forth. Once design criteria are established, the team is ready to move on to the What *If* phase.

WHAT *IF*

In exploring What *If*, designers brainstorm ideas and develop concepts (in other words, they ideate). To many, this feels like the most creative piece of the design thinking process and also the one in which they have the least experience. Some of the exercises may feel silly or extraneous to those used to more linear approaches to solving problems, and there is no shame in admitting discomfort. Yet the more designers can set aside their day-to-day roles (hierarchy has no place in the What *If* process) and experience the excitement of collaborative ideation, the more likely the team will be to converge on a solution or combination of solutions that are truly innovative.

Brainstorm

> *The best way to develop a great idea is to start with a large number of different ideas.*[23]

The What *If* phase of the design thinking process begins with brainstorming solutions to a given problem statement. The purpose of brainstorming is to intentionally generate as many and as varied ideas as possible, from multiple different perspectives, without expectation of viability or feasibility. In this phase, divergent thinking is prioritized: all ideas (no matter how wacky or seemingly impossible) are welcomed, and designers are encouraged to temporarily disregard barriers to implementation, which tend to "constrain problems and restrict choices in favor of the most obvious and incremental."[24] Liedtka and her colleagues encourage design teams to begin brainstorming solutions to a problem through silent, individual idea generation (on paper or sticky notes) before moving on to public sharing, as this ensures that everyone's ideas are considered, not just those of participants who are more comfortable shouting out ideas or taking control of unstructured conversations.

There are numerous techniques for brainstorming and discussing ideas, but none so sticky as the Post-it note (sorry/not sorry for the pun). These colorful, tacky squares are perfect for limiting an initial concept to a few words and for sharing ideas on a wall, board, table, or other large space. They can also be moved around easily, which is quite useful for grouping related ideas, mapping how possible solutions might interrelate, and so forth. Brainstorming (with or without sticky notes) need not be limited to words; quick sketches of ideas or storyboards—visual representations of a scenario, experience, or storyline—are also effective methods for generating ideas.

In addition to brainstorming solutions to a given problem statement, Lewrick et al. offer several other suggestions to get the creative juices flowing. One involves introducing a dark-horse exercise, in which all constraints are lifted and essential elements of a problem are omitted. For example: "How might you build a degree program that doesn't utilize credit hours or grades?" The team would be given an hour to brainstorm what this program might look like and how it would run, after which a facilitator might ask the following questions: "What radical possibilities have not yet been considered? Which solutions are utterly unimaginable in practice? What elements of this solution might be important to keep, even if some constraints (e.g., credit hours) are reintroduced?"

Similar to the dark-horse exercise, the funky prototype technique helps generate and build upon disruptive ideas in order to boost the design team's creativity. In it, a facilitator asks the team to identify one or two of the craziest, coolest ideas brainstormed thus far—those that have clear benefits for target populations—and ignore certain constraints, such as cost of implementation, how it might complement or compete with existing programs, which department or faculty members will have ownership, and so forth. Without considering these potential complications, how might these ideas be implemented? What would they look like? How would they affect students or various groups in the community? What could be done to improve them? This exercise—especially useful among faculty and others who have strong ties to the status quo—forces design teams to prioritize the benefits or potential outcomes of a given idea over barriers to its implementation. Often, designers find that they are more drawn to an off-the-wall idea than they initially thought, and because they are more excited by it, they find it easier to reframe budgetary, workload, and other constraints as design challenges instead of impediments.

The Rules of Brainstorming

> *Brainstorming, ironically, is a structured way of breaking out of structure.*[25]

Effective brainstorming takes practice, and there are rules. The first of these is to encourage wild or out-of-the-box ideas. Even the craziest ideas can lead to aha! moments that may alter the way a design team thinks about a problem, and ultimately, unrestrained thinking about possibilities is necessary for true innovation to occur. The second rule is to defer judgment or suspend disbelief—this applies to one's own ideas as much as the brainstorms of others. Self-censuring can be just as detrimental to idea generation as judging others' contributions.

Rule three: embrace ambiguity. Rarely will an initial idea have received enough thought to have a bullet-point defense against every conceivable hinderance. Nor should it; if only ideas that are fully thought out are allowed in brainstorming sessions, radical new solutions or approaches to a problem are unlikely to emerge. Fourth: stay focused on the topic. It is easy for community college faculty and staff to respond to an idea with "but how will that affect what we are doing over here," but that kind of what-about-ism detracts from the purpose of the original exercise. So does "That brings up a great point; I think a bigger problem is that . . ." Setting boundaries for brainstorming sessions—perhaps designating a space to jot down important but unrelated thoughts—is crucial to their success.

The fifth and most important rule of brainstorming—Tim Brown puts it on the same pedestal as *Thou Shalt Not Kill*—is to build upon the ideas of others. One way to ensure this is to enforce the *yes, and* rule of improv comedy, in which designers accept as true what another designer has stated, and then work to expand upon that idea. In improv, an actor might start a scene by saying, "Hello! Welcome to my store!" The second actor then has a responsibility to accept that he or she has walked into a store and build the plot from there, perhaps by responding: "Oh! I see you sell ladies footwear. Do you have anything in a men's size eleven?" The audience laughs, and the actors continue exploring a congruent—and hopefully funny—story line. If, however, the second actor responded to the first by saying, "This isn't a store, it's an alien planet," the story is no longer congruent (or funny), and the audience is left wondering why they paid $10 to see such terrible improvisors.

The same is true in design thinking; following the *yes, and* rule helps designers maintain congruity in extending initial ideas. It also helps to reframe constraints as design challenges and think creatively about how perceived barriers might be overcome. For example, in brainstorming solutions to a nursing shortage in the community, one faculty member might suggest that the college expand its nursing program to admit the nearly thirty students currently on the wait list. If the other designers respond with "we can't afford to build new simulation rooms or purchase new manikins, let alone hire the faculty to teach these additional students," or "don't you guys know that there is no return on investment for community college nursing programs? We already lose $300,000 per year on ours!" the conversation is over, and the idea is effectively dead.

If, instead, the other designers empathically listen to the faculty member and respond in a *yes, and* manner, the team might start making progress toward a solution. For example, "I agree that it is important for our college to train more nurses to work in the community, but hiring new faculty is expensive: how might we think about collaborating with local hospitals or clinics to jointly employ an instructor?" is a productive response that keeps the initial idea alive. So is "Since the hospital will ultimately benefit from our training more nurses, perhaps they would be willing to donate manikins and other equipment to use in simulated nursing bays." Even "If we are to train more nurses we really need to think about instituting a differential tuition policy so that our nursing program can start to pay for itself" does not kill the initial idea, yet still manages to provide a different perspective.[26]

Develop Concepts

> *In concept development, we take the most innovative ideas from brainstorming and thoughtfully combine them to generate creative bundles of solutions.*[27]

After an initial brainstorming of possible solutions has occurred, design teams will want to identify the best ideas and "synthesize them into packages of solutions that, together, achieve an impact that no single solution could."[28] At this point, designers shift from divergent to convergent thinking; Intuit's design thinkers call this going broad to narrow. The first step is to select ideas to develop further. There are numerous ways of doing this (nearly all assume that solutions or ideas are written or sketched on sticky notes tacked to a large, accessible surface such as the walls of a room). One popular and democratic approach is the butterfly method, in which designers—armed with small stickers or dots—flutter about the room affixing their "votes" to concepts that they believe are deserving of additional consideration. Using different colored dots each time, the butterfly method can also be used to evaluate how possible solutions meet various criteria, such as desirability, viability, and feasibility (desirable ideas get a blue dot, easily feasible solutions a green dot, and so on).

Another method is to organize the solutions according to various criteria. Lewrick and his colleagues suggest that design teams group ideas several different ways, taking note of which solutions appear most frequently in the targeted clusters. For example, ideas might be grouped by the extent to which they match the problem statement; by how exciting, new, and different they are; by their likelihood to generate revenue for the college; by their potential to provide new or greater benefits to students and communities; and so forth. Design teams may also choose to evaluate various ideas by discussing where each solution might be located on a given matrix. Axes of such matrices might include ease of implementation, potential to generate revenue for the college, benefit for students, incremental versus radical, and so on.

Ultimately, all ideas or solutions selected for further consideration should meet the design criteria specified in the What *Is* phase and, in some way, balance desirability (what offers the greatest potential benefits to students or communities), viability (what is likely to become part of a sustainable organizational or business model), and feasibility (what is functionally possible in the foreseeable future).[29] Rarely will any one idea fit perfectly into all three categories; designers will have to embrace some constraints to find the sweet spot that brings them into balance for each possible solution.

Once the team has converged upon a few good ideas, designers work collaboratively to further develop each concept. Brown suggests utilizing the phrase "How Might We . . . ?" to build upon initial ideas. For example, if the idea is to build a new school of public safety for the region, such as that being constructed at Valencia College, designers might ask, "How might we build upon existing fire science and criminal justice programs to create a broader public safety program? How might we work with law enforcement agencies to support students and help pay for their education? How might we access state and local revenues that currently go directly to public safety to help pay for training programs?" "How Might We . . . ?" questions can be incorporated into any phase of the design thinking process but are especially useful at this stage of the game, as they ensure that the creativity practiced in brainstorming sessions is recreated in the process of further developing concepts.

Create Napkin Pitches

> *The term napkin pitch derives from the notion that a good idea can, and should, be communicated simply—as on the back of the napkin.*[30]

The final step in the What *If* phase involves taking the handful of concepts that have been developed and creating what Liedtka and her colleagues call napkin pitches: essentially summaries of new concepts or solutions that follow a standard template so that side-by-side comparisons can be made. Templates can be modified to suit each design team's purposes but will likely include a short description of the idea, why it is needed and/or its benefits, how it will be executed, and the business rationale for it. Napkin pitches serve two purposes. First, they distill the design team's thinking about a given idea. Clearly, not every detail will have been worked out, nor every potential constraint removed, but the team should have clarity about what it is proposing and how it might work. The second purpose of the napkin pitch is to prevent designers from zeroing in on one concept before other stakeholders have had a chance to weigh in and validate (or not) the team's thinking. Returning to the concept of empathy, napkin pitches should be shared with stakeholders—especially those most likely to benefit from or be affected by a proposed idea—in order to gather feedback and ensure that the solutions will indeed have a positive impact on students or communities. Sharing napkin pitches with various groups—faculty, for example—also provides design teams with an early glimpse into where they might meet pockets of resistance as they move toward prototyping and testing their ideas.

Establish Design Teams

> *Empathy coupled with collaboration . . . helps move an organization past silos and toward radical collaboration, rather than incremental improvement.*[31]

Before moving on to the What *Wows* phase, a few words about effective design teams and the importance of creative space. In community colleges, design teams should include a mix of faculty, staff, administrators, and perhaps community partners who are knowledgeable about or will be involved in solving a problem. Simply staffing a project with representatives from diverse backgrounds or various corners of campus is not enough, however; design teams should intentionally utilize individuals who have the capacity and disposition for collaboration across disciplines. Harvard's Dorothy Leonard-Barton named these *T-shaped people*: those with skills and knowledge that are both deep and wide. As Brown writes, T-shaped people possess a "depth of skill that allows [them] to make tangible contributions to the outcome," as well as an ability to empathize and communicate with those from other cultures, disciplines, or systems.[32] T-shaped people make the difference between truly interdisciplinary design teams—in which everybody takes collective ownership of and responsibility for ideas—and multidisciplinary teams, where each individual becomes an advocate for their own specialty or perspective and solutions look more like unhappy compromises than innovative new ideas.

The core design team should be relatively small, perhaps four to six T-shaped people representing the most obvious stakeholder groups (faculty and administrators, for example). Yet the group might swell considerably during brainstorming phases and feedback loops to invite a greater diversity of perspectives and to validate the core team's initial ideas. And, of course, any number of people might be involved in implementing an idea. But throughout much of the What *Is* process, and during the convergence phase of What *If*, smaller teams function more effectively. When tackling more complex, system-level problems, Brown advises creating interdependent networks of small teams, each specializing in a certain aspect of the issue, rather than one large team, as "more often than not this leads to a dramatic reduction in speed and efficiency as communications within the team begin to take up more time than the creative process itself."[33] The iterative and empathic nature of the design thinking process ensures that all stakeholder perspectives and experiences are taken into account, even if not every group has a representative on the core team.

Regardless of who the primary designers are, the goal should be to engage in collaborative decision making and to co-create solutions that benefit students, colleges, and communities. Such collaboration can also reduce the need to secure buy-in from various constituent groups after an idea or solution has been generated, as stakeholder needs have been foregrounded from the start. Lewrick et al. offer several rules for collaboration on interdisciplinary teams. These include formulating a common vision, adopting shared values (these might be based on the brainstorming rules noted previously), respecting the expertise of individual participants, seeking and accepting extensive feedback, and sharing common processes and quality standards.[34]

The Importance of Creative Space

> *Throughout the past two decades, multiple studies have been conducted on the effects of light and nature on human creativity and problem-solving. People in environments with plants, natural light, and better views not only perform better, they also experience less stress.*[35]

Design thinking thrives in creative spaces in which "people know they can experiment, take risks, and explore the full range of their faculties."[36] Design teams should have access to project rooms that look and feel quite different from the offices in which they carry out day-to-day duties—and that can be left in various states of creative disarray while designers develop concepts. Open space for participants to move around and kinetically work through ideas is essential, and thus chairs, tables and other furnishings should be mobile or stackable. Chairs of different heights, including bar stools, are useful for people who think best on their feet, as are height-adjustable workstations. And whiteboards, windows, or glass walls on which designers can jot down ideas, comments, sketches, and storyboards should be plentiful. Plants, views, and natural light have all been shown to increase creativity, and coffee, water, and other refreshments provide fuel as well as a way to take short breaks without losing too much momentum.

Project rooms or designated spaces for creative collaboration should also include basic supplies to aid in brainstorming and developing concepts. These include sticky notes in various colors and sizes, whiteboard markers, adhesive dots or stickers, tape to hang flip charts or storyboards, and markers, pens, and pencils to write or draw with. Balls to toss or toys to fidget with can help kinetically minded people generate new ideas, and Legos, Play-Doh, colored sheets of paper, string, pipe cleaners, and other crafts are not only useful in prototyping ideas, but can also help get the creative juices flowing during other phases of the process.

WHAT *WOWS*

After receiving feedback on the napkin pitches shared with stakeholders in the What *If* phase, designers seek to figure out What *Wows* by iteratively prototyping and modifying solutions to the problem at hand and, ultimately, seeking a balance between what the stakeholders want, what the college can deliver, and what is economically sustainable over time.

Prototype and Surface Assumptions

> *A successful prototype is not one that works flawlessly; it is one that teaches us something—about our objectives, our processes, ourselves.*[37]

Prototyping involves quickly and inexpensively testing the assumptions underlying various ideas, setting up an iterative process in which ideas fail, are refined, fail again, and so forth. Brown calls prototyping *thinking with your hands*. It should be quick, cheap, and dirty: the point is not to build a beautiful model of the solution with all its associated bells and whistles; it is to make an idea tangible so potential users and other stakeholders can react and provide feedback as soon as possible.

The prototyping phase often begins with designers reviewing their napkin pitches and identifying the assumptions underlying each one. In other words, what would need to be true to make each solution a good idea? How does the concept create value for students or communities? How might it help generate new revenue for the college, mitigate costs, or improve internal processes? How might the solution be implemented in practice, and how could it be scaled and sustained over time? These thought experiments will likely utilize readily available data and can help designers learn more about how an idea might function in practice.

Step two involves making and executing a plan to prototype and test the ideas in progressively more realistic ways. At first, prototypes will use the simplest available materials and be created in as little time as possible. Ensuing prototypes might incorporate more complexity and require a bit more time to plan and develop. Prototypes can take many forms. As Brown writes, "[P]rototypes need to be testable, but they do not need to be physical."[38] While they might be made of cardboard, Play-Doh, Legos, or other cheap and easy to build materials, prototypes can also be sketches or mock-ups of ideas. They can be illustrated through improvisation, role-playing, or acting out scenarios; by storyboards of student experiences or descriptions of a customer journey; by illustrations or summaries of a business concept; and through short movies that describe an idea. Liedtka et al. believe that in designing solutions to problems faced by public and social-sector organizations, visual or narrative approaches to prototyping—images, stories, and skits—provide "vivid experience[s] of a new future," and thus are enormously successful in eliciting accurate stakeholder feedback.[39]

Prototyping organizational structures such as a new noncredit training program can sometimes be difficult because of their interconnectedness with existing structures and traditions. For all prototypes, but especially these, it is essential to visualize multiple options and create choices for the stakeholder. This can be accomplished by role-playing various scenarios and asking users to select which option they like best. It can also be achieved by setting up a sample office, classroom, or other space (perhaps using cardboard boxes as tables, desks, or large machines, bedsheets as walls, and so forth) and asking potential students, faculty, and staff to utilize it as they would in their daily lives. Designers can then shift the makeshift equipment and walls around and ask stakeholders to interact in different ways to gather feedback about what works best. These prototyping activities can be incredibly useful in allowing stakeholders to *pre-experience* a new program or offering, which not only provides designers with a more accurate sense of what excites users, but also indicates areas where the team might experience resistance from various groups.

Mitigate Risk by Failing Fast

> *The risk of an iterative approach is that it appears to extend the time it takes to get an idea to market, but this is often a shortsighted perception . . . fail early, succeed sooner.*[40]

There is a tendency to speed through the prototyping phase in order to generate results faster, but this is ersatz logic. Prototypes "slow us down to speed us up. By taking the time to prototype our ideas, we avoid costly mistakes such as becoming too complex too early and sticking with a weak idea for too long."[41] Most often, prototypes fail in small, modifiable ways that provide opportunities for the design team to learn and make important course corrections. Yet, sometimes when prototyping an idea, designers will realize that their hypothesis does not hold up as expected in the real world. This can be a blow, especially if the team has become emotionally attached to the idea, but as Liedtka and her colleagues point out, "exposing and disconfirming false assumptions may be the most valuable activity of all," as it allows designers to abandon or radically change a bad idea before investing too much time, effort, and money. [42] Lewrick and his coauthors have a motto: "love it, change it, or leave it." [43] Sometimes walking away from what you thought was a great idea is actually the best way to arrive at a solution that can drastically improve service to students or communities. There is nothing wrong with failure as long as it happens early and becomes a source of learning.

Gather Feedback through Rapid Experiments with Stakeholders

> *Prototype in hand, you now return to your key stakeholders to seek their feedback. Seek, and hear—especially the bad news. If your prototype is crude, they will fill the "emptiness" with ideas on how to improve it.* [44]

Asking for feedback on prototypes can occur in myriad ways. One simple approach is to ask stakeholders to finish two sentences: "What I like about the prototype is . . ." and "I wish that the prototype . . ." This method ensures that the design team elicits both positive and critical feedback about the idea. Another approach is to ask stakeholders, especially college faculty and students, probative follow-up questions such as, "Can you talk about how this feels to you?" or "How might we improve this so that it works better for you?" In all likelihood, these types of questions will be asked numerous times as the team iteratively rethinks and refines its prototype.

In asking for feedback, it is important to observe stakeholder reactions at least as much as you listen to their words; nonverbal cues and body language often provide important insights into how the prototype affects peoples' lives. Design teams should also turn their powers of observation inward: Lewrick et al. suggest using a feedback capture grid to document how designers' own thinking evolves during the prototyping phase. As they iteratively test ideas, teams should be continuously asking themselves: What do we like (what resonates with stakeholders)? What wishes do we have (constructive criticism)? What questions keep cropping up? And what ideas were generated during prototyping and testing this idea with others? This grid—which can be drawn on a whiteboard and populated with sticky notes—will evolve throughout the prototyping phase; taking a photograph of it after each experiment can help design teams document their progress and identify when their stakeholders become as invested in the idea as they are. When this occurs, teams are ready to create what Liedtka and her colleagues call a *learning launch*: essentially a final, detailed prototype that is ready to be tested under real-world conditions. There's more on this in the What *Works* section, but first, a few words about how design teams might deal with stakeholder resistance.

Dealing with Resistance

> *No one knows, or perhaps can even anticipate, what will stall the innovation process when there are vocal and diverse stakeholders, competing definitions of the problem, entrenched politics, and risk aversion at play.*[45]

Design thinking gurus talk a lot about the *pull factor*: the sense of empowerment that comes with participating in a design thinking project, either as a core team member or an involved stakeholder. Kevin Lee, Visa's vice president and head of design, described it thusly: "Once they experience design thinking, people get evangelized and converted."[46] Yet as powerful as design thinking's pull factor may be, it is not a panacea for creating change in complex social-sector organizations such as community colleges, and not all stakeholders will immediately become converts to a new idea, especially one that bucks long-standing traditions or ways of serving students or communities. Resistance is to be expected and can come from both anticipated and surprising corners. For example, a design team might justifiably predict that some faculty will resist a new approach to training students that falls outside traditional credit-based degree programs because the new courses might compete with existing sequences or because they will be taught by instructors from industry rather than college faculty, which could endanger professors' livelihoods. The design team will likely have encountered many of these reservations during the stakeholder discovery process, but it might not have considered that back-office staff may also push back on the idea, as it would mean asking already overextended personnel to create completely new administrative forms and processes. Dealing with resistance—from faculty, staff, or others—is never fun, but finding ways to allay stakeholder concerns about a new program or process is key to ensuring that the idea can be implemented and sustained in the long term. In other words, the more designers can welcome critiques and reframe opposition as constructive feedback, the more likely their idea is to survive.

A common form of resistance to new ideas in community colleges is what Lewrick and his coauthors call the "Not Invented Here Syndrome," in which those not involved in the development of a certain idea disregard it—either because they already have their own ideas about how to solve the problem or because they believe the idea is not transferrable to their campus, program, student body, and so on. Not Invented Here resistors can be incredibly frustrating—especially if it feels as if they are pushing back on an idea just because it didn't originate with them—but it is important not to dismiss them outright, as often they surface obstacles to implementing or scaling a solution that the design team may not have considered. Valencia's president, Sandy Shugart, commented:

> There are issues in design that really are seen differently by people in different contexts, and they need to design for those differences if they can. So for example, if you design something on West Campus and think it's going to spread to Osceola, but you haven't counted on the fact that 40 percent of the students are heavy Spanish speakers because that's not true [at West] . . . Or if you're Osceola and you are designing a summer bridge program . . . around the Latino community and the community organizations that support youth there, and you haven't included the Boys and Girls Clubs because that's kind of more [influential] up here at West, you have totally missed the boat.

Because resistance to new ideas is a given, design teams in the prototyping phase of their project would be well served to identify who might put obstacles in the path of a new idea and involve them in brainstorming, testing, and providing feedback. This way, even if those stakeholders remain nonplussed about the solution in general, they will feel as though their objections have been heard and—hopefully—they will see how the idea evolved in response to their concerns. For example, Valencia College recently entered into an agreement with CFE Credit Union to be the institution's preferred financial partner. The contract stipulated that Valencia would put a CFE branch on one of its campuses, and in return CFE would pay the college and teach financial literacy skills to Valencia students. To Jeff Filko, Valencia's director of auxiliary services, the agreement seemed like a win-win. But he ran into resistance from numerous faculty and student development staffers when he suggested bringing CFE representatives to new student orientations in order to introduce the students to the credit union and to provide some basic financial literacy tips. "Traditionally there is nothing commercial" at these orientations, he was told. But "CFE is paying us to do this!" he replied. "CFE is paying us for the privilege of providing these student services!" Despite believing that this arrangement would ultimately benefit Valencia's students, Filko understood why his colleagues were wary and backed off his plan until college stakeholders felt more comfortable with the CFE collaboration.

The key to overcoming resistance to an entrepreneurial idea, said Kathleen Plinske, Valencia's executive vice president and provost, is highlighting the values that you share with your stakeholders and illustrating how those principles are aligned with the new initiative:

> I think that working from a place of meeting students' needs and the community's needs is really critical. We have always been able to say . . . "That feels like Valencia," or "That doesn't feel like Valencia." I think that you could very quickly lose your institutional culture if it ever feels like it's a money grab. And so things like our accelerated skills training program, no one says, "Oh, that's just about getting revenue." That is never part of the conversation because it's so clear what community

need that we're trying to meet. And then similarly with our partnerships with employers. I mean, we have to do things that make sense financially, but at the same time we're working with a partner to meet a need, not just go after dollars.

As Plinske indicated, reiterating *why* you are doing what you are doing—clearly communicating to stakeholders how the idea connects to the college's mission to serve students or communities—can help to quell resistance, as can acknowledging stakeholder fears and asking them to suggest ways to accomplish the objective that may be better aligned with their lived experiences. Chapter 6 offers several examples of how community colleges have used these and other tactics to overcome opposition from faculty and others on campus.

WHAT *WORKS*

In *Design Thinking for the Greater Good*, Liedtka et al. conceptualize the What *Works* process as an extension of the What *Wows* phase, a continuation of the iterative prototyping and testing phase leading up to full-scale execution of the new idea. In their book, constructing learning launches and planning for implementation—what the authors call designing the on-ramp—are the primary components of What *Works*. I think it is also important, however, to more broadly consider how a college's organizational structure, culture, and relationships may affect the long-term success and sustainability of any new initiatives. As such, I include the role of college leaders—especially as it relates to the cultivation of an entrepreneurial culture and the development of external partnerships—as a critical element of this phase of the design thinking process.

Run Learning Launches and Design the On-Ramp

> *The most accurate kind of experiments are live, 4-D experiments conducted in the real world by offering higher-fidelity prototypes. We call these experiments "learning launches."*[47]

As the preceding quote illustrates, learning launches can be considered the final prototype of an idea. They involve exposing the concept to as many different stakeholders as possible, over longer periods of time (perhaps thirty to ninety days), in order to "determine whether your napkin pitches will fly in the real world."[48] Though similar to pilot studies or initial roll-outs, design teams will want to stress the *learning* that comes from learning launches. This is not the first phase of implementation; it is the last phase of testing the team's assumptions and ensuring that the solution still meets the design criteria established back in What *Is.* Liedtka and her colleagues suggest that design teams plan a series of learning launches—each specifying concrete variables such as length of time, number of stakeholders, features, and geography—and refine each launch based on what was learned in the previous one. Ultimately, they write: "Learning launches result in decisions. If you decide to move ahead with the additional development, the learning launch should tell you how. Continue your learning launches until all issues and assumptions have been addressed (and, you hope, solved) and you're ready to move into implementation."[49]

The next step, of course, is designing the on-ramp for the new idea and generating awareness of and—hopefully—excitement for it. Similar to a marketing plan, designers seek a strategy to make users aware of how the new concept meets their needs, convince them to give it a try, and in an ideal world, become advocates for it. This likely means sending emails and newsletters to faculty and staff on campus letting them know about the forthcoming new process, program, and so on; advertising the offering to various student and community groups online and in publications that reach the target populations; meeting with businesses or communities that can help market the new initiative; giving a "heads-up, this is rolling out soon" to back-office personnel and other staff who will need to provide administrative support for the new program; and so forth.

After a year or more of working through the design thinking process and seeking feedback from numerous stakeholders, a team might reasonably expect that most people on campus know about their new concept, but due to the fragmented and specialized nature of community college work, this is frequently not the case. For example, Terry Allcorn, dean of business and hospitality at Valencia College, and his team spent nearly three years designing and planning for the implementation of a new bachelor's degree program in business. Finally, the courses were added to the catalog, and just before the program launched, Allcorn sent an email to all faculty: "Hey, just want to let you know that we are launching! This is very exciting, and please let your students know that when they finish their AA or AS they can come into our degree program." He was shocked by the number of responses he received along the lines of: "This is amazing! I never heard of this!" As Allcorn related, "Undoubtedly many of these were part-time faculty, but they stand in front of at least one classroom of people and had no idea that their students had a bachelor's degree option when they finished their AS or AA."

Similarly, Allcorn and his team realized a little late that they probably should have sent out a notification when their new program was added to the course catalog. They didn't think to do so because in their minds, "Who's reading the catalog anyway?" But after bachelor's degree applications increased something like 700 percent when the new bachelor's of applied science in business and organizational leadership launched, they realized that they should have given a heads-up to back-office staff who would need to add the program to the college's IT systems, make sure it appeared on the change of major form, and so forth. Were he given an opportunity to redesign his program's on-ramp, Allcorn said, "I think what I would do differently is that I would find a way to communicate more."

Role of College Leaders

> *What is needed is a serious commitment from the top of the corporate pyramid, and it will be repaid by better ideas from the base. Any promising experiment should have a chance to gain organizational support in the form of a project sustained by appropriate resources and driven by definable goals.*[50]

Design thinking is often conceptualized as a grassroots approach to innovation and change, but the process can only flourish when college leaders buy into it, advocate for it, and reward faculty and staff for engaging in it. As Lockwood and Papke write, "The level of commitment and support shown by leaders for the use and integration of design thinking . . . is *the* key factor to success."[51] College leaders can support design thinking within their organizations by role-modeling and reinforcing associated behaviors, including using empathy to understand the experiences of others; demonstrating an ability to be vulnerable or wrong; accepting failure as a necessary component of learning and organizational growth; relying on the wisdom and insight of others instead of always knowing best; and focusing on creating mutual benefit for students, faculty, staff, and other college stakeholders. College leaders can also support design thinking—and the innovations that result—by establishing incentives for collaboration across business units; by integrating design thinking into faculty professional development and leadership development opportunities; and by providing funding and organizational support for design teams at all stages of the process. As Brown writes, effective leaders help their employees see collaboration and innovation "as a path to success rather than as a career risk."[52] Finally, college leaders can develop partnerships with nearby businesses and community organizations in order to mitigate costs of new or existing programs, provide scholarship and other support for students, and expand into new workforce training verticals. These partnerships should be structured in ways that provide mutual benefits to students, communities, partner organizations, and the colleges themselves.

Cultivating an Entrepreneurial Culture

> *Design thinking, like other ideas and strategic solutions, can fail. In the vast majority of cases, this is not the result of them being bad ideas. Rather, they fail to stick because they do not fit the culture of the organization or are not implemented in a manner that aligns with the organization.*[53]

As the preceding quote indicates, design thinking and the innovations it produces must be adapted to meet the culture of an organization or that culture will eat it for lunch. But design thinking can also be utilized to shift a college's culture to one that is more entrepreneurial, innovative, and tolerant of organizational change. Much has been written about how corporations can utilize design thinking to create cultures of optimism and innovation—Lockwood and Papke offer a set of twelve considerations; Lewrick and his associates list seven—but at the core of cultural transformation is a commitment to practicing what you preach and creating opportunities to innovate and lead from any corner of the organization. Doing so, as Kate Smith, interim president of Rio Salado College, learned, is infectious:

> When I stepped in, I started meeting with every department right away and I would ask them, "Share something you like about your job." Then I would ask, "What would you do if you were president?" to try to learn from their lens. "What do we need attention on? What don't I know? What are the things that you see as really important?" And it was so interesting to meet with facilities and have them talk about how they really miss the days when Rio was pushing the envelope and doing all of these innovative things! And listening to the guy who is painting and the plumber and all these people who were a part of that . . . This culture loves feeling like they are all a part of something that's a little on the edge.

Entrepreneurial, innovative cultures are exciting. They empower all sorts of people to identify and focus on what is important and to seek new ways to do it better. Perhaps the most important step in creating an entrepreneurial community college, then, is teaching all employees—faculty and staff, full-time and contingent—to think like design thinkers, to role-model what that looks like, and to create a culture that values, supports, and rewards an entrepreneurial mind-set. As this mind-set becomes more deeply ingrained in the college culture, more and more faculty and staff will take risks to create something different that has a positive impact on students or communities, and more of their ideas will be successful and sustainable over time.

WHY DESIGN THINKING?

> *People feel threatened by work they think is going to disrupt their job. You have to help them to see themselves in the future . . . use their stories, their insight, and their expertise so that they hear their voices reflected in the future state. You co-create so that they feel like they helped build this new model. There's an old adage that change is painful when done to you but powerful when done by you. If you can just tap into that, you're golden.*[54]

This book recommends design thinking as a framework for practicing entrepreneurship in community colleges, but there is substantial overlap between design thinking and creative problem solving, the four stages of design (often used in architecture), the Entrepreneurial Learning Initiative's (ELI's) eight mind-set lessons, and the Kern Family Foundation's Entrepreneurial Engineering Program, which foregrounds curiosity, connections, and creating value as the central elements of an entrepreneurial mind-set. Indeed, the four colleges highlighted here all utilize one or more of these processes to guide their entrepreneurial efforts, at times drawing from more than one framework at a time. For example, Valencia College's Collaborative Design Center (described in detail in chapter 5) pulls from both design thinking and creative problem solving to guide groups through the design process. Sandy Shugart bases many of his processes on architecture's four stages of design, which as he described, guides designers through identifying what they want to accomplish (architectural program), ideating various ways to achieve that goal (schematic design), developing the idea further (design development), and finally, figuring out how to implement it (construction drawings).

Similarly, NIACC president Steven Schulz sees a lot of crossover between design thinking and continuous quality improvement (CQI) as it has been practiced by the Higher Learning Commission colleges for years. As he and his colleagues work to instill an entrepreneurial mind-set across campus (see chapter 5), they are pulling from design thinking, CQI, ELI's teachings, and the Entrepreneurial Engineering Program, not only stressing the commonalities across all of these approaches, but also utilizing their various perspectives to attract faculty and staff who may not initially see how their disciplines or day-to-day responsibilities align with entrepreneurial thinking.

So why utilize design thinking and not one of these other frameworks? The short answer is, you don't have to. Follow whatever processes make the most sense to you, can be most easily integrated into your college's culture, and result in improved (and sustainable) ways of serving students and communities. Furthermore, follow the examples set at NIACC and Valencia and incorporate elements from several different approaches into design projects as needed to engage stakeholders and achieve desired outcomes. With that said, because design thinking in many ways mirrors all of these processes, and because Liedtka et al.'s four-question framework is simple and easy to use in complex social-sector organizations such as community colleges, I find it to be a practical and unintimidating way to introduce the concepts of entrepreneurship and innovation to sometimes reluctant audiences. Furthermore, because design thinking forces institutions to relentlessly empathize with students, faculty, community members, and other stakeholders and keep their needs at the center of any new idea, it ensures that all solutions are closely aligned with the college's mission.

Design thinking has numerous other advantages as well. One major benefit lies in its ability to eliminate aspects of the innovation process that are frequently burdensome. As educator Peter Boylan points out, design thinking eliminates the need to ensure buy-in from stakeholders once a product or idea has been developed, as stakeholder needs have been foregrounded from the beginning. Similarly, there is less of a need to sell the idea to constituents; because they were involved in the ideation and prototyping processes, stakeholders have already pre-experienced the benefits and drawbacks of the idea and have provided input into how it can be improved—this may be especially powerful for college faculty. Of course, the final program or idea may not look exactly like what stakeholders were expecting, but because the design thinking process is transparent and inclusive, constituents will be able to see how their needs have translated to the new venture.

As Liedtka and her colleagues explain, design thinking also addresses critical flaws in the decision-making process:

> These flaws include overoptimism (the planning fallacy), inability to see disconfirming data (hypothesis confirmation bias), attachment to early solutions (endowment effect), and a preference for the easily imagined (availability bias). Design thinking's hypothesis-driven approach mitigates the impact of these biases by stipulating that innovators develop multiple concepts, create prototypes, surface unarticulated assumptions, and actively seek disconfirming data.[55]

Design thinking also helps to manage conflict, especially in distributed and specialized organizations in which certain groups may feel that their work is not valued or that they do not have a voice in shared governance. Per Lockwood and Papke:

> Design thinking is a valued process for confronting disagreements and misalignments among functions, and their leaders, and effectively breaking down unhealthy silos ... Because design thinking is a way of leading with curiosity ... people come to understand the value of listening to one another, allowing for the creative process of building one idea upon another ... a necessary element in effectively resolving conflict.[56]

Design thinking's ability to resolve intra-organizational conflict is one reason why Lockwood and Papke believe that it is a lasting approach to transformational change. Other reasons include the fact that it is occupation independent, that it works (!), that it links to our basic needs as humans and helps fill some big gaps in education, and that it can be applied to any kind of problem. Furthermore, the results of design thinking can be measured, the process can be applied across an organization, and as they write, "[I]t's pretty cheap to do, and can save lots of money too."[57]

Perhaps the greatest advantage of design thinking as a framework for mission-oriented change, however, lies in its ability to engage the collective imagination and involve all community college constituents—faculty and staff, students and community members, businesses and universities—

in imagining and creating a future that is not confined to the realm of what has always been done but is instead grounded in local needs and limitless in possibility. The idea is intoxicating. William Coppola, president of TCC's Southeast Campus, described it thusly:

> What I always found in making transformational change . . . is really just being transparent and letting people know why you are doing what you are doing. It's very comfortable sitting in your office and having these students come to you, but . . . it's a whole new world. We know that 65 percent of positions need some type of postsecondary degree, credit or noncredit. We know that 70 percent of the jobs in 2030 don't exist yet. Third-graders today, the jobs they will go into don't exist. It's really about educating folks about the responsibility we have to serve that population, and what that does, it creates more value with what they do. And once the value-add is clear, people really feel like "I have something to contribute; I'm not just here to collect my paycheck and teach my class." They get energized. They feel like: "This is mine."

PART II

Stories from the Field

4 : Exploring What *Is*

When somebody comes to me and says, "Hey! I've got that great idea!" the first thing I'm gonna ask is: have you talked to your customers and is this what they want? Go find a problem before you ask them if this is the solution. Because their problem is not going to be what you think it is.[1]

Good ideas—especially those that have the potential to transform the lives of students and communities—do not emerge out of the ether. They develop from a willingness to examine the human needs of college and community stakeholders and the courage to focus the magnifying glass on ourselves, asking if our institutions have or might develop the capacity to meet those needs in new or different ways. As the authors of *Design Thinking for the Greater Good* remind us, transformational change begins by asking What *Is*.[2] This chapter offers four stories of how Valencia College, TCC, NIACC, and the Maricopa Community Colleges have implemented components of this first phase of the design thinking process—empathizing with stakeholders, identifying unmet needs, defining problems, and establishing design criteria—as they seek to serve students and communities in entrepreneurial ways. The diversity of these stories reflects the varied nature of community college work, but the commonalities among them—an emphasis on stakeholder inclusivity, a gradual shift toward third-wave entrepreneurship, and the sense that community colleges are vehicles for solving community problems—are striking. Two of these shared approaches—an unwavering adherence to institutional mission in setting design criteria and a reconceptualization of service to community—are considered in detail at the end of the chapter, as they undergird all four colleges' ability to remain mission-oriented in pursuit of entrepreneurial opportunity.

A TALE OF TWO CITIES: IMPETUS FOR VALENCIA'S CENTERS FOR ACCELERATED TRAINING

> *The soft underbelly of our economy isn't just that there are people in low-wage jobs; it's that people are stuck in low-wage jobs and can't get out of them.*[3]

Valencia College kicked off its 2014 strategic planning process by asking: "What is the intersection between Valencia's capacity to serve and our community's most significant vulnerability or problem, or most precious aspiration? Where do those things intersect?"[4] President Sandy Shugart knew, of course, that there would be a thousand "good things to do," and that everyone would "want their pet project to be recognized in the plan." But he held firm to the notion that the college's intention needed to be focused on the *impact* of a given idea: what impact would it have on students, and perhaps more importantly, what would be the impact on the community? In asking these questions, he forced his colleagues to seek greater understanding of the unmet needs in the surrounding area and use those as starting points for generating possible solutions. He shared, "If we don't answer the question, 'What is the intersection between their need and our capacity?' we've missed the boat." Shugart described the process of developing Valencia's impact plan this way:

> We looked at a number of problems, and the one that came to the surface we called "A Tale of Two Cities." It was an analysis that showed tremendous prosperity and growth in high-wage, high-skill jobs and the economy they generate, largely in technological areas. But also

> business services, manufacturing. Manufacturing here is much more robust than people imagine, but it's in a space that doesn't try to garner attention because it's largely military. Laser photonics, simulation, software development, like that. All that is huge. A third of our payroll is in that area.
>
> But you've also got this other part of the economy . . . We knew we had a lot of low-wage people. We knew we had a lot of low-wage jobs, and we knew that they didn't sustain very well . . . But we discovered that the issue wasn't just that they were low wage, it's that the jobs are contingent. And so the problem with contingent jobs is that they get interrupted, a lot. About one-third of all hourly employees in America . . . have their work involuntarily disrupted for three months a year, or more. So even if you're making $15 an hour and you can make it paycheck to paycheck, once the paycheck stops you tumble into oblivion.
>
> So we said, okay, that's the problem . . . how would we solve the problem? We have taught ourselves what strategic thinking means, and it begins with a working theory of reality. What's your theory about what happened? And our theory was that while it's okay for people to start work at $9 an hour parking cars or whatever, it's not okay to stay there. And what keeps them there is not the cost of education, it's the *opportunity cost of education*. What could we do about that?

As Shugart's story illustrates, Valencia faculty and administrators experienced three crucial revelations about their community—one might call them problem statements: (1) There is a growing high-wage, high-skill sector of the local economy that needs more trained workers than are being produced. (2) Although low wages are themselves a problem, the contingent nature of many low-wage jobs is actually a bigger threat to the economic stability of families. Indeed, as Shugart pointed out, most part-time workers have no sick pay or leave, no personal or vacation days, no job training, and no pathways to promotion. Furthermore, only 3.1 percent of those employed full-time for at least a year are considered "working poor," compared to 12.2 percent of part-time workers.[5] (3) The direct costs of training programs—fees and materials—are less consequential to potential students than the opportunity costs of enrolling in traditional degree or certificate programs, which take at least two years to complete. "We learned that," Shugart said, "by looking at the proprietary sector. Why are people paying $5,500 for this thing we do for $500? And the answer was, because they can! There is somebody wanting to pay it" because they think it will lead directly to a better-paying job and they won't have to spend years in school first.

The final puzzle piece that shaped what would eventually become Valencia's Centers for Accelerated Training (CATs) emerged from intensive study of the local Orlando economy, which in the early 2010s was in a period of transition. Shugart and his team theorized that if they could understand the nature of this change, they might uncover new opportunities for the college. As he shared:

> We've got a moment in history . . . where there are such pervasive shortages of skilled people that employers are going to be willing to be a lot more innovative . . . they are going to try stuff. And the first thing they began to do was unbundle jobs. So when I was a kid, my dad built a house. He hired two guys who were master masons, and they built everything. They could do corners, door jambs, chimney flues, rock, stone, brick, lock, tile, they did it all. They were master craftsmen.
>
> If you go to a house-building site now, you'll see ten guys that can lay brick to the line. That's all they know how to do. And they bring a guy in to finish the corners and door jambs. They unbundled the jobs. And turns out, you can teach a guy to lay brick to the line in about two or three weeks. And while he's not a master craftsman, he makes $12.50 or $13 an hour, which is a lot better than $9. So we started looking for examples like that and we found them everywhere. And the notion of accelerated skills training was borne out of that theory. The theory is that we have a lot of people stuck in low-wage jobs. They can be rapidly skilled to get better jobs. They won't be fabulous jobs; they will be better jobs. Give them economic mobility. And they can do it time and time again if the opportunity cost is low enough.

With these realizations in mind, Joe Battista, Valencia's executive vice president for global, professional, and continuing education, and Carolyn McMorran, assistant vice president for professional and continuing education, began holding brainstorming sessions with industry leaders and thinking about how they could build short-term training into existing associate of science degrees in advanced manufacturing. "What we were told in conversations with industry," Battista related, was, "'You can do what you're doing, but that only gets the student to a 20,000-foot level.' We said, 'Okay, what gets them down to the ground level?' 'Well, you've got to give them a lot of hands-on training. And they've got to have experience.' And we're like, 'Okay, I can do the hands-on, but how do you intend for us to give them the experience?'" What the team learned from industry representatives in manufacturing, construction, and other skilled trades is that what they really wanted was high school students and recent graduates to spend years learning the trades through apprenticeships. Shugart recalled one conversation with the local Associated Builders and Contractors association:

> For the first hour and a half [the conversation] was about "We've got to get more high school kids interested in the trades." And it's a conversation that's been going on since the 1940s, unsuccessfully. And we listened and listened and listened. We were trying to be diplomatic, and finally I asked one of the plumbing guys, I said, "So how long is this apprenticeship that you want to enroll more young men in?" And he said, "It's five or six years depending on when you start it." And I said, "What do they make at the end of that?" "$14.50 an hour." "Well," I said, "nobody in his right mind would do that! It's idiotic!"

Understanding that a five- or six-year apprenticeship presented even more opportunity cost to students than a two-year degree program, Battista and his team came back to their industry partners and offered a solution: "What happens if there is so much significant hands-on training that it really kind of counts for the experience?" With the partners willing to give this model a try, Battista's team put in for a federal Trade Adjustment Assistance to Community College and Career Training (TAACCCT) grant to build an Advanced Manufacturing Training Center in recently renovated manufacturing space near the college's Osceola Campus, and soon and began developing short-term (six- to twenty-week) programs in CNC, electronic board assembly, mechatronics, and welding.

These accelerated skills training programs offer students stackable credentials and "clear pathways to increase career and economic mobility, [as] the sequence of credentials can be accumulated over time to build an individual's qualification and help them continue to move up in a specific career pathway to higher-paying jobs."[6] For example, McMorran noted that while employment of welders in the greater Orlando area is expected to grow roughly 5 percent over the next ten years, and graduates of Valencia's twenty-week Welding I program are highly coveted, "most students leave Welding I and go to Welding II because the number of additional certifications that you're going to receive is huge. And it also drastically changes your starting pay." Yet because the programs are unbundled, students can always enter the workforce after Welding I and come back for Welding II when they are ready to upskill.

Each of Valencia's accelerated programs is 60 to 70 percent hands-on and includes both simulation training and experience with the actual machinery students will encounter in the workplace. McMorran credited the Advanced Manufacturing Training Center's emphasis on simulation as one reason for its success: "If you crash the computer, I don't care. If you crash this [the CNC machine], I do care! So we limit that ability. And what's really great about crashing it on the simulator is they get to go back and see where they screwed up."

Since building the accelerated training programs in advanced manufacturing, Valencia College has identified unmet needs in other industries and created short-term courses in construction and maintenance, clinical medical assisting, and transportation and logistics, and has established two additional CAT locations on the Poinciana and Osceola campuses (with a third planned for downtown Orlando). All accelerated training programs lead to industry-recognized certifications and provide "an opportunity for individuals to earn family sustaining wages immediately upon graduation and enter the workforce in less than six months."[7] Nearly all of the specializations have been developed in partnership with local employers who contribute financially to the programs, donate equipment, provide tuition assistance to students, and—perhaps most importantly—"come in and literally hire all of our graduates."[8]

One of the most innovative aspects of Valencia's accelerated training programs emerged from the design team's understanding of and empathy for the communities the CATs serve. In designing the programs, said Executive Vice President and Provost Kathleen Plinske, the team had two major realizations. First, she said, "At some point you saturate the market for a particular thing. There are only so many folks living in one zip code that are going to go through basic construction training." Second, "One of the challenges we have with our traditional credit programs is that they tend to be campus-based. If you live in Poinciana and you want to study film, sound, and music, you might as well be going to Miami or Gainesville. It's [so] long of a commute that it's not possible" for community college students, who are largely place-bound. "It's very frustrating as a campus leader," she added, "when you have students who want to study a certain thing and they can't."

For Valencia's advanced training programs to be sustainable over time, and for them to be accessible to students across the college's expansive service area, the team realized that it needed to create mobile units that could make the programs "essentially on demand in a community where the need is greatest."[9] Today, most of the advanced training programs are mobile, even those involving heavy machinery, thanks to portable CNC machines, mobile and virtual welding machines, and so forth. "And," Shugart noted, "we have multiple sites that we swirl the programs through so that students aren't asked . . . to commute an hour. It'll be in your neighborhood in a couple of months." And for those programs that cannot be taken on the road (such as those that utilize multiple heavy machines), Valencia is exploring opportunities for students to complete roughly 80 percent of the training at a neighborhood location, then providing transportation to the Advanced Manufacturing Training Center for the remaining 20 percent of hands-on work. By designing the accelerated training programs to be mobile, the college ensures that certain locations are not saturated with prospective new hires who have the same skills and can "target neighborhoods where members experience accessibility challenges to training."[10]

Valencia's CATs have proven to be a successful solution to the problem statements identified in the college's 2014 impact plan, as they provide local employers with roughly a thousand skilled workers for unbundled, high-demand occupations each year, create opportunities for students to earn substantially higher wages (between $15 and $23 per hour) in full-time jobs with benefits, and put students to work in less than six months, drastically reducing the opportunity costs associated with traditional college degree and certificate programs. The direct costs of accelerated training programs—$4,000 to $7,000, depending upon the length of the course and materials required—are not (in most cases) eligible for state subsidy or financial aid, but can be offset by veterans benefits, grants, and tuition assistance provided through CareerSource Central Florida, the Valencia Foundation, other community foundations, and various industry partners. Students can also apply for Sallie Mae loans to help finance their training. As Shugart hypothesized, these fee levels are low enough that they "don't scare anybody," but high enough to cover CAT operating costs and even return a small profit to the college. Over time, Battista and his team hope to operate the accelerated training programs at a 50 percent margin in order to support overall college functioning and infrastructure.

These benefits—for the college, for students, and for local businesses—are substantial, but they are only the first step in what Shugart, Battista, and their team believe will result from Valencia's accelerated training programs. Shugart's long-term vision is far more transformative: "If I can scale those 1,000 certificates with a team to 5,000 per year, in five years 25,000 families will be delivered from paycheck-to-paycheck vulnerability. They will have full-time employment with benefits . . . they will no longer go to the Emergency Room with a sore throat. They will no longer have members of their family who are stealing to survive." The social costs avoided by that kind of transformation, he added, are enormous: "There's about 2.3 million people I think in the greater Orlando area, but the caboose of the train"—by which he means low-income, contingent jobs—"really only has about 80,000 or 100,000 people in it. If you can get the caboose's brakes unlocked, then the engine—that's the high-wage, high-skill [workforce]—can move the train. But as long as the caboose's brakes are locked, nobody is going anywhere." Yes, Valencia's CATs will make money for the college, and yes, they will benefit students and industry partners. But Shugart's aim is far more expansive: "We are looking to change the shape of our community."

UTILIZING DEEP CUSTOMER EMPATHY TO IMPLEMENT A DECADE-OLD IDEA: RIO NATIONAL

> *The deep, deep eyes, ears, heart listening is really important because then you can bring back all of the differing opinions, thoughts, feedback, and really put it all together.*[11]

In 1978, the Maricopa County Community College District opened Rio Salado College, one of the first *colleges without walls.* Transforming its telephone and mail-order distance education model into a premier online institution and virtual campus, Rio now offers Arizona residents access to over 450 online courses in numerous degree and certificate programs. Rio Salado is one of the major reasons why the Maricopa district is considered one of the most entrepreneurial in the United States. As interim president Kate Smith explained:

> It was interesting to come into the Rio culture. There's definitely much more of an entrepreneurial mind-set. You know, how do you diversity your portfolio so that you have different revenue streams so you are not caught in one place when the money dries up? I would say for Rio, that has been embedded. It's a cultural mind-set . . . You have this machine, so to speak, of people that just function that way.

For decades, Rio Salado has demonstrated a willingness to buck educational tradition and approach teaching and learning in new and different ways, including building its own learning management system in partnership with Dell and Microsoft; creating a one course/many sections model that allows roughly twenty-five full-time faculty to guide program development and supervise an army of about fifteen hundred adjuncts, each paid by the number of students they teach rather than the number of sections; providing extensive student support in financial aid, enrollment, and academic advising; and designing academic schedules around students' needs, not those of faculty or administrators (for example, Rio students can enroll in a course nearly every Monday; there are forty-eight official start dates throughout the year).

Although it is not immune to the retention and completion challenges shared by many online learning enterprises, Rio's model has been exceptionally successful as a revenue generator for the district. Smith reported that Rio is allocated only 11 percent of Maricopa's overall operating budget, but accounts for 23 percent of district revenues. A recent study by the Boston Consulting Group and Arizona State University estimates that because of its limited physical footprint, Rio Salado avoids roughly $6 million in operations and maintenance costs each year, "and more than $200 million in upfront construction costs that would be necessary to enable the college to serve a comparable number of face-to-face students."[12]

Roughly a decade ago, under the leadership of former president Chris Bustamante, Rio Salado began exploring the idea of expanding its course offerings to students outside Arizona. Yet at that time, the state did not have enabling legislation that would allow Rio (or any other Arizona institutions) to enter into the intergovernmental agreements necessary for this to occur. Working together, Arizona's community colleges, the Arizona Board of Regents, and Arizona's private postsecondary institutions pushed for the passage of legislation in 2014 that led to the creation of Arizona SARA: a state council governing each institution's participation in the national State Authorization Reciprocity Agreement (SARA), which enables the provision of distance education across state borders.[13]

When Smith was appointed interim president of Rio Salado in August 2018, Arizona SARA reciprocity agreements had been hammered out, and the college had commissioned a study to explore what building a national online education platform might look like. Believing that Rio needed to slow down and ensure that this idea—eventually titled Rio National—would truly meet stakeholder needs and be competitive in a market dominated by online programs at Southern New Hampshire University, the University of Phoenix, and Arizona State University Online, Smith embarked upon a process of seeking deep customer empathy and establishing design criteria. One of her first steps was to ask, "How does this help students? I can't do it just because we have to see if we can make more money. There has to be real purpose in what we are doing." In considering this question, Smith and her colleagues reminded themselves of the main reason for creating Rio National: ensuring that the 11.2 million students in "education deserts around the country"—defined as living sixty miles or more from the nearest institution of higher education—have access to accredited degree and certificate programs that are both affordable and transferrable.[14]

The next step was engaging in market research to learn about the needs of potential students. As part of this process, the team collaborated with a digital marketing firm to create five different personas or target groups of students, and for each persona researched what program(s) would be most impactful (and would also meet the requirements for SARA). Smith and her colleagues decided to launch Rio National with eight degree/certificate programs that would best serve the five target groups. During this process of identifying future students and empathizing with their needs, the team realized that a lack of high-speed internet in many rural parts of the country was a major stumbling block; a substantial number of potential learners simply could not access Rio Salado's (or any other online provider's) courses. The Rio team added this problem statement to their business plan (what design thinkers would call the design brief) and are currently working with local internet providers and philanthropic organizations to build the connectivity necessary to enroll in Rio National.

Feeling that she better understood her most important stakeholders—students—Smith turned toward those a little closer to home. In late 2018, she closed the college for a day and held an institutionwide retreat to share information about what Rio National would be and to engage faculty and staff in "looking back at who we are, what we are about, how we engage as employees, where we are headed," and so on. As she told them, "Not everybody is going to be a part of Rio National directly, but everybody is a part of building this. We're all doing this together. And it's a little scary, right? So it's going to take all of our minds and all of our energy to create something that really reaches those 11.2 million people . . . in a way that is meaningful." For Smith, taking the time to empathize with and understand the needs of Rio National's future students, as well as Rio Salado's existing faculty and staff, was an essential step in preparing the college to embark upon an entrepreneurial idea that had been a decade or more in the making.

GATHERING INFORMATION ABOUT STAKEHOLDERS' NEEDS: TCC'S OPPORTUNITY CENTER

> *My team's #1 charge when they meet the client is to listen. Academics tend to tell people what they need, and we do it to businesses all the time. And we've got to be able to step back and really listen to what they are saying their needs are.*[15]

TCC's Opportunity Center is located in a nondescript, gray-and-white building on the outskirts of Fort Worth, Texas, and serves as the college's primary base for customized workforce training. For over twenty years, the Opportunity Center has partnered with area businesses to design and deliver short-term (half-day to multiweek) training programs in communications, computer skills, technical job skills, management and leadership, job safety, and other subjects. While much training is delivered at corporate locations, minimizing drive time for employees, the Opportunity Center itself has classrooms for soft-skills training (all with movable furniture and walls to allow for any size group); computer labs; a composites lab, complete with an autoclave; a call center; and technical training areas for supply chain and logistics, electrical machine repair, welding, precision machining, and so on. The Opportunity Center also has mobile maintenance, mechanic, and hydraulics trainers that can be set up in a client's parking lot so "we're on-site but we aren't pushing buttons on their machines and messing things up."[16] While it receives some funding from the district, the Opportunity Center is primarily supported by grants from the Texas Workforce Commission (which supplement training dollars for incumbent workers in certain industries), the US Department of Labor, private foundations, and of course, the corporations whose employees or potential new hires receive training.

As the quote at the beginning of this section attests, TCC's Opportunity Center has long understood the advantages of empathizing with and gathering information from stakeholders; indeed, its success as an economic development service to the community is entirely dependent upon its ability to understand the needs of area businesses. As Jennifer Hawkins, director of corporate solutions and economic development described, each new idea begins with an environmental scan: what companies are moving to the area, which are expanding, what industry sectors are growing the fastest? Armed with labor market information and following discussions with the local workforce board and chamber of commerce, she and her team reach out to business and industry partners and community nonprofits to ask about their training needs and suggest ways that the Opportunity Center might collaborate to build a more robust regional workforce. Opportunity Center staff research and tour local businesses, speaking not only to CEOs and vice presidents, but also to line supervisors and others who can give them a sense of where the organizations are struggling to hire, where interns might be useful, and so forth.

In addition to training workers in the skills central to the success of certain industries (for example, composites manufacturing for the aerospace industry), Hawkins and her team also investigate needs related to internal processes that help businesses run more smoothly. For example, in conversations with a local health-care company, Opportunity Center staff concentrated "on the usual things you would think about with healthcare-focused occupations," but they also noticed that there are certain "processes that have to happen" for the hospital to run smoothly and began asking about the company's needs for workers trained in logistics and supply chain management.[17] (Turns out they had some, and the Opportunity Center was able to help.)

Through these conversations, the health-care company also realized that one of its biggest challenges was hiring people with call-center experience, which it believed was necessary to improve customer service and communication with patients after discharge. The company was thrilled to learn that the Opportunity Center already had a call-center curriculum and classroom—developed in partnership with JP Morgan Chase several years prior—with customizable modules that could be added, removed, tweaked, and so forth to meet the organization's training needs.

Similarly, in developing the Aerospace Manufacturing Training Program (AMTP) with its inaugural partners Bell Textron and Lockheed Martin, Opportunity Center staff realized that providing training was only one part of preparing students to be successful workers; they also needed to provide potential employees with experience working in an environment that mimicked Bell's and Lockheed's to ensure a seamless transition to employment. To facilitate this, the Opportunity Center designed and built its AMTP shop floor and break room to look just like those at Bell: the walls were painted bright, helicopter blue; the furniture was exactly the same as at Bell; and "there was a buzzer, just like at Bell, and if the buzzer drove you crazy, don't go to Bell!" Bell and Lockheed helped to finance the AMTP program, knowing that it would result in employees who had not only the necessary technical skills but also experience working in a comparable environment.

While an excellent example of how a community college gathers information about stakeholders' needs in order to deliver on its mission in an entrepreneurial manner, TCC's Opportunity Center has also been, for much of its existence, a good example of second-wave entrepreneurship, as it had been operated on the margins of the institution with little connection to TCC's core academic programs. Under the leadership of TCC chancellor Gene Giovannini, however, that is beginning to change. Opportunity Center staff have begun collaborating in regional economic development efforts, actively sharing lab and classroom space with other TCC campuses, and working closely with TCC faculty to identify new opportunities, refer partners, and ensure that short-term training programs articulate to credit-based degrees and certificates. Under TCC's new One College approach (discussed in chapter 5), the Opportunity Center is now "able to talk to things that we haven't talked to before. And we're going to have to kind of sniff around and find different opportunities that may not just be for us, but for the college as a whole."[18] In other words, it is strategically moving away from its formerly siloed existence into third-wave entrepreneurship.

INCUBATING AN ENTREPRENEURIAL APPROACH TO BIOSCIENCE WORKFORCE TRAINING: THE CENTER FOR ENTREPRENEURIAL INNOVATION AND LABFORCE

> *We are taking business incubation and applying it to, you know, a new educational initiative. Because in all respects, it's the same. It has to stand alone. It has to generate a profit. It has to serve a need and do it very well. And we want to have a really big growth potential.*[19]

Maricopa's Center for Entrepreneurial Innovation (CEI), based at the district's GateWay College, is a business incubator that provides space and support services to high-growth, technology-driven companies in the early stages of their development. The idea for CEI emerged from a 2003 Flinn Foundation study that proposed a road map for how Arizona—and the Phoenix area in particular—might collaborate to serve the bioscience industry. As former GateWay president (and subsequent chancellor of the Maricopa and Tarrant County districts) Gene Giovannini wrote, "From this study came recommendations that specifically spoke to entrepreneurship—the need for wet lab and rentable research space and a business incubator for start-ups in varying industry sectors such as technology, energy, biosciences, and software . . . all with the goal of job creation at its core."[20]

Sharing a "deep-rooted desire to address a regional issue with an innovative solution," Maricopa, the City of Phoenix, and the Economic Development Administration began collaborating on what would eventually become CEI, investing $6 million and securing a corporate donation from Blue Cross/Blue Shield of Arizona to build the center and recruit clients.[21] CEI's 18,000-square-foot facility, opened in 2013, encompasses fifteen furnished offices or suites; three convertible light manufacturing spaces; a 3D printing and design center; commercial-grade biotechnology equipment for rent at a reduced cost; eight wet labs with fume hoods; medical device maker space; and numerous other spaces for collaboration. Its incubation services, however, are what set CEI apart. For each client, most of whom are in the bioscience industry, CEI staff offer strategic growth planning and tactical business advice, pro bono mentorship from leading industry professionals, ongoing market and competitive intelligence research, collaboration with like-minded entrepreneurs, and access to many other discounted services, including legal work to secure patents. CEI executive director Tom Schumann explained: "Researchers come over from ASU to develop out the technologies that they've been creating there. They need that neutral environment to come and do that. Most of them are PhD scientists coming over here who know absolutely nothing about the rule of business. So our role at CEI is to help them build a business around their technology." Schumann and his team called it concierge-level service: "always anticipating what our clients' next set of needs are going to be before they know it themselves . . . We know where everybody is on their development road map, and it's like okay: in a month they are going to need a branding expert. So let's get that branding person ready to help them."

For Assistant Executive Director Patti DuBois, CEI's approach to business incubation in many ways mirrors the design thinking process. Researchers often come to CEI, she shared, with a solution to what they believe is a widespread problem. Her first task is to guide them through customer and stakeholder discovery processes in order to confirm that enough people have that problem for the solution to make sense from a business perspective. Then begins an iterative process of ideating, prototyping, and testing: "We have to live in a way where trying fast and failing is supported. We have to. I have to get to the point of okay, you tried that and it's not working. I mean, the first couple years of any business is really how do we get in, who do we get in with, what problem are we actually solving. So you have to play quick. You have to play efficiently."

To date, companies incubated by CEI have created over five hundred jobs in the community, raised nearly $70 million in capital, and have over $100 million in combined annual sales.[22] Unlike many other business incubators, CEI does not take an equity stake in its clients. Instead, Schumann said:

> Our sustainability is built around a sales royalty agreement . . . The majority of our companies will not have a large equity event where we'd be able to cash in. They will be small, privately held, and we'd own some stock in something that never has a market value. What good would that do us? So what we do is just before a company is graduating, we have *the talk*. About paying it forward and such. And we ask them to voluntarily—if they wish—make a commitment of either a percent of their sales royalty stream or a fixed amount that they amortize, usually based on sales. And our idea is if you've been with us for three years and we haven't shown you any value, then don't give us anything 'cause we don't deserve it.[23]

On the other hand, for the companies that believe "if it weren't for CEI, I wouldn't be in this position"—roughly one-third of those incubated, Schumann estimated—a sales royalty agreement feels like a fair way to compensate CEI for their services and contribute to the incubation of future entrepreneurial efforts. All royalties go to the Maricopa Community College Foundation (as tax-deductible donations) and CEI, in turn, utilizes the funds as needed for operational support.

• • •

A few years ago, Schumann, DuBois, and a small group of bioscience industry advisers sat down and asked how CEI might build upon its early-stage incubation services and better assist its clients and the community. In particular, they considered what CEI's companies need after graduating from the incubator. As Schumann shared, "So growing, scaling companies have two big needs. One is continued access to growth capital. Nothing we can do about that. There are bigger players in the state that are working on that. And the other is a trained workforce. So we decided we would start focusing on that and we created an initiative called LabForce." LabForce will be Arizona's first workforce training center focused on the state's bioscience and life science industries, which have grown by 9 percent since 2015—more than twice the US growth rate.

As Schumann related, his team initially planned to provide workshops and lab training for the clinical technicians employed by bioscience companies. But as they went through their customer discovery process, they "found out that the biggest problem—and this is why you do customer discovery!—is the quality systems. Across the industry, across all the levels of jobs and classifications inside a company, they need more and more skills training because our industries operate either under FDA, ISO, Global Manufacturing Best Practices, and those types of regulations." What Schumann and his team learned through six months of CEO interviews, stakeholder surveys, conversations with economic development and city planning officials, and market research on thirty different private-sector bioscience training companies was that there was an unmet need for bioscience certification and credentialing in Arizona that was not being addressed by anyone, including Arizona State University.

As a result, CEI staff decided to incubate LabForce as it would any other early-stage entrepreneurial venture. Schumann's team wrote a business plan (similar to a design brief) that summarized what it learned from customer discovery, defined the problem it hoped to solve, and specified that the team would develop and prototype LabForce curricula and delivery mechanisms by testing "five different products to five different personas with five different delivery methods," and then engaging ten companies to pilot the curriculum and provide feedback via focus groups. Armed with this plan, Schumann convinced Maricopa's governing board to invest $5 million in the venture in order to build a new learning management system and construct a 6,500-square-foot training facility in the recently developed downtown Phoenix Biomedical Campus. By 2021 LabForce will begin working with bioscience companies to directly provide "workshops and lab training for everyone from lab technicians, scientists, executive teams, and quality systems managers in the industry. The workshops can be onsite and hands-on, or be participated in virtually through online courses."[24] Eventually, LabForce will offer more than four hundred industry-related courses in lab science, quality assurance, and regulatory compliance, many of them certified by the Arizona Bioscience Association.

The LabForce business model, Schumann noted, is essentially a content aggregation strategy: it builds, buys, or licenses content for each course or workshop, taking a "slice of each piece of content that moves through the system." Schumann hopes that LabForce will hit the breakeven point within the first few years of operation, thereafter providing revenue to support CEI and future efforts to grow Arizona's bioscience workforce. But more importantly, he argued, LabForce will "demonstrate to the community that the community college *is* responsive and we will come up with solutions . . . we are a partner with them." Schumann and his team are also working with Maricopa faculty to explore opportunities for LabForce courses to articulate to new associate degree programs preparing students for jobs as quality technicians or quality systems managers. These pathways would more closely tie the innovative and revenue-generating work done through CEI to Maricopa's traditional teaching and learning enterprise.

ALIGNMENT WITH INSTITUTIONAL MISSION AND OTHER CRITERIA FOR EVALUATING ENTREPRENEURIAL IDEAS

> *Great idea, but is it aligned to the mission of the colleges? Is it feasible? Do we have the resources or can we get the resources? And who's going to benefit? At the end of the day, we need to serve the community here.*[25]

The stories presented in this chapter offer illustrations of how community colleges have empathized with stakeholders, identified unmet needs, defined problem statements, and created design briefs or business plans to address issues of importance to their communities or student bodies. In these examples—as well as many others not described here—college faculty and staff carefully considered the criteria by which they would evaluate new programs or ideas. Although many criteria were project-specific, in every instance the primary criterion was alignment with college mission. Rio Salado's Kate Smith put it this way: "We don't exist just to find revenue streams, right? We exist to make a difference in society . . . It's about students, people! And communities." Former Maricopa chancellor Maria Harper-Marinick echoed the sentiment: "You have to keep that focus on the right thing. And that is the students or the community . . . it has to come from that lens."

This criterion—positively impacting students or communities—sounds simple, but is not always so, and college leaders often must dig a little deeper to ensure that entrepreneurial ideas do indeed meet fundamental human needs. For example, the state of Iowa has a substantial shortage of certified nursing aides, and in recent years both the health-care industry and governor's office have been pressuring NIACC to expand its certified nursing aide (CNA) program, offering training funds for doing so. At first blush, this appears to be a win-win scenario: the health-care industry gains more workers to meet an unmet need, the community has access to better health care, more students have a pathway directly to employment, and NIACC receives some additional financial support. The problem, however, is that certified nursing aides do "the hardest work in the industry and they are paid [next to] nothing."[26] According to NIACC president Steven Schulz, "There is great pressure for us to do more and more and more of this, but I can't look your child in the eye and say this is a great career for you." NIACC ultimately turned down funding to expand its CNA program because doing so would not help students earn a livable wage. Maricopa, TCC, and Valencia leaders all shared similar stories of declining new revenue streams because the associated activities would not be in students' best interests.

Although benefiting students or communities is the most important criterion used to evaluate entrepreneurial ideas, the four colleges highlighted in this book also ask faculty and staff to consider the financial implications of any new initiative. As the following quote from Sandy Shugart illustrates, financial savings or return to the college are never the primary reason for embarking on a new project, but they are important nonetheless:

> Every plan has a business plan as well as a mission plan . . . The process is one of solving problems on our mission. And the business part of that is subservient to the mission. So we wouldn't do that to make money. We *do* make money doing it, because that whole arm of the college [continuing education] is expected to make a return to the college. So when they build their models, there is a business model assumption that we've got to make money doing this. But that's not where we start. So we're looking at a gap in the marketplace, an opportunity.[27]

NIACC also asks faculty and staff to consider revenues and costs when proposing new ideas. Schulz explained: "We're getting a lot better at return on investment proposals for everything we do. So before we can add that, you've got to outline your expenses, direct and indirect." Tight budgets, he laughed, "require you to be more thoughtful . . . and have a little more ROI mind-set." And although he often heard, "Well, you don't need to make money on it," he disagreed vehemently. "Yes, we do!" he exclaimed. "We absolutely do. We can't continue to add programs that pull away money from the general fund in terms of a loss, because career and technical programs—the middle skills if you will—those are the high-cost programs.[28]

Of course, faculty and staff are not always wild about the idea of considering the financial implications of each new program, idea, or initiative. Joe Davis, NIACC's interim vice president of academic affairs, put it this way: "I think that's probably the biggest challenge for faculty . . . in evaluating programs, we have to think about the money. Are we bringing in enough to cover what we are doing?" Most faculty are not taught how to assess the true costs of programs, and many are uncomfortable with a growing business ethos on campus. Understanding this, Shugart found a way to reframe Valencia's commitment to entrepreneurship:

> Rather than thinking of our entrepreneurship as how can we make money, it's more like, as we pursue our mission, what's going to be most sustainable? Let's go there first. Sometimes it makes sense to take a huge risk on something that might lose money anyway, and still do it. But most of the time if you've got enough bandwidth for three projects

> and there are thirty competing, let's pick the three that will help us be able to afford the next three.

For Valencia, NIACC, TCC, and Maricopa, the expectation that all new programs or ideas must positively impact students or communities—and that they must, at a minimum, consider how they will be funded and sustained over time—are key to ensuring that entrepreneurship remains mission-oriented. Other conditions may be more project-specific. NIACC's Schulz often prioritizes projects based on the scope of the intended solution: "You don't have to make money on everything you do," he shared, "but at the end of the day you've got to cover your costs. So you have to make some forced choice about where do you serve the largest group of students."

Clint Grant, executive dean of aviation, business, and logistics at TCC's Northwest Campus, has a rubric for evaluating new programs. Because community colleges are always dealing with limited resources, he said, "I kind of rank things [by] how long I think they'll last and what is sustainable." His first priority is programs—either short term or those leading to traditional academic certificates or degrees—that are associated with national certifications: "For example, the flagship program at TCC for the aviation side of the house is the aviation maintenance program . . . the reason that program has lasted as long as it has is because there are very tangible federal certificates that go along with it, and unless you have those federal certificates, you can't do whatever it is you are trying to do." To Grant, federal certificates are the gold standard. Next best are certifications "that mean something to industry and are not going away . . . 'Cause it's gonna be there for a while and it leads to employment." Third on the list, he shared, "would be just our own certifications based on local needs. So that's kind of the way I tend to rank it, and then you prioritize your budgets" accordingly.

Similarly, Valencia's Carolyn McMorran has three criteria for considering new accelerated training programs: (1) "You have to have industry partners who want your students . . . I don't want to run a program where I can't place people in high-wage, high-demand jobs"; (2) "It has to have an industry-recognized credential"; (3) The programs need to be in areas where scholarships for students are available: "CareerSource has like five or six buckets of interest that they want to fund people in. So manufacturing, construction, transportation, logistics, health care, IT. So we try to stay in those areas because . . . funding would be there to support the students." At the end of the day, she related, difficult financial decisions must be made about which industries to pursue, but "we're not going to do a program that won't fit the model we are looking for." Joe Battista concurred: "We still stick to the basic mission of community college."

RECONCEPTUALIZING SERVICE TO COMMUNITY

> *It's our job to find out what are the gaps and the needs in our community and try to fill those. And to serve as a hub for bringing together others that are doing the same thing.*[29]

Service to the community has been part of the colleges' mission since their founding, although there has never been a cohesive definition of what constitutes community work. Edmund Gleazer, longtime president of the American Association for Community and Junior Colleges, saw the institutions as "the nexus of a community learning system," to be used by the general public as an agency assisting with community issues.[30] The 1988 Commission on the Future of Community Colleges wrote that "the term *community* should be defined not only as a region to be served, but also a climate to be created," before listing about fifteen separate ways the colleges can carry out this vision, including acting as "a center for problem-solving in adult illiteracy or the education of the disabled" and coordinating "efforts to provide day care, transportation, and financial aid."[31] Perhaps because we have never quite understood what constitutes community service—Is it lifelong learning? Adult basic education? Making sporting and performance facilities available to the general public? Providing workforce training? All of the above?—this function has become a catchall for any services that fall outside the scope of traditional academic forms such as grades, semesters, or credits.[32] As a function of the community college mission, community service frequently has been attenuated in comparison with its education and training counterparts.

Yet the most recent wave of community college entrepreneurship has spurred a reconceptualization of what it means to serve the community, and this new understanding has the potential to elevate this function to the utmost mission priority, one by which all other education and training activities are evaluated. Harper-Marinick put it this way:

> We've had to acknowledge how the community has changed, how the expectations have changed, and that we need to serve the business community and the community at large in different ways than historically we have. So historically, it was more of: "Here's the college, here's the menu. Choose. Come to us if you want, and if you do come, choose from the menu and if we don't have it: oh well." So we're shifting that to: "What's the need? And in which ways do we respond?" So then that's leading to different ways to approach the services . . . Lots of it is based on partnerships with municipalities, and businesses, and the groups in town like the economic development groups or the governor's office.

As Harper-Marinick made clear, serving the community now means much more than providing social services or benefits to individuals. To Maricopa and other colleges, service to community has been reframed as collaborating with businesses, industries, municipalities, economic development agencies, workforce boards, and community organizations in order to improve the economic health and welfare of the community writ large. This reconceptualization—a critical component of third-wave entrepreneurship—not only affects the colleges' ability to act in innovative or entrepreneurial ways but is leading to a fundamental change in how the institutions define success. Valencia's five-year impact plan, for example, is titled "The Power to Serve: Building Community by Serving Community." In it, Shugart writes that the focus on "student outcomes, on learning, will continue to be central to our work." Nonetheless, he continued:

> We have discovered new opportunities, in fact, new obligations to serve. Our community needs us and we can have an impact beyond

> anything we have yet imagined if we focus the same energy and imagination that has fueled our impact on student learning on making an impact in the quality of life in our community—raising educational attainment levels, increasing economic opportunity, growing the economy, and helping our community to flourish.[33]

This shift toward serving the community—as opposed to individual members of the community—has been met with mixed reactions. On one hand, Harper-Marinick noted, "The work we are doing to shift how we approach service—and I mean service in a big, broad way—is welcomed and supported by this community." Yet critics may fear that it opens the door for community colleges to prioritize the desires of business and industry over the needs of students. According to Lourdes Ramboa, faculty chair of business, entrepreneurship, and small business management at TCC's Northwest Campus, "Off-campus the community has embraced it: 'Yes! That's exactly what we have always wanted!'" But "on campus there has been a little bit of pushback." To combat this resistance, Sasan Poureetezadi, Maricopa's former chief strategy officer, argued that students also benefit from this reconceptualization:

> Instead of chasing FTSE [full-time student equivalents], I think we need to chase completion around the areas where there's gainful employment, economic impact . . . The vast majority of people, not only in our local municipality but in this country, this state, this nation, and globally, are engaged in education because they want a leg up. They want to be successful. And . . . we have to understand that's why they are coming to us, and acknowledge and build and structure our programs [accordingly] . . . There's this idea that sometimes you are selling out to industry, but that's not really the case. That's where most of them want to go, by the way. *We* work in the academy, so we love it. We love teaching in and of itself and love the Socratic method. Still valuable today, I believe that. But that's not why most of the students are here . . . So if there's a big demand in the market, it would make sense for us to respond to that, right?

Still, Poureetezadi noted, some faculty are distrustful of Maricopa's new orientation toward a more broadly defined community. When this occurs, he typically empathizes but points out that it is possible to serve students *and* communities. "I agree," he might say, "you're right." There is intrinsic value in education in and of itself. "But then there's this too, and we can do both."

Nassar Hedayat, Valencia's assistant vice president for career and workforce education, also believes that a reorientation toward community benefits students. Under his and Shugart's leadership, the college has focused on decoupling enrollment—and the per-student funding associated with it—from strategic planning and decision-making, developing new workforce programs only in areas where there is a demonstrated need so that "as soon as a student graduates, they are placed." No longer, Hedayat stated, will Valencia offer a program just because it generates enrollment. And while that may indeed be a step away from serving students' desires, it is a step *toward* serving their needs. (For more on Valencia's approach to "dethroning the idols of community colleges, which [are] enrollment and money," see chapter 7.[34])

• • •

Central to this reconceptualization of service to community is looking to partnerships with business and industry from a strategic engagement standpoint rather than a service orientation. In other words, focusing less on providing training and other services if and when local businesses or community groups demand it, and instead seeking collaborations that result in wins for both the partner and the college. Ramboa described this shift at TCC:

> We have a new chancellor and a new president at Northwest. So with both of them coming on board, it's a new set of eyes looking at, what does community engagement really look like? So Dr. Blankenbaker [president of Northwest Campus], I've seen her really take more of a business approach to community engagement, saying "Let's not just be engaged for the sake of being engaged … Let's make sure that we

> understand what is the return on investment." It's really about understanding how we can partner strategically with community partners that are going to be beneficial to both partners. They are going to gain something of value and we can also gain something of value by supporting them.

William Coppola, president of TCC's Southeast Campus, described how the perception of his college has changed as TCC has approached community partnerships in a more strategic way: "The community and the chambers and the cities and even the city of Arlington [didn't] see us as the economic engine that they need for the development, the education, and the training of their citizens, for business and industry to move here." It wasn't until Amazon started looking to community colleges for trained workers "that the mayors started realizing that we have to partner with our community colleges as a training pool." Community colleges are partly to blame for this disconnect, Coppolla believes, because "we never asked people to pay in! We always did things where, this is part of our community service, to do this noncredit, free training. To get people out of poverty. And that's always been our mission." The community college's role hasn't changed, he said, but the perception of them is changing. "People are finally starting to look at us—we've always had the red-headed stepchild thing—they are looking at us as a value-added to the community."

Robin Lasher, director of TCC's small business development center, views this shift as central to the college's ability to be a strategic partner in regional economic development. Until about 2007, she recalled, entrepreneurship at TCC "was very academic." Since then, entrepreneurship throughout the Fort Worth area has exploded. "But the difference here, with [chancellor] Giovannini coming on board, the *college* has become entrepreneurial . . . it's allowed TCC to position itself to be a core part of entrepreneurship here instead of another resource. It's part of the ecosystem."

Approaching business and community partnerships from a strategic engagement standpoint makes much sense, as it helps to ensure that collaborations are both mission-oriented and financially sustainable, but what does it actually entail? Community college faculty and staff shared several perspectives on this question, noting that some things are already occurring—for example, focusing on win-win collaborations that lead to greater economic vitality for both the college and the community—as well as others that might be considered next steps. Ramboa, for example, believes that a strategic partnership approach must be role-modeled so that faculty can see how it applies to teaching and learning. Still, she thinks, this may be an uphill climb:

> It's not what they [faculty] do on a day-to-day basis. I think we reach out to the community as guest speakers, bring them in, but the idea that I may need to be in tune with what they are talking about and their priorities, and then I adapt and shift my classroom and my curriculum to meet those needs, I think sometimes—and don't take me wrong—I think that there's a group of faculty who see that as a priority and are working toward it, but is it the majority? I don't think so.

Harper-Marinick hopes that continually reminding people that this reorientation is important "because the expectations are different" will reinforce to faculty that a broader understanding of service to community is necessary if the colleges are to be successful in the future. She said, "The business community is pretty clear about what they need. And there's urgency in the state of Arizona for more talent development and the companies are looking for people today or tomorrow. Not next year, not in five years." Understanding that they have a role to play in how the colleges respond to community expectations, Harper-Marinick noted, has led faculty to "some creative ideas" about how to adapt their practices to fit the new paradigm. Rewarding them for doing so, she laughed, also helps.

TCC's Grant believes that faculty are not the only ones who need to be shown how community colleges can play a critical role in economic development. To him, the institutions must also market their services to business, industry, and community leaders, proactively positioning the colleges as strategic partners in entrepreneurial ecosystems. He shared:

> Everybody needs help. They are looking into the not-too-distant future and wondering where the workers are going to come from. And I don't just mean the bodies, I mean the skills. And Dr. LeBlanc [TCC's executive vice president and provost] said something to me at one point. We were in a meeting and I was whining about marketing or something, which I do a lot around here, and she said, "You know Clint, Coca-Cola still advertises." Which made the point to me that the school has to constantly let—and I think the chancellor is doing a good job—the community know that we are here and we are their school.

Transitioning from the colleges' historic approach to serving communities—providing services to individuals and groups, often at little or no cost and without any expectation, as Coppola put it, that communities "pay in"—to a strategic engagement paradigm where colleges, community, and business groups collaborate to improve the economic health and welfare of the region *and* the institution will not be easy or seamless. Faculty, especially those in disciplines more closely aligned with liberal arts and transfer preparation than skills training, may fundamentally disagree with this reorientation or simply fail to see how it applies in their courses. That is okay. We should always have checks on new ideas, as they keep the colleges tethered to historic (and important) purposes, such as ensuring access, providing for social mobility and second chances, and educating students for participation in a democratic society. Yet in many ways, this broader understanding of service to community is a critical component of ensuring that colleges pursue entrepreneurial opportunities in a mission-oriented manner, as it keeps communities and the students within them at the center of all institutional decision-making.

5 Asking What *If*

Our purposeful focus on creativity influences the culture at multiple levels . . . And that culture is helpful in creating an environment where ideas can surface . . . and divergent thinking is encouraged.[1]

Despite a historic responsiveness to societal needs, a willingness to provide something for everyone, at many community colleges, traditional structures and systems constrain entrepreneurial thinking about how to best serve students or communities. Creative, divergent ideas are not cultivated or rewarded, faculty and administrators are encouraged to stay in their lane, and as a result, new programs or practices frequently look more like updates to old ones than innovative solutions to pressing problems. Faculty and staff at NIACC, Valencia College, TCC, and the Maricopa Community Colleges have turned this stagnant paradigm on its head, instead creating cultures where constituents feel comfortable asking, *What if . . . we did something different?* This chapter shares five stories of how these colleges have engaged in the second phase of the design thinking process, brainstorming creative ways to meet stakeholder needs and utilizing a *yes, and* mentality to develop concepts to their fullest potential. The chapter concludes with two sections exploring how these institutions encourage divergent as well as convergent thinking and how they have created spaces on campus for innovation to occur.

WHAT IF . . . WE COULD ESTABLISH AN ENTREPRENEURIAL MIND-SET ACROSS CAMPUS?

> *If we're going to say that we want our students to do this, that's awesome. We have to do it too. We have to be able to fail. We have to be able to ideate and prototype and take risks and micro-experiment. It would seem odd to ask the students to be able to do that and then not have that be part of your culture.*[2]

The idea of establishing an entrepreneurial mind-set across campus had been floating around the NIACC campus for years. Several faculty had received training in entrepreneurial mind-set learning through the Entrepreneurial Learning Initiative (ELI) or the Kern Family Foundation. Others had begun incorporating elements of design thinking or ELI's eight mind-set lessons into their courses. But in 2019, several disparate factors came together in a perfect storm, propelling the establishment of an entrepreneurial mind-set to the top of the institution's priority list. First, the strain of fewer state dollars and lower enrollments (due to a declining population in north Iowa) meant that NIACC needed to be more entrepreneurial in everything it did, from identifying new revenue streams to evaluating new and existing programs. Second, President Steven Schulz became convinced that learning to think in an entrepreneurial manner was critical to NIACC's long-term success and sustainability. As he put it:

> The winners—those that are going to come out on the other end of this as successful, sustainable institutions—are going to take the principles of entrepreneurship and really embed them into all walks of their lives. 'Cause it's really about innovation and grit and all those things that we know are the tenets of entrepreneurship, whether you are a business owner or whether you are just a successful person.

And third, NIACC faculty decided that it was time to revamp the college's student success course, required for all developmental students, as it did not seem to be improving persistence or attainment rates. All of these factors combined meant that NIACC was primed for a change, and receptive to college leaders' strong sense that establishing an entrepreneurial mind-set across campus would not only benefit the institution, but also improve students' lives. Tim Putnam, director of NIACC's John Pappajohn Entrepreneurial Center, described it this way: "When you have a group of staff and faculty who are collectively working together, and the president, when those visions are colliding, then you triangulate with stuff that we are trying to do, and we've got that perfect formation to really try to make something happen."

Understanding that faculty and staff may respond to (or resist) different aspects of the entrepreneurial mind-set, NIACC identified several different approaches to introduce the concept to campus constituents. The first and broadest tactic emerged somewhat organically when the college's common read committee selected *Who Owns the Ice House? Eight Life Lessons from an Unlikely Entrepreneur*, published by ELI, as the book that all faculty and staff would read over the summer and hopefully incorporate into their classes during the 2019–2020 school year. Lindsey Dalrymple, director of NIACC's Auditorium Leadership Series, shared the process that the common read committee went through to select the book, saying that she and her colleagues really responded to the notion—set out in the preface to *The Ice House*—that "[e]ntrepreneurship is a mindset that can empower ordinary people to accomplish the extraordinary."[3] This would resonate, she believed, with community college students who frequently have to overcome enormous odds just to attend classes and graduate. Thus, the committee convinced each freshman composition instructor to teach the book, and Schulz arranged for its two authors to visit the campus to speak with students and staff. Dalrymple shared:

> One thing we've asked with the common read is that even if you don't require them [students] to read the book that you read it yourself as a faculty member. And find a way to maybe bring something up from it. You don't have to change your curriculum, just reference the book and use an idea from it . . . This one actually has some training that goes along with it for some of our faculty, so they'll get real concrete ideas of what they could do and how this could be more than just a book, but also a common ground of things that we can connect on.

The goal was for everyone on campus to connect with the eight entrepreneurial mind-set lessons outlined in *The Ice House*, so that "even after this book is done this year, it's going to have a long-term effect on what we are doing."[4] By summer 2019, excitement for the book and the lessons it contained was palpable on campus. Dalrymple shared, "I'm beyond thrilled with how the support has kind of come from the rest of the campus. I'm really excited to see kind of the long reach that this has."

Around the same time the 2019 common read was rolled out, NIACC faculty began restructuring the college's student success course around ELI's eight mind-set lessons, believing that helping students to think and problem solve in an entrepreneurial manner would be far more empowering than simply orienting them to the college and teaching them study skills. Putnam related, "I think this entrepreneurial mind-set, honestly, is the best way to get our students motivated . . . It's not about business per se, it's about solving a problem and then how do you get that solution to those who can benefit from it."

To acquaint faculty—both those teaching the revised student success course and others—with the basics of entrepreneurial mind-set learning, in 2019 NIACC offered a three-day professional development training on the topic. Although roughly forty faculty attended, not all were immediately convinced that it was the right approach for the college's student population. Kelley O'Rourke, NIACC's school partnership entrepreneurial coordinator, recalled some instructors' doubts: "I don't think this is going to fly with some of our students," they'd say. "They are first-generation, they have low grades, high school grades coming in, they have low standardized test grades."

Other faculty were unsure that developing an entrepreneurial mind-set would apply to their discipline. Heather Rissler, a biology instructor, admitted that coming in "I had probably a negative view of entrepreneurs because I always thought of that guy who runs Amazon and makes a bazillion dollars. Who needs that much money? So in my mind I had this negative connotation and I hadn't really associated it as a mind-set for really discovering opportunities and solving problems." But then Rissler had a major aha! moment:

> I kept thinking, this is the scientific method! You can call it what you want, we are doing the same thing. So to me that iterative nature of the process: this is what we do in the lab with our students . . . Recognizing a problem, having that hypothesis—your ideation, your hypothesis: the same. The prototype: your experiment. The iterative nature of it . . . it's just a parallel. It feels like you're doing science when you're coming up with these projects that they [the students] are working on, and they prototype and realize that no, that's not going to work, I need to go back and ideate again . . . And I was just caught. It was like, I'm in a cult! If there's a cult, I'm in it! I'll drink the Kool-Aid, whatever. This is awesome.

Rissler was not the only convert to entrepreneurial mind-set learning. Agriculture professor Joel Morrical also became a believer. "I loved sitting in on the training," he said. "What this person is saying in sharing with us is deep, thought-provoking, profound." According to O'Rourke, after the training, "a lightbulb has really gone off" for NIACC faculty. Not because "we want to create a bunch of people doing startups," but because it became clear that the skills students gain in developing an entrepreneurial mind-set in many ways mirror the competencies that they will need in the job market. As Rissler emphasized, "Who wouldn't want an employee who is curious? Who creates value? Who makes connections? I mean, who wouldn't want that? I just feel like it will set them ahead when they go out to the workforce."

Since the ELI training, Rissler—who also attended entrepreneurship training through the Kern Family Foundation—has worked to incorporate design thinking and an entrepreneurial mind-set into her classes, finding that its practical application actually connects students more deeply to the subject matter. She shared her experience with a biotechnology class:

> Almost every student who takes the class is an Ag [Agriculture] major, so we would—as an example—one of the projects we did, we looked at nematodes that infect soybeans. So we were looking at the ways that we are currently dealing with this; how can we use biotechnology to solve this problem? And if you were to recommend to the local bean

> growers' association, what . . . would be your recommendation of how we should mitigate this problem?

Rissler was blown away by how her students responded: "This population of students," she said, "they are problem solvers . . . and having that more practical application can draw them into the science." Rissler has lots of ideas about how she will tweak the class next semester—she applies the same iterative approach she teaches to her own process—but she's very encouraged about how the entrepreneurial mind-set lessons resonated with her students. "The engagement was different than what I saw before," she noted. "And I learned things from them. They were coming up with solutions that—in my mind, I thought, here are some possible solutions—but they were coming up with things that were outside of the realm of what I was thinking."

Morrical has also incorporated an entrepreneurial mind-set into his teaching, especially in his Introduction to Entrepreneurship class, which every agriculture student must take. To him, helping students learn to think in an entrepreneurial manner is imperative:

> I push really hard to try to teach them how to think and how to be problem solvers. And when they come from K–12 anymore, they don't have those skills very well. They want to know what they need to know, what's going to be on the test, what do I need to study . . . that's all they want to know. They don't really want to learn and think . . . especially for Ag kids who are more conservative, more stuck in their ways, so to speak. And if you get them to have to do some different work that they are not used to, it kind of helps, I think. In the long term.

Morrical stresses to his students how an entrepreneurial mind-set "can work for you in the workplace or in your everyday life. We spend a lot of time on creativity," he said, which pushes students out of their comfort zones:

> Today we did the little Stanford Design School crash course: interview your partner back and forth. Which is fun to watch because they don't like it at first . . . I set the timer and I walked out for a little bit. I came

> back in and they were at the point where they were supposed to sketch all their different ideas of prototypes, and they were actually all sitting there pretty into it, drawing. I was like, "See! It works every once in a while!" So that's kind of where I push the course more, I would say, as a mind-set that you can use to benefit you in anything you do. Like your personal life. Like so many times we are so afraid to take risks because we are afraid to fail. And talking about, "Well, why is that such a big deal?" . . . And then as we go along, they have to come up with a bug list—things they wish were different in their life, or problems that they have—and then narrow that down to something they want to work on.

In speaking with Morrical about how transformative entrepreneurial mind-set learning has been for his students, I was reminded of a passage from comedian Trevor Noah's book *Born a Crime: Stories from a South African Childhood*:

> People love to say, "Give a man a fish, and he'll eat for a day. Teach a man to fish, and he'll eat for a lifetime." What they don't say is, "And it would be nice if you gave him a fishing rod." That's the part of the analogy that's missing . . . You need someone from the privileged world to come to you and say, "Okay, here's what you need, and here's how it works." People say, "Oh, that's a handout." No. I still have to work to profit by it. But I don't stand a chance without it.[5]

For Morrical and his colleagues at NIACC, simply educating or training students in a discipline—teaching them to fish—is lovely, but not sufficient. Colleges also need to provide students with Noah's metaphorical fishing rod: the skills and capabilities they will need to succeed in a rapidly evolving workforce. As Morrical said:

> My job is not to make sure that my students understand the physiology of lactation. Yeah, that's fun to learn about if you're an animal science geek, but most of them don't care. How do I teach them, how can I be good enough to engage them so that they want to learn about that, but then also teach them things along the way that are going to help them

be successful later? If I don't do that, or if *we* don't do that, we're not doing our jobs.

• • •

When I visited in early summer 2019, NIACC was just embarking on its efforts to establish an entrepreneurial mind-set and still figuring out how college leaders could support and reward faculty and staff for adopting the new paradigm. Nonetheless, many small entrepreneurial ideas were being enacted across campus, including several creative approaches to stemming enrollment declines. One of the more inventive is a show-pig operation in which Morrical and NIACC students raise prize hogs on the college's farm and then sell them to children in 4-H and Future Farmers of America (FFA) programs throughout Iowa and southern Minnesota. Doing so, Morrical shared, not only brings in a few dollars, but allows him to connect with "4-H and FFA kids who love showing and breeding livestock" and recruit them to NIACC's agriculture program. Morrical views this strategy as akin to building a winning athletics team: lots of students come to NIACC to run track or play baseball, he said. The show-pig operation is no different: "There's sixteen community colleges in Iowa, and we all—almost all of us—have an ag program. So how do you differentiate yourself and get students to think about you?" It has become imperative for faculty to think about where their students will come from, Morrical argued. In an era of declining enrollments and diminishing funds for community colleges, "One of the biggest things you have to do is try to create opportunities and programs kind of above and beyond your program of study or your department that interest or entice students."

Unlike many community colleges, NIACC is able to recruit students from outside its service area due to another of the college's entrepreneurial ventures: four hundred recently renovated student dormitories. These dorms—open to all students, but catering especially to those who live beyond or at the far reaches of the college's 3,700-square-mile service area—also enable the institution to enroll international students; offer overnight summer camps to local youth, familiarizing them with the campus and its programs; and widely recruit athletes for its numerous successful sports teams. These initiatives not only help to boost NIACC's enrollment, but also create additional connections between the college and its community and can be scaled to generate additional revenue for the institution.

Although NIACC leaders are optimistic about these and other ventures, including the common book read and new curricular emphases on an entrepreneurial mind-set, it will likely take several more years to institutionalize a culture of innovation and entrepreneurship across campus. Joe Davis, NIACC's interim vice president of academic affairs, put it succinctly: "I wish we were farther along in the process. Right now I just have high hopes for it. We haven't seen it actually work yet" at any sort of scale. Heather Rissler agreed: "We have to find ways to infuse that [the entrepreneurial mind-set] into our classes so that students, they are not just learning it one time. Because it's like with anything: if you do it one time it's great, but if you don't have that reinforcement, then you might forget the skills that you learned." The real push, she believes, will be "to think about how we can incorporate this throughout the curriculum so that by the time a student has left NIACC . . . they will be entrepreneurial minded." Luckily, Morrical noted, "If you really dive into entrepreneurial mind-set, I think it's really hard not to get hooked on that thinking."

WHAT IF . . . VALENCIA'S BACHELOR'S IN BUSINESS AND ORGANIZATIONAL LEADERSHIP HAD NO PREREQUISITES?

> *The entrepreneur, as I understand them, spends less time focused on what can't be done and looks for things that can be done. So I can't tell a student when they show up as a first-time-in-college learner that "Hey! You are in a bachelor's program," but I can tell them, "Get that associate degree in any field you are interested in and I'll be here waiting for you."*[6]

There had been talk of developing an applied bachelor's degree in business at Valencia College long before Terry Allcorn became dean of business and hospitality in 2013. And when, a few months after his arrival, he and his team began meeting with Orlando business leaders, all of them cited a need for more students with four-year degrees in business. The University of Central Florida (UCF) had a program, of course, but the university alone couldn't meet the demand for graduates. Thus in 2015, Allcorn and his colleagues initiated a series of conversations with UCF officials, Valencia College leaders, and faculty and staff at nearby community colleges to "make sure that our stakeholders, and even what someone from outside of Orlando might see as our competition, is at least moderately comfortable with" Valencia developing a new applied bachelor's degree in business.[7] Given the clear need from the business community, there were only a few sticking points; Valencia's plan was widely supported. The next step was approaching the state of Florida for approval. According to Allcorn, all of the initial work coordinating with other institutions—and demonstrating how Valencia's new degree would complement, not compete with, UCF's bachelor's and master's programs—paid off, as UCF vice provost Jeffrey Jones effectively secured Valencia's approval to offer the bachelor's in business by standing up in the meeting and saying, "UCF wholly supports these programs."[8]

Having secured the green light from Tallahassee, Valencia faculty and administrators began designing the program. As Allcorn related, there were several design constraints, the most limiting being that Florida community colleges cannot offer four-year degrees; instead, they had to design a two-plus-two pathway, with the bachelor's degree awarded upon completion of the second two years. Given this, Allcorn's group endeavored to create "the widest door in for a two-plus-two that is imaginable," as well as a degree that prepared students to enter the workforce or continue their studies in any number of UCF's master's degree programs. Allcorn described the process of brainstorming how the program might work:

> We put people in a room and all talked about it. I'm sure everybody does that stuff. But when we first started talking, we had two or three, up to nine hours of pre-reqs [prerequisites] we were going to make the

> students take to get into the program. And we got pretty far into the process with that in place. And we were pretty happy with it because it was way less than a lot of the programs we looked at. But at the end of the day, we—I remember where I was sitting, and I remember who said it—they said, "What if we had *no* common course pre-reqs to get in?"

No common course prerequisites. Allcorn and his colleagues had to sit with that idea for a while. It was outlandish: students would come in from all different disciplines, with various levels of experience and comfort with basic business concepts, and Valencia would need to get them all to the same place within two years! How could anyone design a tight, two-year curriculum without requiring that at least some courses be taken in the lower division? But the more Allcorn and his colleagues thought about it—the more they applied a *yes, and* approach to the concept—the more it began to make sense. As he related, "Even if I had said there is one pre-req, the student views it as a hurdle," especially if they came from an associate degree program unrelated to business. Furthermore, by eliminating prerequisites, Allcorn figured that he would be better able to support enrollment in Valencia's existing associate of science (AS) degrees. At that time, he recalled:

> Students were walking away from the AS in business administration [at Valencia] and getting an AA [associate of arts] with the common course pre-reqs to get into UCF. How can I blame them for that? As a matter of fact, my advisers were advising them to do that. Every time I heard that, I'd just die a little on the inside . . . And several of them would say, "Hey, with nine more credits you can get your AS also," but okay, why?! So for them to be able to legit get an AS and come into a bachelor's degree, in my view, that supports those programs. And so I've gotten no pushback at all. I think if we had required an AA, I would have received and deserved pushback. Because we'd be continuing to erode the AS enrollment.

Yet despite the clear benefits of this idea, the ease of a more traditional arrangement was alluring. No prerequisites, Allcorn said, "causes a lot of work for the advisers. I could have said, get an associate of arts, take these pre-reqs, and then you are eligible. Boom. Easy. And I would have had 100 or 115 students." But because Allcorn's team prioritized a "broad pathway in, broad pathway out" ethos over ease of implementation and followed a seemingly "nuts!" idea to its very logical conclusion, Valencia College now offers a bachelor's of applied science in business and organizational leadership where students "have no concept they are in a two-plus-two. They think they are in a bachelor's. When they finish that associate degree, they know they can walk right into the bachelor's degree. That makes it as smooth as if they would have been at a university."[9] Figuring out how to compensate for the lack of prerequisites was somewhat complicated, but by creating prototypes of education plans for imaginary students with AA and AS degrees in various disciplines, Allcorn's team was able to identify and bypass numerous administrative hurdles and design a system whereby the college utilizes the first semester of students' third year to backfill any general education requirements that AS students might not have completed and/or any lower-division business courses that students in AA programs would not have taken.

Valencia is already reaping benefits from the aha! moment that occurred in Allcorn's brainstorming session. Over five hundred AA and AS recipients enter the bachelor's program each fall—five times the number they had initially expected. Total unduplicated head count nears two thousand. And by 2018, the program was already beating its very aggressive revenue goals, returning a profit to the institution. All because someone asked, "What if . . . ?" and their colleagues took the idea seriously.

WHAT IF . . . EVERYTHING THE COLLEGE DOES COULD BE CONSIDERED IN LIGHT OF THREE GOALS AND EIGHT PRINCIPLES?

> *We have just three goals. This is the only reason we are here. We are here to serve the community. We have to operate as one college . . . and we have to be student-ready.*[10]

Ask anyone at TCC what the biggest change has been since Chancellor Gene Giovannini came on board in 2016, and the answer will inevitably be the college's Three Goals and Eight Principles. TCC's three goals are the lens through which all work at the college is considered, and the principles specify eight areas of focus or ways in which college faculty and staff work to achieve each goal. The Three Goals and Eight Principles are also the driving force behind a unique new administrative structure and the basis for evaluating all new programs, budget requests, and entrepreneurial opportunities. The Three and Eight framework is, to say the least, a significant paradigm shift for the college, yet it occurred because an incoming chancellor had the audacity to ask, What if we engaged in a districtwide visioning processes to agree upon why we are all here, and then to identify how we will work together to carry out our shared objectives? William Coppola, president of TCC's Southeast campus, recalled the genesis of the Three and Eight model: "Like many community colleges in the country, we were part of Achieving the Dream and we had initiative overload . . . we implemented every single initiative that came out. And it just got to be, okay, what am I going to do next semester?" Coppola recalled conversations with then chancellor Erma Johnson Hadley, where he'd say, "Erma, you are not building a sustainable model! You are basically just throwing spaghetti against the wall! So we don't know—when our math scores went up, we don't know what did it! Was it the intrusive advising? Was it the emporium? We don't know!"

Agreeing with Coppola, when Gene Giovannni arrived at TCC in summer 2016, he vowed to simplify things. One of his first steps was to hire Ayers Saint Gross (ASG), a national consulting firm, to help faculty and staff across the district's six campuses engage with the question, "Why are we here?" ASG held twenty-five visioning sessions with over 450 participants, ultimately coalescing around three major goals or mission priorities. The first, Giovannini shared, is to operate as one college. To him, that means coordinating initiatives and programs across campuses and sharing human and financial resources in ways that best serve the college as a whole, not its component parts. As he said, "We have six campuses, but we are really here as one college." The second goal is to be student-ready.

Coppola explained: "That was new for us. Not that we didn't think like that, but we never saw that as part of our mission. To go into the community and say, 'If you want to be successful college students, then *we* have to be ready to accept you where you are.' That was the hardest one to go through." The third goal—to serve and partner with the community—in many ways sets the stage for all of TCC's entrepreneurial efforts. By elevating service to community to the same pedestal as the other two goals, and by agreeing that all new initiatives shall be considered in light of their ability to further one or more of the three, TCC faculty and staff opened the door to new ways of doing business while ensuring that the college remains mission-oriented in its endeavors.

"So that's what came back from all this visioning, all these stickies all over the place," said Giovannini, "Three very simple goals." The next step, he said, was asking "Okay, now that we have the *why,* what do we need to do to deliver on the why?" Over the next eighteen months, TCC continued its visioning process, ultimately deciding on Eight Principles—detailed on the college's website—that identify the specific ways in which TCC will work to achieve its goals.[11] That faculty and staff from six very different campuses were able to agree on eight tactics to carry out their shared objectives was impressive, but to Coppola, the stakeholder-driven process by which they were developed was just as powerful:

> The good part about it is that we have individuals within this college that are, for the first time, being asked, "What do you think?" And there are some—I always call them diamonds in the rough. There are people who never said a word, and now they are shining! They just can't wait. They love it. They go back to the campuses and they can't wait to get to panel meetings. We engaged them, "What do you think we should do?" And we make it very clear: "We aren't doing that if you don't want to do that" . . . So really it's getting the college to be more understanding that you're not just an employee here. You have a responsibility to make what we are doing relevant to the community.

The Three and Eight model also led to some substantial shifts in administrative functioning, which both support the new framework and help to carry out the One College goal. Specifically, Giovannini appointed each of his six campus presidents to be the champion of one or more principles. For each principle, the champion leads a panel of experts: faculty and staff from across the district who have relevant experience or need to be involved in the work of the group, including IT, HR, facilities, finance, and so forth. Giovannini explained, "We don't need any ad hoc committees, we don't need any task forces, everything that comes up goes to a principle. And if the champion and the panel need help, let's say it's a parking issue, well, you bring the police in! More engagement. When that issue is over, they come out . . . If we do our job right," he said, "no matter what comes up in this college, we should be able to put it within one of those that we call principles."

TCC has, in effect, created a process by which all new ideas, entrepreneurial opportunities, and budget requests are vetted, developed, and carried out by the champion and panel responsible for the success of each principle, thus ensuring that all new ideas remain closely tethered to institutional mission and preventing efforts from being duplicated at multiple campuses. This has required some significant changes to top administrators' job descriptions. Coppola explained:

> When I first got here, it was like a typical multicampus president. You are in the weeds; you are running your campus. Nothing happens without your approval. It's changed now. I'm not even on my campus; I'm here [at the district office] most of the time. So everyone's kind of raised up a level. So my chief academic officer, my student services, my team runs the campus. I have a chief of staff who takes care of things. I take care of things at more of a 30,000-foot level, and Gene is up at a 100,000-foot level. So it gives me more of an opportunity to have more resources around all of the campuses . . . And that's how the principles are really getting us to work more as a group.

To Giovannini, these structural changes are integral to the success of his institution: "We've operated in higher education with all of these silos," he said. "You've got the faculty, the administration, the board, the community. And none should they ever come together. Well, what we are doing is taking those silos down and being much more intentful [sic], purposeful, and obvious so everyone can see that connection ... When you begin taking down the silos, you begin changing the mind-set. And when you change the mind-set, new ideas are much more accepted." TCC's Three Goals and Eight Principles—and the organizational structure that supports them—provide a solid foundation for the college to explore new ideas and vet existing processes, enabling it to act in an entrepreneurial manner while safeguarding mission priorities.

WHAT IF . . . WE COULD GENERATE REVENUE BY PROVIDING BETTER SERVICE TO STUDENTS?

> *We start with service first here at Valencia, so it is a student-centric decision.*[12]

Nationally, just under 3 percent of community college revenues come from sales and services of auxiliary enterprises, including vending machines, food service contracts, school stores, and so forth.[13] At Valencia, that percentage is somewhat higher, thanks in part to the creativity of director of auxiliary services Jeff Filko and the college's firm belief that the campus remain "student-focused and student-forward" in making decisions about potential revenue-generating opportunities. Filko is a self-described ideas man; he has "a dry erase board about the size of a television that is full. Organized but full. And I'm always thinking, what else can we do here?" For example, when Filko arrived at Valencia, he learned that the college owned three cellular towers, one each on the East, West, and Osceola campuses. They were, at the time, maintained by the college's facilities team, but Filko saw an opportunity to generate additional revenue and improve students' connectivity. He commissioned a study that showed poor cellular coverage in these areas, and convinced providers such as AT&T, Verizon, and T-Mobile to lease space on the towers for their antennae. He also began leasing television channels for educational broadband. Today, Valencia's three cell towers generate about $1 million per year, all of which supports student programs and services.

Given the success of the three original cell towers, in 2018 Filko began exploring the idea of building two more: one on the Poinciana Campus—"all the carriers have poor coverage in that area"—and one on an undeveloped parcel of land the college owns west of Disney World. College leaders were supportive of a Poinciana tower, assuming Filko could find a way to pay for it, but resisted the idea of putting up a tower in an area that did not directly benefit students. As Filko related, "I was pretty quickly told no. Because we don't want the first use of our educational property to be commercial . . . So there was resistance, but it wasn't 'absolutely never,' it was 'not now. Wait until we get a building up.'" Understanding the college's need to prioritize service to students over revenues, in late 2018 Filko turned his energy toward the Poinciana tower. Not wanting to spend his own budget to build it, he asked, "What if I can get somebody else to pay for it?" He described his idea:

> I approach T-Mobile, for example, and say, "Hey, why don't you build the tower. You do all the FCC and regulatory and I'll let you put your antennae on the tower for ten years for nothing. No rent." 'Cause they are paying me several thousand dollars a month, some of them. I make it sweet for them and as soon as the tower is done, they deed it to me and I can lease it out. I can make my money off AT&T and Sprint. Whoever didn't build the tower, they don't get this sweet ten-year deal.

Filko has applied the same willingness to ask "what if . . ." to improving the college's vending partnerships. When he arrived, Valencia's vending contract paid a guaranteed minimum of $200,000 a year, plus a percentage of sales over a certain amount, although the latter was rarely achieved. Despite being a consistent and relatively large sum of money, Filko received complaints from students and faculty alike: "Oh, the vending is terrible," they'd say. "The food is out of date, it's expired, moldy sandwiches, machines aren't functional." He spent a week auditing all of the college's ninety-two vending machines and found that "about 85 percent of them had either expired food or weren't working. It was appalling." Filko called in the vending company, developed a plan for it to address the problem, and "vending revenues immediately went up. Of course! Because people are buying more. And it's a win-win. I get more commissions, they get better sales, everybody wins. I have happier students, happier faculty and staff."

But Filko didn't stop there. Noting that in several locations, demand was outpacing supply—especially at East Campus, where two side-by-side vending machines were grossing about $4,000 a month and constantly running out of products—Filko began exploring the idea of replacing the machines with unattended retail kiosks called Smart Markets. He approached the vending company with his idea, saying, "Here's the data; I've analyzed it. It's gonna sell a ton of stuff just if we keep what's there, but I think there is an opportunity. But I know the [Smart Market] equipment costs $50,000 to $60,000. I don't want to pay for it. Why don't you pay for the equipment? I'll pay the installation costs, $13,000 in plumbing and electric and all that stuff." Filko's intuition paid off. He negotiated a lower overall commission rate to incent his vending partner to pay for the Smart Market equipment, but because sales have been so much higher—the first month the East Campus Smart Market opened, revenues went from $4,000 to $14,700—Valencia is earning $330,000 per year from its vending contract instead of $200,000. Furthermore, the Smart Markets offer a greater variety of healthier food options for students, as well as a communal place to gather. As Filko described, "We are not just feeding them. We are not just giving them food. We are giving them an environment in which they can engage with their peer cohort. They can maybe spend a little time. Maybe they are going to spend a couple of bucks, but primarily they are there for other reasons and we happen to make money off some of it."

Of all the entrepreneurial ideas and ventures highlighted in this book, Valencia's cell towers and Smart Markets are the most obviously commercial and the least tied to the curriculum or students' academic experiences. And for many who are concerned about an increased market orientation, they may well represent the kind of entrepreneurial activity that has the potential to shift community colleges away from their commitment to providing a public good and toward the slippery slope of profit-driven decision-making. Yet I include these examples precisely because they sit on the razor's edge between revenue generation and adherence to institutional mission and values and because they illustrate how Valencia (and other colleges) can maintain this delicate balance by insisting that all revenue-generating activity remains fundamentally student-focused. If it doesn't benefit students, don't do it. But if it does—if it provides greater connectivity or healthier food options, for example, and it also helps the institution's bottom line—college leaders might be remiss to ignore such opportunities. In Valencia's case, increased sales from vending contracts and cell towers have been critical to supporting the college's ambitious infrastructure projects. "If I brag on something," Filko said, "it's that I put $2 million into the downtown campus. So when you are complaining about your $1.75 Mountain Dews, realize that about $0.50 of that Mountain Dew went into the downtown campus to directly benefit our students." Similarly, when people say, "I spent $10 in your Smart Market," Filko replies: "Thank you for putting $3 back into our college. 'Cause it's almost linear." Through its Smart Markets, cell towers, and numerous other auxiliary enterprises, Valencia has found a way to generate revenue by providing better service to students.

WHAT IF . . . WE UTILIZED A CREATIVE PROBLEM-SOLVING PROCESS TO ENVISION A SCHOOL OF PUBLIC SAFETY SERVING THE CENTRAL FLORIDA COMMUNITY?

> *The successful creative problem-solving process and the divergent and convergent thinking strategy created a positive and inclusive experience for all internal and external stakeholders . . . The process not only defined a clear vision and mission for the School of Public Safety, but also established . . . a new distributed and collaborative education model.*[14]

Like many community colleges, Valencia had for many years offered training leading to state certification in law enforcement and fire and rescue, as well as an AS degree in criminal justice. But in 2013, President Sandy Shugart, Executive Vice President for Global, Professional, and Continuing

Education Joe Battista, and Jeff Goltz, executive dean of Valencia's School of Public Safety, sat down to discuss how the college might better meet the education and training needs of Central Florida's law enforcement, corrections, fire and rescue, 911 telecommunications, and private security organizations. These agencies, Goltz noted, are responsible for the safety and well-being of Orlando's rapidly growing population, as well as that of the nearly 70 million visitors to the area each year. Plus, he added, there is a direct correlation between public safety and economic development, which presented a clear opportunity for Valencia College to expand education and training in a way that would benefit students, public safety organizations, and the community.

To ensure that the new public safety model would meet the needs of these stakeholders, Shugart outlined a plan to be executed in four phases. Phase I centered around the intentional service integration of existing criminal justice and fire institute programs. The most important design criteria during this phase was a seamless public safety student experience, and to accomplish this the team "created new synergies and multidisciplinary public safety programming," integrating noncredit training leading to state and industry-recognized certifications into existing AS degrees and working with faculty across Valencia's campuses to develop and align the curricula.[15] The team also created an entirely new organizational structure, providing administrative support for both criminal justice and fire programs "in the middle . . . so there's no duplication of efforts."[16]

For Phase II, "Expand the Vision of Public Safety Education and Training," the Valencia team utilized creative problem solving to guide visioning exercises with college and external stakeholders. In early 2014, the team brought over forty faculty, administrators, and staff to the college's Collaborative Design Center (described later in this chapter) and engaged them in a series of exercises. The first was meant to encourage divergent thinking: participants were asked to brainstorm definitions for a School of Public Safety. These fell into seven themes, including regional emphasis, multidisciplinary, and collaborative. In the second exercise, which focused on convergent thinking, "small groups discussed facts and evaluated the local public safety industry, regional population and demographics, the central

Florida service population and tourism, and college-wide safety programs."[17] For the third exercise, participants prioritized divergence once again, each sketching their vision for the School of Public Safety.

Following the internal meetings, Valencia hosted a visioning summit with forty stakeholders representing thirty Central Florida governmental, public safety, private security, healthcare, educational, and entertainment agencies. Thirty-six college representatives, including public safety faculty, also attended. Each participant was assigned to one of twelve public safety groups and—drawing on the themes identified in the internal visioning sessions—tasked with identifying public safety challenges; suggesting education and training solutions; confirming, modifying, or enhancing the college's public safety vision and model; and identifying future programming areas.[18] Goltz recalled the experience:

> We brought all the public safety community in. All of our stakeholders. And we had this big visioning session in our events center. A big auditorium, a big open room. And we started to think about, what is public safety? What programs do they want? And that's where everything really started the ball, based on their input . . . We defined the School of Public Safety. We looked at programming; what does multidisciplinary mean? . . . What does it really mean for our communities?

By the end of Phase II, Valencia's stakeholders had converged on a vision and mission for the new enterprise, and in December 2014 Valencia's board of trustees unanimously commissioned the School of Public Safety. Goltz and his team immediately embarked upon Phase III, "Expanding Public Safety Programs." Adding a new safety and security curricular focus, and drawing heavily from the Phase II visioning sessions, the team designed a "collaborative and distributed model" in which the School of Public Safety acts as the master hub for programming, and all of the other campuses that have public safety programming on them function as spokes. To solicit feedback from campus faculty and staff about the new model, Battista and Goltz went on a listening tour, meeting with "every senior team at every campus."[19] This was especially important, Goltz noted, because the associate degree program in criminal justice offered at East Campus needed to be exactly the same as that at the Osceola, Poinciana, and West campuses so that law enforcement agencies know exactly what they are getting and the college can still provide multiple, convenient locations for public safety education and training.

To coordinate Valencia's distributed model, the college expanded the collaborative organizational structure developed in Phase I and created a public safety core team that meets quarterly to "talk about all the public safety issues, collegewide issues, and programming issues." The core team comprises deans, chairs, faculty members, and administrators from each campus and is, as Goltz explained, "really the glue, the collaboration, that keeps us all together." Supporting the core team are various subcommittees and industry advisory committees, which "review all aspects of the criminal justice and fire programs on a regular basis to make sure that the curriculum meets the needs of the local public safety community."[20] The multidisciplinary nature of the core team reinforces Valencia's commitment to intentional service integration and is a major factor in its success. Goltz shared, "It's not just about law enforcement, it's not just about fire, it's about everybody working together . . . Because public safety is so complex now, everybody has got to work together because of what we are dealing with in society."

Another key to the School of Public Safety's success, said Battista, is "how we've integrated continuing education into the model so . . . it's a wide breadth of programming, whether you are pursuing a degree or whether you're doing something in the continuing ed area," like the fire, law enforcement, or corrections academies. Indeed, all continuing education and certification courses are now integrated into specific tracks in Valencia's degree programs. The idea, Battista shared, is to "articulate credits in everything we do." For example, "In fire, a high schooler comes out, spends two years with us, they walk out of here with their degree in fire science, their EMT certification, and their firefighting certification." Similarly, he said, "we've just developed one in law enforcement. They come out of high school, spend two years with us [getting their AS in criminal justice]; their last semester, they go to the police academy and articulate college credits."

In Phase III of the design process, the School of Public Safety also incorporated opportunities for education and training beyond the associate degree. For example, graduates are encouraged to consider transferring into Valencia's new bachelor's of applied science in business and organizational leadership. Current public safety professionals (as individuals or in groups) now have access to advanced specialized training to refresh and upgrade their skills. And in addition, the school offers a Public Safety Leadership Development Certification Program in which leaders from law enforcement, fire, corrections, and other organizations come together for four weeks to "anticipate and meet the challenges of the future," including gaining "insight into fostering innovation within their agency while exploring leadership theories and practices that apply specifically to public safety professionals."[21] Although the leadership development program is fee-based, Valencia and other colleges award undergraduate and graduate credits upon completion of the certificate.

By all accounts, the School of Public Safety has already been a huge success, thanks in large part to the creative problem solving and inclusive stakeholder-driven approach used to develop it. Goltz related, "I think we crafted this strategy almost perfectly. I really do. The way that the team has worked together at the college and with the community." Enrollment and revenue numbers support his assertion: between 2015 and 2018, enrollments more than doubled from five thousand to eleven thousand students, and fees generated through continuing education certifications and academies help to support traditional associate degree programs. Riding these accomplishments, by late 2018 Goltz and his team were well on their way to completing the fourth and final phase of the process: "Expanding Public Safety Facilities." Goltz explained:

> We have about forty acres at the School of Public Safety site that's woods right now . . . We started in May of 2016 with an architect, and . . . we spent a year going through visioning exercises with the locals. With the stakeholders, internal and external. We had several different workshops, and then I went out and met with leaders and asked them what their priorities are, and we came up with this master plan that is in this

> document here. It's a $170 million project. To me it's the most important project in Central Florida right now because public safety is a huge priority. So here's our master plan. Right now we are in this yellow building. Everything back here is all future: big classroom buildings, firearms range, tactical building, tactical village . . . fire training facility.

When we last spoke, Goltz had raised about $10 million of the $170 million needed to enact the School of Public Safety's long-term facilities plan. But, he noted, he had also applied for a $5 million infrastructure grant; "the Orlando Economic Partnership has taken this project on as their number-one priority this year"; and there were multiple other opportunities for federal and state funding. "I'm very optimistic that this thing will get funded in the not-too-distant future," Goltz asserted. "I can really feel it . . . The public safety leadership, they are so in. They respect the college, they respect what we are doing." Battista concurred: At the end of the day, "this is a community asset. This is for everyone."

HOW MIGHT WE . . . SUPPORT DIVERGENT AND CONVERGENT THINKING?

> *It's really clear to me from Sandy [Shugart] that you can't just do things the way we've always done them. That's not good enough. So the campus presidents hear that, and then the deans have that expectation from their campus president . . . which in turn creates that expectation of: You need to try something different. And let's see what the results are. If it doesn't work well, then we'll try something else.*[22]

The four community colleges highlighted in this book have all made intense, public commitments to entrepreneurship, and thus it is no surprise that each is working to support divergent thinking among faculty and staff and that they have all established processes by which they can converge upon and develop the most interesting, impactful ideas. At TCC, incorporating a *yes, and* attitude into program evaluations has been key to encouraging creative thinking and risk taking among faculty and staff. For example, when Clint Grant, executive dean of aviation, business, and logistics at TCC's Northwest Campus, approaches his president or provost with a new idea, "rarely am I shut down. They are open to anything I have to say, and our little motto is . . . 'We Go until Someone Says No.'" Sometimes he has to go back and refine an idea, of course, but as he tells his own faculty, "Assume that it's going to happen and get things in place to make it happen."

For William Coppola, giving staff permission to change processes without prior approval has been critical to encouraging creative solutions to problems. He recalled a day when roughly eight hundred students were standing in line to register for classes. At many colleges, he said, staff would process the registrations one at a time because that is the way they have always done things. Instead, looking at the long line, his staff "quickly said, Okay, let's do this. Let's put people here, let's move people around, let's do a triage." According to Coppola, no one was afraid to act because the campus had a history of celebrating innovative solutions and rewarding staff for taking the initiative to implement them.

Kathleen Plinske, Valencia College's executive vice president and provost, believes a similar ethos exists at her institution. "I think that perhaps one of the biggest challenges that we confront is our traditional structures and ways that we make decisions," she said. "And so in order to be entrepreneurial, it causes you to ask: Why is it that we do that? Why do we require that? And is that something that we must continue to do?" Plinske shared how she came to this understanding:

> A couple of years ago, I was in one of my regular meetings with Dr. Shugart and he said, "Do you feel free to break our rules?" And I was like, Wow. What is the appropriate response to this question?! What is the right answer? But I came to discover what he was trying to get at, which is, Do we have a culture where the machine sort of runs and nobody is actually paying attention to why we are doing things the way we do them?

For Plinske, this realization was transformative and underscored the importance of encouraging new ways of thinking, new approaches to solving problems, so that inertia doesn't take over and the college doesn't revert back to an attitude of, "Well, this doesn't work well for students, but it's the best we can do." Faculty and staff must be empowered to break the rules, she said, because "there are certain instances where the boxes or boundaries that have been set up actually don't meet our students' needs or our communities' needs well." In addition to giving employees permission to draw outside the lines, Valencia also works to encourage divergent thinking by sending deans and administrators to workshops at the college's Collaborative Design Center to learn how they can implement design thinking and creative problem solving into their departmental processes. For Terry Allcorn and other faculty leaders, this training has been incredibly "helpful in creating an environment where ideas can surface."

Valencia's Shugart, TCC's Giovannini, and the innovative faculty and administrators working for them were not born knowing how to lead in this way; establishing a culture where divergent thinking is encouraged and rewarded is learned behavior. Rufus Glasper, former chancellor of the Maricopa Community Colleges, came to understand the importance of such a culture early in his career by watching how his predecessor sought out diverse voices and opinions in institutional decision-making. Glasper had just moved from Chicago to Tempe, Arizona, to take the position of Maricopa's director of finance under then chancellor Paul Elsner. Within his first few weeks, he was asked to sit in on a Chancellor's Executive Committee (CEC) meeting. He recalled:

> I was the only one at the CEC who was director-level. And Paul was asking a question of the CEC members, and almost to a person, everyone says, "Yeah, Paul, I think that's a good idea." Then he came to me and . . . he said, "Rufus, what do you think?" and I'm sitting there thinking, you know, you've got fourteen people in front of you saying the same thing. So I said, "It sounds like it's a pretty good idea, Paul. I'm sure you can make it work." So he went on for another twenty minutes or so and came back to me again. And I said, "You know, I think if we talked to some of the folks at the colleges, we could tweak a few things, but it can work." He came back to me a third time. And finally I'm

> thinking, does he *really* want my opinion? And I gave my opinion. And I said, "I've actually talked to the colleges and there are better ways to do this, and this is how you could do it."

As you might imagine, Glasper's immediate superior was not happy with his performance and "accused me of insubordination and not following the group." But when Glasper asked Elsner, "Why did you do that to me?" he received a response that still resonates with him nearly thirty years later. "I supported you coming here because of your background and your experience," Elsner said. "I want you to use it. I don't want you to sit in on these meetings and just give me what you think I want."[23]

Elsner went on to demonstrate his commitment to divergent thinking—from all levels of campus leadership—by repeatedly asking his employees to share their opinions and ideas, support them with data, and think creatively about how the district might improve the lives of students and communities. Elsner's only rule was to "be consistent and do it for the right reasons." For Glasper, this permission to take risks was empowering, and as he—over time—ascended to chief financial officer and, eventually, chancellor, he incorporated the same philosophy into his leadership style. Very quickly, he recalled, things began to change. Long-standing policies, such as "if you don't spend all of your money by May 1, then we will take it away from you" or "you can't spend any more than 10 percent of a certain line item at one time" were eliminated, as Glasper felt that they limited each campus's ability to strategically invest its budget in new programs or initiatives. Even small changes such as these can have an outsized effect on institutional culture. From Elsner, Glasper learned that empowering faculty and staff to think critically and creatively about how to do their jobs better not only makes for more engaged employees, but also enables the college to more effectively accomplish its goals.

• • •

As Intuit's design thinkers like to say, *after you go broad, you've got to go narrow*, meaning that in order to be truly innovative, colleges need a process for combing through all the beautiful, creative, divergent ideas their stakeholders have generated and converging on those few that have the most promise for improving the lives of students and communities and/or increasing the financial sustainability of the institution. At Maricopa, each college has its own process for *going narrow*, and the district has also developed a way to identify and fund those ideas that require additional support or that can be scaled across the district.

For example, GateWay College utilizes its vacancy savings—dollars committed to faculty and staff positions that are temporarily unfilled—to invest in entrepreneurial ideas. According to former president Steven Gonzales (now Maricopa's interim chancellor), with an average of twenty to thirty vacancies at any time, and mean annual salaries between $60,000 and $75,000, the college has $100,000 or more just sitting around each month. "Rather than just letting that money dissipate . . . we play the come line"—meaning college leaders essentially place a low-risk bet with those dollars. Faculty and staff are encouraged to submit entrepreneurial ideas to the president's office, which commits up to $25,000 per year to funding at least one of them. To date, GateWay has utilized its innovation fund to explore new community education courses, develop a pro bono community health clinic, and support a long-term educational partnership with First Place, an independent living organization for individuals with autism. The goal for all innovation fund projects, said Gonzales, "is undesignated revenue for the college. But it is also to get people here. It goes back to recruitment and retention."

At nearby South Mountain Community College, President Shari Olson annually sets aside $100,000 for innovation grants—half of which is dedicated to faculty-driven projects and half for initiatives coming out of student development or organizational effectiveness units. South Mountain's grant competition is built into the college's annual action planning process. Each division submits a yearly action plan, identifying between three and five goals that are tied to South Mountain's Five Pillars and Nineteen Strategies (similar to TCC's Three Goals and Eight Principles). Within those goals, divisional action plans specify new or changes to existing programs and initiatives, identify necessary resources and/or possible cost savings, and detail how the college might provide financial or other assistance.

Each divisional action plan is vetted by its appropriate vice president, who prioritizes the ideas that they believe will best serve students, the college, and the community. The vice presidents then come together to lobby for what they want to fund from their divisions, using "each other for push-back and challenge," and ultimately deciding on one or more projects in which to invest that year's innovation dollars.[24]

This process is mirrored at the district level, where the CEC works with faculty and staff at each of Maricopa's ten campuses to more fully develop promising entrepreneurial ideas, establish an expected return on investment, and present them to the board of governors. LabForce was approved and funded this way, noted Maricopa chief of staff Darcy Renfro, as was the Maricopa Information Technology (IT) Institute, a collaboration between Chandler-Gilbert, Mesa, and Scottsdale community colleges that meets an emerging workforce need for talent in the areas of blockchain, app development, big data, gaming, cloud computing, and mobile and wearable technology. (Maricopa's IT Institute is discussed in more detail in chapter 6.)

A similar innovation fund exists at NIACC: each year the college's division chairs identify two or three promising entrepreneurial ideas, and together with Steven Schulz select one strategic initiative to present to the board. After providing feedback and suggestions, the board commits to three years of funding at $50,000 per year. Schulz explained, "At the end of three years we assess it and we either decide to bring those expenditures into the general fund or we stop."

As you might expect, some of NIACC's strategic initiatives have been more successful than others. For example, efforts to double the number of international students at the college "were marching right along"—international student enrollment was up 40 percent and the college had hired a part-time international adviser to provide support on campus—until, as Schulz recalled, "the [2016] change in the federal administration really restricted visas, student visas." Since then, he said, "We've seen a dramatic decrease in the application process and the ability to get [visas] in a timely manner." Nonetheless, because the initiative still has the potential to increase tuition and student housing revenues in the future, and because it helps to globalize a campus where nearly 90 percent of students are white, NIACC opted to incorporate the international adviser's salary into the general fund, even though the program has yet to meet its revenue goals.

NIACC's strategic initiative to develop and expand summer camps—many of which utilize the college's on-campus housing—has been far more successful. As part of this initiative, faculty and staff were invited to submit proposals for youth camps, the best of which were funded for three years and then expected to become self-sufficient. "Honestly, I don't care if we make money on [summer camps]," said Schulz. "But we at least want to cover the faculty costs and the staff costs and the food and whatever else the students need. Because we know that youth camps in this area, they are just not available. Parents are dying for things for their kids to do in the summer besides sports." Each summer camp—whether it is sports-related, academic, or focused on entrepreneurship—culminates with a campus tour so that every one of the 1,500 to 2,000 kids visiting each summer develops a personal connection to the college.

The crown jewel of NIACC's summer camps is the two-week overnight Verizon STEM camp for sixth- through eighth-grade girls. This camp—developed in partnership with Verizon Innovative Learning and NACCE—is designed for middle school girls in rural areas, half of whom must qualify for free or reduced lunch. By engaging girls in projects utilizing virtual and augmented reality, coding, 3D printing, and other exciting technologies, the Verizon STEM camps seek to show young women that there is place for them in the STEM workforce. At NIACC's Verizon STEM camp, middle school girls learn about design thinking and utilize the framework to develop a solution to a problem related to one of the United Nations' global sustainable development goals. Each camper works alone or in teams to identify a need and then brainstorm and prototype a technology-based solution that will make a social impact. "I think this world needs to be thinking entrepreneurially," said Kelley O'Rourke. NIACC's Verizon STEM camp helps "our kids to be thinking that way," while also generating summer revenue and creating additional pathways to the college.

Like NIACC and the Maricopa colleges, Valencia also has a structured process for generating innovative ideas and then converging on a few of the most impactful. Adapted from a model utilized by early-stage investors, Shugart calls Valencia's approach the "innovation funnel." As he described it, across campus, there are:

> A thousand flowers blooming. A climate of innovation, [everyone] trying wacky stuff. It doesn't cost very much . . . Once in a while you have a project that is really worth scaling a little bit. So they come into the funnel and say, "We need some resources." I'll call that Level I. And somebody close to them has some resources to say, "Yes, let's do some more of that. Let me give you release time or funds to go to a conference. Let me give you $5,000 in equipment, whatever you need."

Valencia has set aside money to support these Level I ideas, and for those that have the potential to be developed further, they move through the funnel to Level II, which incorporates, as Shugart said, "a little more rigor, evaluation, and some more money." Subsequently, "if it looks successful and looks like it has the potential to be scalable, then you move down the funnel to Level III and now you are talking about the Big Bucks. This is a pilot at scale. And that might mean a Department of Labor grant, Title Five, Title Three, or it might be a college investment. But at this point we're saying: pretty high standard of proof, established a priori." At any given time, Shugart shared, Valencia may have a hundred small-scale innovations occurring across the institution, fifty at Level I, twenty in Level II, "probably only about five" at Level III, and one or two at Level IV, where they are "getting institutionalized across the campuses." The Centers for Accelerated Training (discussed in detail in chapter 4) came out of Valencia's innovation funnel, as did the School of Public Health described earlier in this chapter.

For Shugart, the funnel is important for two reasons. First and foremost, it encourages divergent, innovative thinking across all of Valencia's campuses, letting faculty and staff know that there will be support for their ideas as long as they are grounded in data and tied to the college's mission to serve students and the greater Orlando community. Second, the innovation funnel ensures that all investment decisions are transparent. Pet projects are not financed from secret accounts known to only a few administrators; faculty and staff know that each funded idea went through the same process of establishing need, identifying necessary resources and possible returns to the college, and being iteratively refined and improved based on stakeholder feedback. As a result, there is much less resistance to innovation, as constituents understand that each project is simply another way Valencia is working to accomplish its shared objectives.

HOW MIGHT WE . . . PROVIDE CREATIVE SPACE FOR INNOVATIVE THINKING?

> *The purpose of this space is disruption. To disrupt our normal practices in order to really be able to focus on the work.*[25]

All four colleges highlighted in this book have considered how they might provide space for innovative thinking. NIACC, for example, has a technical room—originally built for STEM learning—where participants can write on tables and whiteboards and ideas or images from anyone's work space can be projected to a central screen in order to facilitate collaboration. TCC's Opportunity Center and Maricopa's CEI (both described in chapter 4) each have several rooms where walls and/or furniture can be rearranged to accommodate different size groups and encourage creative thinking. In addition, CEI offers numerous informal spaces where people can collaborate over coffee and snacks as well as "more formal meeting spaces and writable walls so you can get creative." As Executive Director Tom Schumann said, "A lot of what we are trying to do is build community . . . so we use food, we use meetings, coffee, to bring them together. And we're amazed sometimes at the amount of collaboration that goes on."

Valencia College has made a much larger investment in creative space, setting aside eleven thousand square feet of a new building on West Campus for a facility dedicated to inquiry in design, a place where faculty, staff, and community stakeholders can come together and be, as Shugart put it, "designers of a solution, not advocates for constituents." Valencia's Collaborative Design Center (CDC), described in the following pages, is an inspiring place, and in a perfect world, all community colleges would have the means to create similar spaces for creative problem solving. Given resource constraints at all or most institutions, however, I offer this illustration of the CDC less as a best practice that should be replicated elsewhere and more to stimulate thinking about how elements of the CDC's physical space—as well as the activities that occur within it—can be adapted to support innovation on any campus.

Katie Tagye, an energetic former speech and communications professor, is director of the CDC. While giving me a tour of the facility, she stressed that "the space itself is really just a physical manifestation of the work we do at the college." As such, she said, several metaphors are integrated into the design of the space. One of these, physically depicted on a large poster in the CDC entryway, is that of a ship, signifying that Valencia faculty and staff are all in the same boat and must rely on one another to navigate unfamiliar waters. Another metaphor, this one painted on a long hallway, is a bridge. Tagye explained:

> At the time we were building, Sandy [Shugart] was reading a book on the Brooklyn Bridge, and just the innovation, collaboration that went into it represented a connection to our work. And Felicia Williams, the campus president on [West] Campus, she loves it because it really represents what we are as a community college: we are the [bridge], not the destination, for students to reach whatever destination they are aiming for.

The other metaphor used in designing the CDC, Tagye said, is "right brain, left brain. So the rooms on this side were designed to be more convergent. And the rooms on this side were designed to be more divergent." Walking through the divergent, or right-brain side of the building, Tagye pointed out the characteristics of numerous creative spaces: "Everything that is white is a whiteboard. So the tables, the walls, the boards. And the board on the wall over here is also a digital space where you can do digital Post-its and that kind of thing. And then we have, you know, all the technology in here." Some rooms in the CDC have movable desks and chairs. Others "are more lounge-y," furnished with large comfortable armchairs and ottomans, all on wheels. Each room has multiple mobile whiteboards and a smorgasbord of sticky notes, markers, crayons, stacks of construction paper, rolls of butcher paper, and other supplies for participants to use in brainstorming or prototyping.

During the tour, Tagye pointed out that "different spaces are designed to evoke different feelings." For example, the CDC's three design studios were constructed to let in as much natural light as possible. The two smaller studios each have floor-to-ceiling windows, extra-high ceilings, and views of a green space abutting the college's culinary arts facility. "These rooms are more expansive," Tagye noted. They are "for small groups working on a project [where they] might just spend the day in here mapping things out. Or it's used as a breakout space for divergence or convergence." The largest of the three studios features electronic collaboration tools, as well as a large table in the middle that can be pulled apart to make smaller standing desks. Like Maricopa's CEI, the CDC also incorporates informal spaces where visitors can enjoy coffee, water, and light snacks. "What we try to do," Tagye noted, "is take care of those underlying needs so that you're not focused on, 'Oh, if I could just leave here and go get a coffee, I could focus.'"

At the back of the CDC are several smaller rooms, similar in look and feel to the design studios, that faculty or staff can reserve for longer periods of time. For example, when I visited the CDC, two different faculty and administrative groups had recently come together to improve the way that the college onboards faculty and staff. They had held several ideation sessions and had reserved one of these rooms for a month in order to "map out the details of how it's going to work." Evidence of the group's progress was visible everywhere: lists of previously brainstormed ideas were jotted down in pink marker on a large whiteboard, as were green checkmarks and symbols denoting various categories or reactions to the ideas. Yellow and pink sticky notes, connected by arrows, illustrated a potential new onboarding process and identified the campus unit that would be responsible for each action. Having space to let ideas percolate, Tagye said, is important: "And then in that way it also doesn't take over your life. It's here; come work on it here. Away from the distraction of your office. And do some deep thinking on it."

Valencia's CDC provides physical space for innovation, but perhaps just as important, Tagye and her colleagues actively facilitate collaborative decision-making using a combination of design thinking and creative problem-solving techniques. "When people ask to use the space," Tagye explained, "we ask them two basic questions. One is 'What problem are you working on?' and the second is 'What's your design plan?' So when the answer to the second question is 'I don't know what you are talking about,' then I'll jump in" to help guide the process. "What we always want to have—what we set a deliberate practice for—is really great dialogue . . . What's most important in this space is an exploration together."

As Kathleen Plinske shared, Katie Tagye "has an inventory of different techniques and strategies and ways to make sure that you're hearing from everyone and not allowing certain voices to dominate . . . So if you're really trying to figure out 'How do I get input from across the college on this topic,' she's just a tremendous coach that can help convene those really important conversations." Tagye attributed much of her success in helping diverse groups engage in collaborative decision-making to the fact that in the CDC, everyone is equal, everyone's perspective equally valid. She elaborated: "This is a different space, so we will act differently here together. It makes it a little easier to ask for that than if we are sitting around a conference room, or somebody is standing up and everybody [else] is sitting. Trying to create spaces that put people physically on the same level as well as asking them to look at each other on the same level." To that end, CDC participants are asked not to use titles or salutations, relying instead on first names. To be truly collaborative and creative, Tagye argued, you have to "set the hierarchy aside," at least for the time you are in the room together. During the design process, the perspective of a facilities manager or administrative assistant is just as important as that of the president or a senior faculty member.

This leveling of power also helps to break down silos that frequently exist in institutions of higher education. "I see other institutions struggling not to have an 'us and them' [mentality] in the room," Tagye said. "And 'us and them' inhibits good, collaborative, creative thinking. So I think that we have a culture that supports that, and a space that encourages something different." Also important is having someone in the room reminding participants that "yes, that's part of your job. Part of your job is to maybe be silly. To write on the wall. Part of your job is to question everything that we do with a sort of innocence that you might not have if you are stuck in an expert role . . . We are going to leave all that behind. And it's all up there together: it's not your idea or my idea or Barbara's ideas. It's just ideas."

Most of the groups utilizing Valencia's CDC are connected to the college itself: faculty and staff working to improve certain programs or processes, or collaborations between campus constituents and external stakeholders. According to Tagye, because everyone at Valencia is aware of the CDC, groups know that they can come in when they hit that place in their decision-making where "we seem stuck: let's get a third-party perspective." However, the CDC also offers workshops and seminars to introduce college leaders to ways they might encourage innovation in their divisions and think creatively about how to solve to current challenges. As Tagye described, "we have about an eight-month program where faculty, staff, and administrators join us. A cohort, and they meet once a month and we cover topics like creative problem solving, design thinking, systems thinking, wicked problems . . . The intent of that program is changing your own way of thinking and practice."

Valencia's CDC is certainly a next-level response to the question: *How might we provide creative space for innovative thinking?* But Tagye was quick to point out that an eleven-thousand-square-foot facility is not necessary to encourage collaboration, creativity, and entrepreneurial thinking. Creative space must be tailored to each college's needs and resources, but more importantly, it must align with an institution's values and commitment to shared decision-making. "I think that even without this space, the college has a pretty good discipline of collaboration. And I think that's a really important foundation for an organization: to think creatively. So I think that even without this space, we would have done great things that way. But," she said, "I think the space in and of itself invites something different to happen."

6 Seeking What *Wows*

There's always this evaluation and the continuous evolution of what works, what doesn't work—a continuous improvement process and making adjustments accordingly.[1]

As Jeanne Liedtka, Randy Salzman, and Daisy Azer remind us in *Design Thinking for the Greater Good*, in seeking What *Wows*, designers iteratively prototype and refine their innovations based on stakeholder feedback. The goal of prototyping, they write, "is to bring concepts to life in others' minds in order to reduce the risk of innovation failure by learning from and adapting to the best feedback we can get."[2] At Valencia College, NIACC, TCC, and the Maricopa Community Colleges, faculty and staff have approached prototyping in numerous ways, including launching new courses or programs as pilots in order to prove a concept before engaging in lengthy curriculum approval processes; testing new courses as noncredit offerings before moving to credit; utilizing target personas to test the attractiveness of new courses, sequences, or delivery methods; implementing a process such as Valencia's innovation funnel to iteratively test, expand, and invest in new ideas; and creating education plans for various imaginary students to uncover possible administrative or advising hurdles associated with new programs. In addition, the colleges have experimented with innovative new approaches to workforce training and public-private partnerships by testing concepts in areas with demonstrated industry demand before expanding to other disciplines. Two examples of this—one at NIACC and the other at Maricopa—are described in this chapter.

Prototyping can be a humbling process, as it requires viewing everything as a work in progress, fighting for what you believe will best serve students or communities, and doing your best to view resistance or negative feedback as a design challenge instead of a setback. It necessitates near constant communication and collaboration with college constituents. It also requires a willingness to let an idea go—at least for the time being—when it becomes clear that it no longer satisfies established design criteria. In prototyping, you try, fail, try again, step on some toes, figure out how to accomplish your objective without doing that again, learn some tough lessons, celebrate a few early successes, and somehow, some way, work your way toward a solution that leverages college assets to meet stakeholder needs in new, economically sustainable ways. It is, said Rebecca Corbin, president and CEO of NACCE, "messy work."

The first half of this chapter offers four stories of how community college faculty and staff have gotten their entrepreneurial hands dirty: soliciting and reframing stakeholder feedback about a new idea, fighting to serve students in a new way, and prototyping new partnerships and workforce training models. The second half of the chapter considers how colleges might set themselves up for success during this phase of the design thinking process, highlighting the importance of widespread communication and collaboration and exploring how leaders can understand and overcome resistance from faculty and other college constituents.

LISTENING TO WHAT PEOPLE MEAN, NOT WHAT THEY SAY: SOLICITING AND REFRAMING FEEDBACK ABOUT MARICOPA CORPORATE COLLEGE

> *The pushback is: are we a competitor to the colleges? . . . We try to say: "We are not a competitor. We are offering these micro-skill, noncredit programs that aren't the mission of the colleges."*[3]

The early days of Maricopa's Corporate College (MCOR) provide an example of how community college leaders can gather feedback about a new idea from college constituents and translate what at first blush feels like opposition to a win-win scenario for all. In 2013, believing that there was "a geographic mismatch between workers and available jobs" in Maricopa County, Gene Giovannini—then president of GateWay College—secured approval to pull all noncredit training from the district's ten colleges and offer it instead through the newly created MCOR, modeled after the global corporate college developed at Cuyahoga Community College in Ohio.[4] Centralizing training for business and industry, Giovannini believed, would reduce competition among colleges and decrease the amount of time it took the district to respond to proposals from industry (which had averaged four to six months).[5] Most importantly, Giovannini believed that a centralized model would provide better training and support for businesses across Maricopa County and in the process generate more revenue for the district.

However, Giovannini soon ran into resistance from Maricopa faculty and staff, who saw the move as a district power grab and feared a reduction in revenue to their campuses. Rufus Glasper, Maricopa's chancellor at the time, empathized with the colleges but also saw the promise of the MCOR model from both community service and revenue-generation perspectives. After listening to their concerns, Glasper realized that college leaders were much more worried about the loss of noncredit training dollars than they were resistant to the idea of centralizing the delivery of that training. He asked each college how much they earned per year in contract training. What if, he asked, "we guarantee that we will give you that same allocation each year?"

This seemed like a pretty good deal to campus leaders: they receive the same amount of workforce training dollars as in previous years, but do not actually have to provide the training. It is also a good deal for the district and for local businesses. Under the MCOR model, Maricopa brings in more money—roughly $1 million in 2018—which can be used to support district priorities. Furthermore, MCOR's centralized design and increased efficiency means that the district can now respond to industry proposals in roughly two weeks, providing businesses with streamlined access to noncredit training. In short, Glasper was able to quell much of the initial resistance to the MCOR model because he worked to understand the fears and human needs behind his stakeholders' concerns and found a way to address what they meant, not necessarily what they said.

• • •

From 2013 to 2017, MCOR focused on building its centralized business, creating customized training opportunities for local employers, offering workshops to address common workplace challenges and skills, providing industry-sponsored bootcamps, and the like. However, like TCC's Opportunity Center (see chapter 4), in recent years MCOR has moved toward third-wave entrepreneurship and is now collaborating much more intentionally with Maricopa's ten colleges to connect credit and noncredit programs and meet employers' needs in a more holistic manner. As MCOR director Patti O'Brien said, we are trying to "communicate to the system that we are here for you, we are not separate . . . We'd love to partner with you if there's some business in your region that you feel like you could have a strong relationship with. We'll come to the table with you."

For example, MCOR has worked to engage at least one big employer located close to each college who will pay for a cohort of their employees to engage in credit or noncredit training through the nearby institution. MCOR collaborates with participating businesses to survey workers about their education or training needs, and then organizes college faculty to teach the course(s) on-site. For the most part, employees never need to set foot on the college campus; MCOR provides all enrollment and advising services at their place of employment. Furthermore, MCOR centralizes all billing for employers, which allows them to contract with more than one community college without any added headache. Currently, most employers utilize this model—MCOR calls it "corporate learning concierge"—for noncredit training, but Amazon and other companies have also begun offering employees access to credit-based courses in communications, English, and computer and information systems.[6] And for State Farm Insurance, MCOR and Rio Salado College have created entire insurance studies certificate and associate degree programs, all delivered on-site.

Hearing from employers that they also need help identifying prospective employees, MCOR has recently initiated a "digital alumni recruitment" service wherein staff reach out to Maricopa graduates and students nearing program completion and say, "Hey, these employers are looking for someone like you; they love Maricopa students." In this way, MCOR provides a centralized recruiting service to local employers and, in the process, helps students across the Maricopa system find jobs upon completion of their program. As O'Brien noted, this has been "pretty popular with businesses right now"; recruited students are pleased as well. For O'Brien, the centralized nature of MCOR's business model, combined with its new distributed method of course delivery and employee recruitment, has been critical to the unit's success: "We consider ourselves pretty agile. We feel like a start-up . . . we can listen to what [employers'] needs are and pretty quickly adapt our product to serve what they are looking for."

FIGHTING TO SERVE STUDENTS IN A NEW WAY: VALENCIA'S INTENSIVE ENGLISH PROGRAM

> *We wanted advertising in local papers, in Spanish-language papers, to promote our [intensive English] classes. We were told Valencia doesn't do that. That's not part of our vision of how we market ourselves, because again, degree-side thinking.*[7]

In 2001 Valencia College recognized a need in the community and among international students for low-cost, intensive English language and culture programs. Had the staff of what was then called Valencia's Center for Global Languages limited their understanding of the unmet community need to this simple problem statement and designed the intensive English program to function like nearly every other higher education offering, the program might have taken off and achieved moderate success. Yet because staffers spent time empathizing with members of communities who might enroll in these programs, because they applied their business acumen and a client service model to their work, and because they never stopped fighting to serve their population in a new way, the program has grown to become Valencia's second-largest profit generator, bringing in $3 to $4 million per year.

For example, former director Jennifer Robertson (now executive dean at Valencia's Poinciana Campus) and former program manager Lisa Eli (now assistant vice president for global and continuing education) realized in the early 2000s that advertising for the program—which was primarily online and in English—was not reaching target communities. Part of the problem, they realized, was that potential students did not or *could* not read the publications in which Valencia's language courses were being marketed. This aha! moment led to a decision to advertise in print versions of local Spanish- and Portuguese-language papers and to provide all information sessions, registration and intake processes, and student support in students' primary languages. This decision was controversial at first, as it did not align with how the college advertised for other programs and because enrollment and registration personnel had to modify many of their processes to accommodate students with little or no English proficiency. "That's where we got that pushback," Eli explained, "because it didn't fit the model" to which staff were accustomed. Yet Eli and her colleagues held fast to the promise of multilingual marketing and student services, and eventually the grumbling died down.

Another early challenge, Eli related, "was that we felt like we needed to have a discount plan." Like many in the Orlando area, Eli's background before joining Valencia was in hospitality, so she was "very used to doing discount plans and programs." She thought a discount plan might be useful for the intensive English program, as at that time, most students did not have access to credit, lived paycheck to paycheck, and would wait until the last minute—often a week or so after classes began—to register and pay. "This was quite untenable," Eli shared, because "we would never know whether a class was going to make it or not. Or on the flip side, when the start date happened, we didn't know if these teachers were going to have a contract, a job." Offering an early registration discount two weeks before the start of classes, she thought, would motivate students to register and pay early, and allow for more accurate planning and enrollment management. Yet differential pricing based on registration date is rarely used in public higher education, and Eli's immediate superiors were nonplussed with the idea. "We do not do discounts," Eli recalled being told. "That's just not done." Nonetheless, Eli and Robertson persisted, asking their bosses, "Are we committed or not to this program? These are going to be the things that are going to make a difference . . . we could just give it a try."

The hardest part, Eli shared, was receiving approval to test the discount program. Yet "the minute it was implemented, it was immediately successful. And we've kept it to this day, as it is a huge motivator for our students." Building on this success, Eli's team implemented a longevity discount, offering lower prices if students signed up for a year in advance. Once again, staff more familiar with traditional higher education pricing models resisted the idea, but complaints died down after it became apparent that persistence rates increased exponentially among students who prepaid for their classes.

Emboldened, Eli and her team kept trying different ideas to recruit, retain, and serve students, sometimes irking faculty and staff who identified more with what Eli called "degree-side thinking," but more often than not achieving success. Over time, intensive English staffers implemented fully multilingual registration and intake processes, offered courses at night and on the weekends to accommodate working adults, and began working with agents in other countries to recruit potential students. All of these ideas were initially met with resistance, Eli related, as they conflicted with higher education's long-standing attitude that (to paraphrase the famous line from *Field of Dreams*) "all we need to do is build it, and they will come." To effectively provide short-term instruction in personal, professional, and academic English, Eli knew, she and her team needed to be more "entrepreneurial, nimble, and flexible." The model, she said, has to be "find out what the client needs and then deliver on that," followed by "aggressively marketing" the courses to prospective students.

Although Valencia's intensive English program still faces challenges—including recent difficulties in transferring and articulating students' continuing education coursework to the college's credit programs—Eli attributes much of her program's success to the level of trust she and her team were able to establish within Orlando's immigrant and international communities by reaching out to potential students in their native languages and designing a program around their needs. The team had to fight to implement all of their ideas, Eli recalled, but it was worth it: "Having multilingual staff, being flexible with the [registration] deadline, advertising in local papers, and the registration discount—those made the difference in our growth."

PROTOTYPING A NEW SCHOOL/WORK PARTNERSHIP: NIACC'S INDUSTRIAL MECHANICS AND MAINTENANCE PROGRAM

> *So oftentimes these conversations begin with the employer asking, "Why aren't you graduating more maintenance technicians?" And I'll say, "We are graduating everyone that's here. And they all have five job offers. How do we get more? How can you help us get more?"*[8]

In recent years, NIACC incorporated what President Steven Schulz called "an investment component" in its program reviews in order to create an iterative process for examining low-enrollment programs and experimenting with the changes necessary to keep a program running and justify the resources dedicated to it. Schulz commented, "If your enrollment is not hitting your targets, then we put you in a bit of an intensive assistance plan." In particular, NIACC has created a structure whereby a group of faculty, staff, and other stakeholders connected to the program consider, "What do we need to do to either change a program, increase enrollment, change marketing, increase marketing? What are the potential solutions?" After a year of pursuing the agreed-on course of action, Schulz said, the college will evaluate the program once more and either "you might have to make some difficult decisions or you may have solved a problem."

NIACC's industrial mechanics and maintenance program has gone through this new program review process and, as a result, emerged as a successful prototype for new school/work partnerships. According to Laura Wood, chair of NIACC's agriculture, business, and industrial division, industrial mechanics and maintenance has long been "the hardest area for us to encourage a student to pursue," despite the fact that employers are consistently asking for more graduates with these skills. Part of the problem is the program's title; when students hear industrial maintenance, they tend to think of janitors and other similarly unskilled workers. This couldn't be further from the truth, shared Schulz. Industrial mechanics and maintenance technicians "are the people that run infrastructure for a large facility." They need to be skilled in "programmable logic, electronics, pneumatics, [and] robotics."

The first step in revising the industrial mechanics and maintenance program, Wood shared, was approaching local businesses and having "a long conversation about . . . what does the industry need." From there, she and the program's lead instructor—who had twenty-five years of industry experience and several more teaching at NIACC—revised the curriculum and began recruiting students. In the first year, only five enrolled, but Wood was not discouraged. Rather than simply opening the doors and saying, "We are here, come if you want," she realized that NIACC needed "to be much more intentional about recruiting students to programs, not just to campus." Thus, she and her colleagues started meeting with representatives from local businesses, saying:

> You know, we can't make students. We can try to attract as many as we can, but it's a fixed number and once we get the students that's all there is for us. So we need your help to come up with students. Why don't you take your employees that you already have, and train them to become—to fill these positions that you need? Because they have already started with you, they are already committed.

The first company to take Wood up on her offer is located in Hampton, Iowa, about thirty miles away from NIACC. Identifying a current employee whom it wanted to upskill, the company agreed to enroll him in NIACC's industrial mechanics and maintenance program, cutting the number of hours he needed to work to about twenty-five per week. The company would keep him on full salary, pay his tuition and fees, and provide him with the tools necessary to complete the program. The only sticking point was the schedule. Wood explained, "We run these programs in the morning, five days a week, so that we can enroll high school students. Well now that became problematic, because they didn't want him coming thirty miles away, five days a week, because that really cut down on [his] work time." Understanding that a traditional model would not work with this new school/work partnership, NIACC rearranged the industrial mechanics and maintenance course schedule so that all classes could be taken on two days each week, allowing working students to dedicate a full three days to their jobs. In order to accomplish this, the college extended what had been a two-year sequence of courses into a model for a three-year, fully employed, associate degree and apprenticeship program.

As Wood shared, once this prototype for a new kind of school/work partnership was up and running, "others are wanting to follow suit." NIACC created similar partnerships with other companies needing industrial mechanics and maintenance technicians, and together the college and local businesses have refined the model to include progressive pay increases for apprentices and agreements that workers remain with their sponsoring employer for a certain amount of time after graduation. These collaborations have bolstered enrollment in NIACC's industrial mechanics and maintenance program and are being used as models for similar school/work partnerships in the college's welding and tool and die programs.

PROTOTYPING NEW WORKFORCE TRAINING VERTICALS: MARICOPA'S IT INSTITUTES

> *Through this approach we think we can leverage and focus on those verticals that have the highest demand and the greatest propensity for employment. And it's going to have a greater economic impact.*[9]

The greater Phoenix area, said former Maricopa chief strategy officer Sasan Poureetezadi, "is a growing tech hub. It's not Silicon Valley yet, but it's a growing tech hub. And there are literally thousands of open jobs in fields like app development, information security. And those jobs pay about twice the average for most middle-skill jobs. Most of them require either an associate [degree] or a certificate. They don't necessarily require a bachelor's degree." For example, Poureetezadi noted, there are roughly ten thousand openings for coders and programmers in the greater Phoenix area, many at three large financial services companies that recently relocated from California to the growing tech corridor in Mesa, Arizona (the state's third largest city, located in Phoenix's East Valley). Many of these employers, said Maricopa chief of staff Darcy Renfro, "were coming to us and saying, 'We need help filling these jobs!'"

Maricopa stepped up to the plate. The district began by examining current programs to identify which might be modified to meet the demand from industry. While many of its ten colleges offered associate degrees in computer information systems and related disciplines, Poureetezadi noticed that "we had programs that had two completers in the last three years" and that "some of the stuff we are teaching . . . while it has value, it's not aligned with where the greatest demand is." Furthermore, these programs were scattered across the district and not necessarily concentrated in areas where jobs were plentiful. This was "nobody's fault," Poureetezadi said, but "we have to own it as a system. We have brilliant faculty, we have a lot of committed staff, but as you saw, there's this big gap." It became clear to Poureetezadi and his colleagues that Maricopa needed to rapidly adapt and build a model that could respond to the need for workers trained in information technology (IT) by producing a large number of completers in a short time. So, he said, we became "really laser-focused on an opportunity in a single vertical" and began looking to external stakeholders to design a solution.

To create what would eventually become Maricopa's first IT Institute, located in downtown Mesa and anchored by Mesa Community College, Poureetezadi and his colleagues "flipped the model. Instead of coming up with programs that *we* think industry and our community needs, and our students need," he shared, "we engaged the community. We engaged our stakeholders and the private sector and the IT vertical. We focused specifically on that vertical. And really structured a plan around their feedback."

Under Poureetezadi's leadership, faculty from Mesa and nearby Chandler Gilbert and Scottsdale Community Colleges met with the East Valley Partnership (a regional economic development group), staff from the City of Mesa, and industry partners from Apple, Hewlett-Packard, CenturyLink, Blackboard, and other corporations. Together they formulated a plan to develop courses leading to certificates in the areas of blockchain, app development, big data, gaming, cloud computing, and mobile and wearable technology—all areas "that were in the highest demand in that vertical."

The team iteratively vetted and validated the plan, working "internally though the chancellor's office and the chief of staff and provost" and incorporating feedback from external partners. Then, said Poureetezadi, "we reached out for letters of support from those industry partners, including the mayor's office and the East Valley Partnership, and so we brought the whole package forward to the chancellor's office" along with a request for $2 million to start the Institute. Once approved, this investment anchored a public-private partnership between Maricopa, the City of Mesa—which offered a very attractive lease-back deal to house the Institute—Apple, Hewlett-Packard, Blackboard, and numerous other corporations that have contributed their own dollars, provided in-kind assistance, or helped to fund scholarships for students.

The first IT Institute went from initial idea to its first course offering—Apple's Everyone Can Code Swift coding system—in one year. A nine-credit, three-course blockchain sequence followed soon after. Poureetezadi said, "In business terms that's not real fast, but in academic terms, everybody's like, 'That was lightning speed!' It took about half a year for the planning cycle, but implementation in a year." His team was able to move so quickly, he said, because it set up each course as a pilot, which allowed it to bypass traditional program approval processes. It also allowed the team to "take that vision and tweak it," asking, "You know what? We can improve it this way, let's modify it that way, expand it this way."[10] This flexibility and willingness to move quickly paid off; of the six institutions chosen to prototype Apple's Everyone Can Code curriculum, "we were the first ones to graduate completers."[11]

Despite the fact that the IT Institute was designed to function much more like incumbent worker training offered through MCOR or noncredit accelerated certificate programs such as those at Valencia College (see chapter 4), Maricopa has committed to offering all IT Institute courses for credit, which ensures that credentials are stackable and will apply toward both an associate degree and transfer to universities. This is important, Poureetezadi explained, "because what the data show is that, let's say you start working as a programmer. You do pretty well, you're making a decent salary, $70,000 to $80,000 a year. That's about the average for a lot of programmers and app developers." But somewhere down the road, "you realize you want to manage a whole team. Well, to be a manager you have to have a bachelor's degree. Well, those credits I took count toward an associate degree and a bachelor's degree! So that's a leg up for our students." The only difference between the institute model and Maricopa's traditional academic programs, Poureetezadi argued, "is quick turnaround. Rapid response. And they need a larger number of completers" in very specific areas.

Using the IT Institute in Mesa as a prototype, Maricopa is working both to scale the programs—primarily by launching online sections and offering the courses to dual-enrollment students—and develop new institutes in different verticals. Poureetezadi said:

> So we are looking at a second IT Institute, version 2.0 with improvements, in Central Phoenix with Phoenix College as the anchor institution . . . [because] the other hotbed of tech is Central Phoenix. So version 2.0, we just had our first major roundtable. Industry partners showed up. And this time we worked with GPEC, the Greater Phoenix Economic Council, because that's who is in Phoenix. And we solicited feedback from the community, our IT stakeholders, our faculty, and it became apparent that the approach around this institute, while it's similar in being rapid response, quick turnaround, industry-relevant programs that are in the highest demand, there's a lot of underserved communities in that area. So the real focus is gonna be on underserved communities and getting connected to our local K–12 partners.

The approach for the Central Phoenix IT Institute has resonated, Poureetezadi said, with industry partners who share a similar commitment to diversity and innovation. A third institute—this one focused on financial services, banking, and insurance—is being developed in Tempe and the Southeast Valley, and a fourth, anchored by South Mountain Community College, will focus on the construction and skilled trades vertical.

According to Renfro, the district is taking a regional approach to developing each institute, asking community colleges that normally work in silos to collaborate and share facilities and resources. Each institute, she shared, is located "in strategic locations where the employer—where the bulk of the employee jobs are," but just because most of the start-ups and tech companies are in Mesa doesn't mean that it's "a Mesa thing. It has to be a Mesa/Chandler Gilbert/Scottsdale thing and serve the region and the industry, not the college." This, she believes, "is a big culture change," but it is necessary to ensure that the district is not creating redundant programming and that it can respond to workforce needs quickly and in a coordinated fashion.

Shari Olson, president of South Mountain Community College, believes that Maricopa's new institute model will greatly benefit the district and the communities it serves. Not only will the institutes help Maricopa meet imminent workforce needs, she said, but they will also serve to grow enrollment and modernize each college's curricular offerings. Having built something similar at an institution in Minnesota, she noticed that "it also created new energy within the college that influenced technical programs in the college. The welding program got better, the IT program got better." Plus, she noted, the revenue opportunities associated with the institute model "are endless." But to be effective in serving the community in this way, she argued, "you have to be really open and leave your ego at the door. It's all about them and nothing about you." This requires a culture-shift for many community college faculty and staff, however, which can prove challenging.

Helping reluctant faculty and staff see the value of the institute model is not the only challenge Maricopa has experienced. As Renfro noted, one major issue the district needs to resolve is lack of student enthusiasm about working in some of the fastest-growing workforce verticals. "I'm not sure people go to college thinking they want to be an accountant or a finance—some other job in that area," she noted. "They may not see themselves in that industry. I also think you have similar problems in construction, skilled trades. Where people don't necessarily have that vision as their life goal. So getting enough students interested is something we really have to work with the industry on." Poureetezadi agreed: "A lot of students aren't well educated in the sense that they know of the opportunities and see themselves in these positions. That these jobs pay well and are good opportunities." Part of what Maricopa needs to improve, he said, is working "with our K–12 partners through dual enrollment to leverage a ground game . . . You can do marketing and all that, and it matters, but to be connected with those local stakeholders to articulate the value of the different pathways to those students is important."

Poureetezadi's team has also experienced challenges in securing governing board approval quickly enough to close on building leases. In the future, he said, he would work to "get the executives on board" much earlier in the process, "because in the end, there's some resources that you're going to have to leverage, and that's their responsibility." He has also learned that he can ask much more of industry partners. Maricopa relied heavily on corporate partners to design and develop curricula, but in the future, Poureetezadi would think about "leveraging some of their actual on-the-ground services," such as project management during the design phase, in order to reduce the amount of time it takes to develop curricula for new verticals. It would also be useful, Poureetezadi shared, to rely more on industry partners for marketing and awareness campaigns. "While we have a good marketing team, what we spend is not going to equate to something like what Microsoft or Apple can give."

Despite these challenges and lessons learned, Maricopa's institutes are a promising step toward third-wave entrepreneurship for a district long beset by distrust between faculty and administrators and a lack of coordination among colleges. Poureetezadi identified four factors contributing to the success of the fledgling institutes. First, the amount of time spent in roundtables with industry and economic development groups ensured that every course and sequence was designed around stakeholder needs and would lead directly to employment. "You have to really do your homework and understand your regions and your constituents and listen to them," he said. "You have to say, 'Hey, this is a concept' instead of 'This is what we should do.'" The second factor contributing to the success of the institutes, Poureetezadi shared, is the fact that Maricopa faculty were included in the idea from the start and were ultimately responsible for writing the design plan and developing the curricula. "The important thing was having our faculty own it," he said, because while "there were some concerns, and we heard some feedback, overall the faculty was very supportive."

Third, support from district leaders, including Darcy Renfro and former chancellor Maria Harper-Marinick, allowed Poureetezadi's team to capitalize on the opportunity to play a crucial role in regional economic development efforts. They were the "unsung heroes in all of this," said Poureetesadi, as they were "in the loop the whole time and very supportive, but also gave some critical feedback." Finally, the district's iterative approach to designing the institutes has been key to the model's success. We knew, Poureetezadi shared, that our ideas "might not stick or float all the time. It might take a couple of trips." And while that can sometimes be challenging, because his team was "flexible enough to say, okay, we can change that," they were able to learn from their false starts and quickly adapt their strategy to meet immediate workforce and community needs.

HOW MIGHT WE . . . COLLABORATE AND COMMUNICATE ABOUT IDEAS?

> *Innovation is a team sport.*[12]

As the preceding quote indicates, innovation and entrepreneurship are seldom carried out by an individual or small group of people working alone; communication and collaboration with the people for whom you are designing—and all others touched by the idea—are critical to the success of any new venture. Entrepreneurial community colleges understand this. Indeed, in my interviews with faculty and staff at NIACC, Valencia, TCC, and the Maricopa Community Colleges, nearly every person identified communication and collaboration as essential building blocks for entrepreneurship on their campus. Poureetezadi put it nicely: "I'm fortunate enough to work with a lot of innovative people and I think there's a cross-pollination of innovative ideas," he said. "And so everything that I've been able to do . . . has been because who I've worked with and who I've learned from."

For James McDonald, dean of career and technical programs at Valencia, an institutional culture that prioritizes cooperation across campus and divisional boundaries has been critical to Valencia's entrepreneurial success: "The culture of our college is we focus on our students and we collaborate together to get it done. I just think that there's less of an emphasis on ego and more on the collective spirit." Nassar Hedayat, Valencia's assistant vice president for career and workforce, agreed: "As a college we are always connected and always in the conversation."

The four community colleges and districts highlighted in this book strive to engage faculty and staff in the conversation in different ways. Valencia and NIACC utilize collegewide forums (discussed later in this section) to share information and gather feedback. TCC is using its new Three Goals and Eight Principles framework—especially its goal to operate as One College—to "take the silos down" and highlight the interconnected nature of community college work.[13] William Coppola, president of TCC's Southeast Campus, stressed the importance of communication in this effort: "It's really just being transparent and letting people know why you are doing what you are doing . . . And it's asking their opinion. What do you think? How do you think about this?" Kate Smith, interim president of Rio Salado College, echoed this sentiment. Innovation takes "a lot of conversations," she said. "I feel like I'm so old-school when I say that, but it's true! It's 'I've got an idea, what do you think?' [And they say,] 'Well, I don't know' . . . and you learn from the conversation. And the idea gets a little refined. Now, 'I've got this idea, what do you think?' And you go to the next person. And slowly those people start filtering the idea around. And that's kind of how you grow."

The specific mechanisms by which a college communicates and collaborates are less important, said NACCE's Rebecca Corbin, than who is involved in those conversations. As she argued, "Entrepreneurial ventures are much more successful when you have a multitude of people working at it, and [when you involve] certain groups—women, people of color, and others who are not adequately represented in entrepreneurial circles." NIACC's Steven Schulz agreed. It is not enough to develop an idea and then reach out to marginalized groups for buy-in. For an initiative to be truly effective, he stated, "Anybody who's going to touch the program should have a voice at the table."

Buy-in Versus Collaboration

> *When my son was four or so, he had three older sisters. And he would wake up early like I did on Saturday morning and he would want to make pancakes. So I'd get all the stuff out. I'd measure everything. I'd put it all in bowls. He mixed. I'd cook it all. I'd put it on a warming tray, put it in the oven, set the table. He'd lick the bowl. And then they'd come out finally for breakfast and he'd say, "We made pancakes!" That's buy-in. And that's fine for a four-year-old, but not for an adult.*[14]

Design thinkers often discuss the merits of their approach to innovation in terms of how it helps teams bypass the more frustrating aspects of traditional decision-making processes, such as ensuring that all constituents buy into an idea before implementation. Valencia's Sandy Shugart and his colleagues have similarly rejected the notion of buy-in, preferring instead (as design thinkers do) to involve stakeholders early and often in the innovation process. Kathleen Plinske, Valencia's executive vice president and provost, humorously shared how she came to understand the distinction:

> When I started, back in 2010, I was told: "You're not allowed to use the word *buy-in*." With no context. It wasn't by Sandy, it was by someone else: "Sandy hates the word *buy-in*, so you can't use it." So I spent like two years trying to catch myself [before] accidentally saying buy-in. And then I heard him describe the importance of collaborative decision-making. That it results in joint ownership of the decision, so that you

> don't have to worry about getting buy-in later on . . . if only someone had just told me that at the beginning! I totally would have understood!

Instead of designing something and then seeking buy-in, Shugart argued, "everybody needs to be in on the ground floor." As he put it, "There are issues in design that really are seen differently by people in different contexts, and they need to design for those differences if they can." This is especially true for large, multicampus districts. "When something is invented on Campus A and needs to scale to all campuses," he said, "it is just very hard to make that happen unless all campuses are in on it from the beginning."

The *collaborate to avoid buy-in* ethos is now so pervasive at Valencia, Plinske said, that she cringes when she "hear[s] other colleges and institutions talk about decisions being made and then going to the faculty to get buy-in." Of course faculty are going to resist if they haven't been involved in the process from the beginning! Collaboration in all stages of the design process ensures that everyone on campus has joint ownership of new ideas, but that is not the only reason Valencia prioritizes it. "We collaborate," Shugart said, "because when we do, the product is better."

Forums for Collegewide Communication and Collaboration

> *The activity that influenced change or action was convening.*[15]

Although many community colleges value collaboration and communication, few have worked as hard as NIACC and Valencia to integrate these practices into their institutional cultures. As a centerpiece of their efforts, both organizations have implemented collegewide forums to inform and engage constituents. These gatherings are symbolically important, demonstrating that college leaders practice the same collaboration they preach, but they have another, more impactful effect on faculty and staff: making them feel heard and their opinions valued.

NIACC's campuswide meetings—called Cracker Barrels, after the bins in nineteenth-century country stores around which informal conversations might have taken place—occur monthly throughout the school year. The purpose of Cracker Barrels, explained Steven Schulz, is to allow "people to communicate with each other, dream, share, change, without it being an overly threatening environment." He also relies on the monthly meetings to gather feedback about various institutional decisions, especially from faculty:

> Knowing that you can't be an expert in everything, you have to bring the experts to the table when you have an issue. And that's generally the faculty members. And they all want to do more and better. I think they want to make sure their job is here; they want to make sure students are getting what they need to be successful once they leave; they want to make sure they are meeting the needs of the workforce . . . we have those common goals. It's really just trying to create a collaborative structure where that can happen.

Each Cracker Barrel begins with Schulz or other senior leaders presenting updates related to legislative affairs, the budget, enrollment, campus construction, that year's common read, and so forth. As Joe Davis, interim vice president for academic affairs described, "I might get up and talk about where we're at with program review, Terry might talk about how many students have enrolled, and that kind of stuff. And then we take questions and try to answer them . . . I try to inform them of what's going on so no one gets surprised by anything." The Cracker Barrel held each March, laughed Mary Smith, administrative assistant for NIACC's John Pappajohn Center and small business development center, is always one of the most interesting, as that's when we learn, "Are they going to cut the budget or not cut the budget?" As soon as President Schulz knows what the next year's budget will look like, he "shares it with us so that we can be prepared." Faculty and staff are always given a chance to weigh in, she said. "Your input is heard, you know, with the understanding that it may not change [a decision], but at least you are being heard."

At more than twelve times the size of NIACC, Valencia College would be hard-pressed to hold monthly all-college convenings. Nonetheless, every February, Valencia holds what it calls "Big Meeting." Big Meeting,

Plinske described, "is a decision-making technology." Faculty and staff from all seven campuses and the School of Public Safety are invited to attend, and typically several hundred come together to learn about major issues the institution is grappling with and to make "big, collegewide decisions." For each Big Meeting, Shugart and his leadership team identify two or three ideas or decisions on which to focus, and through a combination of presentations and small-group activities, participants identify and make recommendations about how the college might best achieve its strategic goals and objectives. Katie Tagye, director of Valencia's Collaborative Design Center (described in chapter 5), often acts as facilitator in order to ensure that everyone has a chance to provide feedback and engage in the decision-making process.

At each Big Meeting, said Loren Bender, Valencia's vice president for finance, "Sandy is very honest about what is happening, and is not afraid to take big questions." He will often talk about Valencia's budget challenges and what his team is doing to alleviate them, and he has established a "process so that people have a voice and they don't get shut down." This transparency, Bender noted, is critical to building the trust necessary to act in an increasingly entrepreneurial manner. Shugart and other college leaders will talk about innovative new approaches to generating revenue, Bender said, "and he can explain why they are the right things to do ... He's able to tie it together for people, and they believe it because he has delivered in the past and I think they believe in him."

• • •

Valencia's Big Meeting, NIACC's Cracker Barrels, and other structured forums for collaboration and communication are helpful on two fronts. First, they allow for transparent leadership and widespread sharing of how college and stakeholder needs inform campus decisions. Steven Schulz said:

> In this whole innovation piece, entrepreneurial piece, transparency is huge ... Surprises aren't necessary or enjoyed by anybody. So when things are going good, we are going to share that. And when things are

> going bad, I'm going to talk about that, to a point where they get tired of hearing about budget challenges, probably. But you know what? At the end of the day, decisions are going to be made to deal with that, and I don't want anybody to be shocked.

Structured forums for communication and collaboration are also helpful in surfacing assumptions and gathering feedback about new ideas from faculty and staff who may have different perspectives of an issue. As Plinske explained, this is a critical step in the process of implementing or refining entrepreneurial ideas: "Things could appear to make a lot of sense from where we sit in the district office, but when you are actually out talking to an adviser, and you hear from them about what they are hearing their students say, or what their queue is like, that's when you really start to understand that the things that in theory make a lot of sense, in actuality may not work best." Shugart agreed: "The people closest to the work really can contribute a lot more than we imagine. And they need to see a larger picture, and that's our job [as administrators]. But they can really help."

The kind of commitment that NIACC and Valencia have made to widespread communication and collaboration is not easy to accomplish, nor does it stop with monthly or yearly all-campus meetings. Rather, it takes sustained effort, over multiple years, to instill in every division head, department chair, faculty member, and front-line staffer the belief that collaboration is essential in creating ownership of an idea at multiple levels, which in turn is necessary for any new program or initiative to flourish. This kind of deliberate collaboration, Plinske said, "is incredibly challenging, particularly given our size and distribution. Boy does it take time and energy and effort." Understanding this, Valencia has developed a process for gathering input and engaging in collaborative decision-making. Plinske explained:

> We have a habit of identifying a *primus*. So rather than a decision-maker, right, you have a primus who is responsible for making sure that you've gathered input and feedback and involved those who are closest to the work in the process. And that you don't move forward unless the primus is comfortable with the decision you are going, but

> we don't necessarily call that person the decision-maker; they are more of a convener.

Faculty and staff who come to Valencia from other colleges or universities do not always understand the benefits of this collaborative process, Plinske said. "People who are new to Valencia might see our culture as slow—it takes a long time to get things done. But it's because we are really intentional in that process."

For faculty and staff at NIACC, Valencia, TCC, and the Maricopa Community Colleges, the benefits of collaboration and communication vastly outweigh the time it takes to practice them. Indeed, creating a process for stakeholders to provide input and feedback on new programs and ideas is essential to understanding what is working (and what isn't) in a timely manner. Nonetheless, establishing a culture where communication and collaboration across campus, division, and departmental lines are supported and rewarded can be frustrating and time consuming. It also requires leaders at every level to practice what they preach, which is often easier said than done. But, as Robin Lasher, director of TCC's small business development center counseled, "You don't perfect collaboration. You find more effective ways to collaborate."

HOW MIGHT WE . . . DEAL WITH RESISTANCE TO CHANGE?

> *If you're not careful, the institution will throw up roadblocks . . . So understanding from a mission and value perspective that this is important work for Valencia and for the community, and then let's figure out the systems and procedures that support that, not identify our current systems and procedures that would prevent that.*[16]

A section titled "How Might We ... Deal with Resistance to Change?" can easily give the impression that resistance is bad, that it's always led by frustrated academics who never want anything to change or disrupt their Ivory Tower existence, and that effective college leaders are always right in attempting to quell the rebellion. But as any fan of *Star Wars*, the *Hunger Games*, or any other dystopian tale understands, resistors are often the *good guys*, the ones fighting for the people and against autocratically imposed rules or restrictions. Resistance, when it comes from an honest and mission-oriented place, can be very helpful and indeed is necessary in an iterative approach to innovation.

Resistance, for example, often leads to critical course corrections during prototyping and implementation of new ideas. Plinske offered two examples. First, Valencia faculty and administrators recently engaged in a three-year collaborative process to redesign the college's new student experience course. In designing this new course, which is now taken by all first-year students, "there was an interest in having co-curricular experiences outside the classroom be an integral component . . . it was a joint decision-making process, and everyone owned that decision."[17] But just as the course was about to be rolled out, many faculty at the Osceola Campus balked at a clause in the common syllabus, which read: "A student will fail if they do not complete the co-curricular experiences." Understanding that faculty were resistant to the specificity of the words "will fail," not to the idea of co-curricular experiences in general, Plinske proposed modifying the language to say a student "*may* fail if they do not complete the co-curricular experiences." That way, she explained, instead of mandating failure, you "give a faculty member the ability to exercise professional judgment as to whether or not a student ought to fail for missing those required elements." In this example, last-minute resistance led to a small but important adjustment to the common syllabus, avoiding longer-term challenges in implementing the college's new student experience course.

Similarly, several years ago Valencia College implemented block scheduling at its Osceola Campus to better utilize facilities on less-popular days and times (thereby mitigating heating and cooling costs). Faculty and staff at Osceola created cohorts of students in their two most popular majors, psychology and business, and intentionally utilized those faculty whose sections are always the first to fill, betting that the popularity of the instructor might outweigh a less favorable class schedule. Block schedules were then created for Tuesday and Thursday afternoons and Friday mornings when facilities were underutilized. Students did indeed sign up for the cohorts because they offered guaranteed schedules with the best teachers, and the experiment was a great success.

When Valencia administrators attempted to export the model to the new Poinciana Campus, however, they ran into resistance from faculty and staff at that location, who argued that the block-scheduling model would not work for their students. At first, this resistance felt like the "not invented here syndrome" described in the *Design Thinking Playbook* (in which stakeholders resist an idea simply because it did not originate with them), and Plinske's team was tempted to push forward anyway.[18] Instead, however, they listened carefully to resistors' concerns, which centered around their belief that while it may be feasible to find two hundred learners to participate in block scheduling at a several-thousand-student campus such as Osceola, doing so at a campus with a head count of only twelve hundred—especially when most of those students also work to support themselves and their families—is not. After considering the feedback, Plinske's team abandoned the push to implement block scheduling at Poinciana. This experience was humbling, said Plinkse. Fortunately, there's no "penalty at Valencia for trying something and failing. What's more frowned upon is *not* trying or adopting an attitude of, 'Well, that's out of our control.'"

In these examples, faculty and staff opposition led, respectively, to the refinement of a good idea and the abandonment of an initiative that—while desirable—was not ultimately feasible at all campus locations. Put another way, in these instances, resistance was necessary and noble, and because it was narrowly tailored to specifics—the wording of a syllabus or the applicability of an innovation to a new setting—it helped Valencia experiment with new opportunities in a mission-oriented manner. This, however, is not always the case. Sometimes resistance—especially when it comes from faculty or others who are seemingly entrenched and invested in the ways community colleges have always functioned—can feel more as if it is intended to stall the innovation process than help move it forward. As the following sections explore, resistance to change in how community colleges operate is real and can be a significant challenge for college leaders seeking to act in entrepreneurial ways. Most often, the opposition is understandable, but there is no doubt that overcoming it is one of the key challenges in creating entrepreneurial community colleges.

Roots of the Resistance: Historical Attachments, Initiative Fatigue, and Legitimate Fears for the Future

> *There are people who—it doesn't matter what it is, it doesn't matter how much data you have, it doesn't matter how impactful it is—there are people who do not want to change. Period.*[19]

Resistance to change is a palpable feeling on many community college campuses, and it can be particularly pronounced at institutions where a growing emphasis on entrepreneurship is challenging the status quo. This resistance—often from faculty, but occasionally from staff and other stakeholders as well—is rooted in some combination of historical attachment to a bygone era, initiative fatigue, and legitimate fears about what these changes mean for their careers, their students, and their institution's ability to carry out its greater civic and social purposes. For example, as chapter 1 explores in detail, the idea of acting in an entrepreneurial manner is anathema to many who have spent their careers in public higher education. Comments like "We are not training monkeys" and "We are not a business" are familiar refrains at many community colleges, as faculty react to requests to develop new workforce training programs or incorporate cost-benefit analyses into program reviews.[20] Distrust of what many view as a growing business ethos on campus is widespread in the faculty ranks, and as traditional associate degree programs struggle to maintain enrollment while short-term training geared toward specific economic development priorities gains traction, many fear that colleges may be sacrificing the noble aims of liberal education and social mobility for the chance to make a buck. These concerns are legitimate and, when applied in good faith as part of the process of vetting specific entrepreneurial opportunities, can be enormously useful in ensuring that colleges continue to prioritize service to students and communities.

But talk to anyone who has worked in higher education, and you'll hear that faculty often resist *any* new idea, not just those that may be more aligned with the market. The resistance phenomenon may be more pronounced in community colleges with a historic bent toward transfer preparation, as well as those where faculty engage in collective bargaining, but it exists everywhere. In his book *Confessions of a Community College Administrator*, Matthew Reed writes about the culture shock he experienced in transitioning from teaching at a for-profit university to a community college where faculty were unionized and tenured: "It was one thing to make a decision and get it wrong; it was something else entirely to find out that certain decisions simply couldn't be made because someone who had been granted impunity thirty years earlier would pitch a fit if we did. Suddenly, the key question shifted from 'What do the students need?' to 'What will the faculty accept?'"[21]

Faculty have historically wielded significant control over matters of curriculum and pedagogy, but as community colleges grew in size and complexity and as new actors (states, unions, coordinating boards) entered the shared governance process, "a struggle for who should run the organization began to emerge."[22] Some faculty—particularly those who mourn past models of internal governance—are reluctant to cede additional control to administrators, and thus wield what power they have to stall or block any new initiative that impinges on historical precedent. Others resist out of pure initiative fatigue. Heather Rissler, a biology instructor at NIACC explained, "The initial reluctance comes from something new again. Now we have to do this, and we *were* doing X, Y, and Z . . . I think people have a hard time wondering if it's just another fad, because there are a lot of things that come and go in education."

NIACC agriculture instructor Joel Morrical agreed. In general, he said, resistance comes "from folks that kind of feel like they've been there, done that. They've done this for so long, they've tried everything they can to motivate students." Furthermore, he explained, faculty are already exhausted and overwhelmed, especially at smaller institutions:

> You are expected to wear a lot of hats. You are supposed to recruit your students in your department. I'm supposed to manage the farm. I'm supposed to come up with the programs. I'm supposed to serve on committees. They want me to teach outside my department—there's tons. Everybody has that going on. And so it can be really easy to kind of [say], "I'm not going to do anything extra." Or "I'm burned out. I'm going to look to the administration to solve all the problems" . . . It can be hard for people, I think, to sometimes reevaluate how we do things.

Time to participate in new initiatives or implement new pedagogical approaches is also a factor, both for adjunct instructors and full-time faculty who bear the brunt of committee work in addition to their teaching. Tim Putnam, director of NIACC's John Pappajohn Entrepreneurial Center explained, "I think the problem is that in community colleges, faculty have a pretty heavy load . . . So I don't think it's that they don't care, they are just so focused on being the best in the classes they are doing. So it's not that 'I don't care,' but 'Tim, I teach math. And that in itself is a pretty big load for me.'"

Fears about what a new emphasis on entrepreneurship will mean for faculty lives and livelihoods also spurs resistance. As James McDonald explained, opposition arises "sometimes where there is a perceived impact, maybe, on a faculty load. Like if you're starting something new, is that going to impact a program somewhere else in terms of enrollment? That can get very sensitive. I have seen that firsthand. And so you go from what's best for our students to—it really boils down to what's best for this particular faculty member or group of faculty. Fear," he said, "is a powerful emotion." Morrical agreed: "An institution like us is very afraid to look at an alternative solution, because then does it start to unwind or unravel other things around it? And then all of a sudden, this one change causes ten . . . So I think we almost get so frightened of it that we're like 'Agh! We'll just keep it like it is and keep cruising on.'"

These fears are exacerbated when community colleges enact new belt-tightening measures in response to reduced public subsidies. For NIACC's Joe Davis, this is understandable: "I think the resistance is that people become very territorial. I have to justify my existence for having a job—everybody worries about that a lot more than they have in the past." This is particularly true as community colleges develop new programs that more directly address community and workforce needs. "Everybody wants their piece," said Robert Muñoz, vice president for community and industry education at TCC. If the courses they teach are not included in new programs, how will faculty make their loads? "We are very me-oriented in colleges," he said, and faculty understandably worry that new programs or institutional emphases might divert enrollment from their courses, in effect jeopardizing their tenure.

Often these fears arise when colleges attempt to meet community needs through noncredit workforce training. On one hand, faculty may support the idea of prototyping new programs within continuing education departments as a way of testing whether the idea will generate sufficient enrollment to justify a credit program. On the other, faculty fear that new noncredit offerings will drain enrollment from existing programs. Worries that continuing education divisions will "steal our students" are commonplace. One professor said to Fred Schmidt, assistant to the president at TCC's Northeast Campus, "Why would they take credit if they can go noncredit?" Schmidt was quick to explain the fallacy of this argument. "You are absolutely incorrect," he said. "I'm actually growing an army of new students for you who are going to be six times more likely to be successful when they land in your credit program than the student off the street, because," he explained, "I did some research and if you come in with a credential you are more likely—by a significant factor—to be successful in your next attempt than if you just came in cold."

Sandy Shugart has made a similar point to his faculty: "There have been times when the growth and investment we've made . . . in scaling the accelerated training in the noncredit world" has caused faculty in associate of science programs to say, "Well, we are not growing because they are taking all of our students." He's received similar pushback from faculty who believe that Valencia's intensive English program has pulled students from the college's traditional English program. "Of course, it couldn't be further—it's just not true," he responded. The students entering Valencia's accelerated training programs are not choosing between them and a two-year associate degree; they are choosing between the training programs and nothing, or the training programs and an insanely expensive course from a for-profit provider: "The populations are fundamentally different."

Fears for the future and historical attachments to the notion of academic freedom can also lead faculty to resist initiatives that involve some standardization of coursework, including guided pathways, guaranteed transfer agreements, and—in NIACC's case—efforts to incorporate entrepreneurial mind-set learning across the curriculum. "Anything that's rigid, faculty tend to resist," said Joe Davis. He elaborated:

> I have one particular faculty member that talks to me often about how we are McDonald-izing our stuff. He particularly resists anything that is in any way the same, conforming in any way. Common syllabi, common anything. And there's a lot of resistance to that type of thing. Academic freedom has been valued for a long time, so there's—even in places where it makes sense—there's some resistance to it.

TCC's Schmidt has had similar experiences, noting that faculty reluctance to relinquish any amount of control over the curriculum has led to missed opportunities. He shared one example. "We had been contacted by the Western Association of Food Chains [WAFC] to start a retail management certification that had been created in California. And it was very defined. It had been vetted," he said, and WAFC wanted to bring it to Texas. Tyler Junior College, located about 130 miles east of TCC, had launched the program and in the process received both Southern Association of Colleges and Schools (SACS) accreditation and approval from the Texas Higher Education Coordinating Board (THECB), paving the way for a similar program at TCC. As Schmidt shared, the certification required eight classes, "so you could do it as a stand-alone, but it really led toward an associate degree." He created an Excel spreadsheet illustrating the related associate degree programs across all of TCC's campuses, "showed that in three of our associate degrees, you would not have to take any extra classes to get this credential."

Schmidt then returned to WAFC and said, "This is part of a degree program that we already have. Would you award it to anyone who completes the associate degree? And they were like, 'Absolutely.'" Showing that there were three existing pathways for students to earn the certification while working toward an associate degree, Schmidt went back "to the academic team that was assigned to implement this, and they came back to me with ten classes that didn't match" the courses approved by SACS or THECB, saying, "We want them [students] to do these courses before we can adopt the certificate." Schmidt was exasperated: "But it's not our certificate! It's a national certificate!" Unfortunately, he said, "The net result was that we never did it. And it was a gimme. It was a gimme for stackable certifications that were industry-recognized. And I had visited with four separate companies that were going to pay for their employees to come to TCC to do it. They ended up sending them to Dallas [Community College District]." Although TCC lost out on this opportunity, Schmidt reported that many of the chief resistors have since retired, and as a result, "I think we've gotten a lot more responsive."

One area where community colleges still struggle to balance responsiveness with academic freedom and participatory governance is the curriculum review and approval process. At nearly every institution, this is a long, protracted activity, often requiring years to go through the necessary programmatic, technical, and articulation reviews. While the process is necessary to ensure that new courses and programs meet high standards for quality and rigor, abide by applicable rules and regulations, and meet the needs of students, anyone working in community colleges can tell you that curriculum review is frustratingly slow at best and, at worst, can be used to delay or derail programs that challenge the status quo. Eli Mercer, dean of technology, health, and business at TCC's Southeast Campus, shared his experience in creating a new program: "When I walked in, I was told point blank by my peers and by folks both up and down the line that . . . to get any approval for changes or new things was impossible and I should expect to get nothing done for at least two to three years, and it probably wasn't even worth trying. That's what I heard from every level from day one." Similarly, when Clint Grant was hired to develop a new aerospace flight program at TCC's Northwest Campus, "it was like the college had never started a program before. I was like, how is this possible?! There are seventy technical programs, and I'm asking for help, and it's never been done? . . . It was cumbersome. It was difficult. I felt like I fought my own people at TCC more than anything else."

What TCC's curriculum review process taught Mercer is that "bureaucratic blockage or organizational resistance—there are several things you could call it—often is not in the form of resistance. Often, it's with a big smile and all the best intentions, but 'we need to review this for a bit longer.' Or find some absolute technicality a hundred pages deep, and 'we'll have to review the whole thing for one more year.'" Resistance is rarely in your face, said Mercer, but "there's a really strong inclination for whatever culture the institution was founded around to persist over time—regardless of leadership, regardless of circumstance." TCC, he shared, is "squarely in the transfer, academic side, historically. So anything that goes outside of those norms is just culturally uncomfortable."

Faculty Resistance Through Curriculum Approval: The Case of TCC's Entrepreneurship and Small Business Management Program

> *Now you're taking classes from us? How are we going to survive?*[23]

The process of redesigning the entrepreneurship and small business management curriculum at TCC's Northwest Campus illustrates many of the fears, historical attachments, and ways of resisting new institutional emphases described in the preceding pages. In 2015, when Lourdes Ramboa became chair of entrepreneurship and small business management at Northwest, the program was essentially a business associate degree with "a sprinkle of entrepreneurship courses." As a former entrepreneur and management consultant, Ramboa had an inkling that the program—which was struggling to meet enrollment targets—was not adequately meeting the needs of existing or potential students. So she began interviewing students—many of whom were starting new businesses or taking over family operations—asking about their biggest challenges and what they hoped to gain from TCC's program. She learned:

> What the majority wanted was really skills and knowledge about how do I go about doing this [starting a small business]? Many of them already have a degree in some other area. And what they wanted was, "Okay, so how do I form a business? And what about taxes? How do I price the product? How do I know what the right pricing model is?" Those kind of very tangible, knowledge courses. And we were still teaching a business concept as if you were going to go work for a corporation . . . And so I felt well, that's really not what the population is craving or needing.

Ramboa spent the next several months reimagining the program around student needs. The first course they will take, she shared, is on the entrepreneurial mind-set, so students learn how to be creative, resilient, and approach solutions in an iterative manner. Other courses include economic development and the impact of entrepreneurship and small business management on communities; social media marketing; payroll and human resource management; and legal matters for entrepreneurs. Excited about the new program, Ramboa began what she called an "extremely challenging" curriculum approval process:

> When [the redesigned program] was presented to my colleagues in the business discipline, there was this very strong resistance, number one, to change, which I get. Number two, [faculty were] very territorial: "Oh my gosh! You aren't going to offer accounting, managerial accounting, or financial accounting?!" No, but I'm going to offer bookkeeping and QuickBooks, and payroll management, because for a small business, that's what they need. They need to understand how to use Excel to keep the books at first, then they move on to QuickBooks. Then, when they hire people, they need to know how to pay them. So yeah, I'm taking two [courses] but I'm adding three related to the accounting curriculum.

The resistance came, she said, from faculty who saw the new courses as "kind of beneath" the more established business curriculum. As she shared, faculty would say things like, "I teach accounting. I don't want to teach QuickBooks. I don't want to teach payroll." Similarly, she'd hear faculty asking, "How am I going to make my loads in accounting" if the students are all taking QuickBooks and payroll? Their fear was not unreasonable, said Ramboa, but "it was a strong pushback, and it was almost an ugly pushback."

Ramboa countered by offering as much information as possible: about the students enrolling, about their needs, about the needs of local small businesses. "Folks, this is the data," she said:

> This is what I know from polling the students . . . from polling the advisory board. Polling other institutions. Many institutions don't offer this as a credit program because they don't have enough [of a] population, and the reason they don't have the population is because the population doesn't necessarily want the degree, they want knowledge! So how can we meet in the middle of offering a degree *and* the knowledge? And still be successful. So thinking entrepreneurially, I want to continue offering it as a credit program, but I have to get sufficient population in order to continue it. And I have to offer the population what they need. It's sort of like Business 101: who's my target market? I have to meet their needs [and] solve the problem my target market is seeking a solution for. This is the solution.

Sharing data about student needs and playing on faculty fears about losing enrollment to noncredit programs ultimately helped Ramboa prevail, although it was three years before her redesigned program received the final stamp of approval. The curriculum review process for Northwest Campus's entrepreneurship and small business management program—which rolled out in fall 2019—taught Ramboa many things, but chiefly it provided an important lesson about how college leaders must work to overcome faculty resistance to change. She said, "Twenty percent of us embrace change no matter what. We love it. Twenty percent will never embrace it, never gonna do that. And then there's the 60 percent who sit on the fence, and you have to prove to me that change is gonna benefit me, that it's worthwhile."

Strategies and Tactics for Overcoming Resistance

> *Change boils down to really taking a look inside and trying to see why. It's answering the why question. Why should we do this? . . . Because we need to generate revenue to continue doing what we are doing. And if we wait for the state to solve our problems, it's a bad road.*[24]

Community college faculty and administrators shared numerous approaches to overcoming resistance to change (in general) and to acting in an entrepreneurial manner (specifically). Like Ramboa, Steven Schulz advocates illustrating how the new idea, program, or initiative will ultimately benefit faculty. "You've got to build the business case to change the way we behave, or to really think about what we do differently," he said. "Because you've got to remember the training that these folks come from. They are academicians. They love their field of study, whether they are career technical or whether they are humanities, arts, the sciences, whatever it is. That's why they do what they do, but to really have them participate in a new model takes time." Change is scary for many people, so Schulz recommends talking through what it might look like at the end of the day: "Try to paint a picture of what this might mean for them. What's the benefit" to them, to their department, to their students?

Similarly, as design thinkers understand, including faculty in conversations about the need for change—as well as brainstorming what new programs or initiatives might look like—can help to overcome resistance. TCC's Schmidt recommends making the design process as participatory as possible. He explained: "One of the tenets of change management [is], are you involving the people who are going to be affected by the change in the process? And I think that's very appropriate, and that's been my experience here. I have not had a challenge that I wasn't able to get around or work through. But I've also included the right stakeholders in the dialogue."

The specific terminology used to describe new ideas or initiatives can also help to reduce faculty fears (and thus resistance). Faculty will often grumble about requests to incorporate cost-benefit analyses into program reviews but, if asked to illustrate how their program can continue to benefit students in a fiscally sustainable manner, may engage in similar practices on their own accord. Similarly, those who resist calls to be more entrepreneurial and innovative in the classroom, and in the development of new programs or services, might be energized by explicit permission to seek new and better ways of serving students and communities. Joe Davis explained: "Arts and science faculty just don't like the word *entrepreneurial.*" To avoid resistance in NIACC's efforts to establish an entrepreneurial mind-set across campus, he said, it's had to frame the work differently. "We frame it as the skills we want to have in the students . . . If we were to say, 'We are going to have an entrepreneur class,' they would shut down right there, but the skills they agree with."

Heather Rissler follows a similar strategy. In professional development sessions helping NIACC faculty incorporate an entrepreneurial mind-set into their teaching, "I didn't call it entrepreneurial until the very end. I waited and said, 'Look at all these things that you've learned in this class,' and I went, 'By the way, this is what we call entrepreneurial mind-set learning.'" At the end of the day, Shari Olson explained, the nomenclature college leaders use is much less important than the actual work that needs to get done: "What does an entrepreneurial mind-set mean?" she asked. It is simply being "able to take ideas from many and create something as a result of that conversation." Or being "able to solve problems because you are open to the possibilities of the crazy quilt of ideas that come from group work and collaboration." Talking about the need to be entrepreneurial and innovative in a way that feels more congruent with traditional higher education values (collaboration, creativity, service) can make it much less threatening to faculty and staff.

But when this doesn't work, Gene Giovannini shared that he's not afraid to play the bad cop and point out the necessity of embracing entrepreneurship and innovation given the existential threats to public higher education. When faculty complain that his approach betrays the ethos of the academy, he might respond: "Well, guess what? There ain't no academy unless the academy can produce something of value." He shared, "I don't have any problems saying, 'This is our cup of tea now. If you don't like it, find another Starbucks.'" Of course, he acknowledges that this tactic won't eliminate the resistance, "but it begins to diminish." Maria Harper-Marinick has taken a similar approach, framing entrepreneurship as the new normal at Maricopa. "We don't talk about entrepreneurship as an initiative," she said. "As long as you keep it as an initiative, and you talk about it as an initiative," faculty and others believe that they can just wait it out because "initiatives have, by definition, a beginning and an end." Instead, Harper-Marinick shared, "We say, this is not an initiative, this is a new way of doing business," which leaves no room for holdouts.

Giovannini has found it useful to put the community college mission into historical perspective for resistors. "This is where we are today," he might say. "It's not 1967 where we are trying to build a bunch of these institutions so people can have access and transfer, okay? It's not what it is today." He illustrated this point with an example. In the 1970s, "what we knew about medicine doubled every eight years. Today it doubles every eighty days. So how do you train someone to be a physician" when the knowledge they will need upon graduation doesn't exist yet? The same can be said for many of the jobs that community college graduates will enter: "Plumber, medical school—what difference does it make?" he asked. "You are going into a job and it's probably changing." The skills and knowledge that community colleges need to impart must be geared much more toward helping students create, adapt, work with others, and think critically about how to solve problems than toward that which has been taught in colleges for the past hundred years.

Finally, as the quote at the top of this section attests, explicitly naming *why* faculty and staff should support their institution's emphasis on entrepreneurship and innovation—making the connection between acting entrepreneurially and improving (or preserving) service to students and communities—may ultimately be necessary to overcome resistance. As Harper-Marinick said, college leaders need to emphasize "the community component of community colleges." New ventures must be framed in terms of how they further the colleges' mission: "You have to keep that focus on the right thing," she said, "and that is students or community." She counsels college leaders to illustrate how new ideas will help students "transition to employment, to better employment, to transfer. Whatever the outcome is," she said, "if that's the lens, it doesn't make the work easier, it just makes the understanding of why we need to do it a little more palatable."

Kathleen Plinske agreed. It is helpful to show faculty that "it's not losing fundamentally who you are, but being willing to think about, Is the way that we're delivering our services in line with what the community needs right now?" And how "might that be different from what they needed a year ago or ten years ago?" She continued, "if the message isn't clear, if the *why* isn't clear, it can be interpreted as 'Why are we doing this, we are competing with ourselves!' Or 'Why are we doing this, our mission is transfer, our mission is to prepare students for the university!'" Resolving tension within an organization, Plinske believes, comes down to "really good communication and conversations. And a clear understanding of the purpose for why we are doing certain things." Giovannini put it this way: "When presidents hit roadblocks, they should go back to the core mission, the overarching reason why they exist ... if the ultimate goal connects with your college's mission, the idea will likely prevail."

7 Understanding What *Works*

What's truly powerful is that the more a leader engages in design thinking, the more they begin to integrate the behaviors associated with design thinking into their leadership behavior. They become better listeners, better inquirers, and more collaborative in how they coach and solve problems with others. In doing so, they show greater levels of empathy, resulting in a better understanding of how to more effectively engage and motivate employees.[1]

A chapter entitled "Understanding What *Works*" might reasonably conjure up expectations for a litany of entrepreneurial ventures that have worked at some community colleges and are likely to be successful at others. But as Jeanne Liedtka, Randy Salzman, and Daisy Azer caution in *Design Thinking for the Greater Good*, there is a downside to "focusing solely on a 'best practice' approach to innovation," as the most successful entrepreneurial ideas are those that are grounded in local conditions. TCC chancellor Gene Giovannini put it more succinctly: "What works wonderfully at one place will fail miserably at the next."

Thus, instead of definitively stating What *Works* in community college entrepreneurship, this chapter explores the conditions that must be established to enable entrepreneurial ventures to succeed, regardless of local context. In particular, after a brief illustration of TCC Connect's soft-launch approach to curricular innovation, this chapter focuses on the roles and responsibilities of college leaders, including cultivating an entrepreneurial culture, managing governing boards, enabling grassroots entrepreneurship among faculty and staff, and establishing external partnerships that mutually benefit students, communities, partner organizations, and the colleges themselves. Stories and vignettes from TCC, NIACC, Valencia College, and the Maricopa Community Colleges are sprinkled throughout, illustrating various ways that the leaders of these institutions have worked to create environments where entrepreneurship and innovation can flourish.

TCC CONNECT'S SOFT-LAUNCH APPROACH

> *I have used a soft-launch approach rather than seeking perfection because, you know, perfection is the enemy of the good.*[2]

Soft launches—or learning launches, to borrow the terminology used in *Design Thinking for the Greater Good*—are critical components of ascertaining What *Works* in public and social-sector organizations such as community colleges.[3] Carlos Morales, president of TCC's Connect Campus, utilizes a soft-launch approach to iteratively test and refine new curricular offerings. "When I was hired, I was given the opportunity to soft launch, rather than pilot test," he explained. So when a program is roughly 85 or 90 percent ready to go, "we just deploy the project and let it run a cycle. A cycle could be one year, a cycle could be one semester, and we quickly refine and adjust for the next time . . . We adjust for the next iteration that way."

TCC Connect's first official soft launch occurred in fall 2015, when the campus debuted eighteen new online programs: thirteen certificates and five associate degrees. These initial programs (there are now over thirty) were selected based on regional economic development data, information about what would articulate to nearby bachelor's degree programs and, Morales laughed, some educated guesswork about which programs might give TCC Connect an early win. Having commissioned a study of all previous hybrid or online learning courses offered through TCC, he took "the low-hanging fruit approach" of launching with those that were already between 95 and 97 percent online, betting that these prototypes would see fewer hiccups in in the transition to Connect Campus. His intuition paid off, and TCC Connect's eLearning programs have since "been on a trajectory towards growth"; in spring 2019 head-count enrollment was roughly twenty-two thousand, with a nearly 10 percent semester-over-semester growth rate. Connect Campus also launched a five-week summer term open to both TCC students and those at nearby four-year universities, which reduces learners' time-to-degree and provides a new source of revenue to TCC.

The second offering Morales and his team soft-launched was TCC Connect's Weekend College, an accelerated, eighteen-month program—split into seven-week terms—in which students can earn an associate of arts degree or complete the transferrable core curriculum in associate of science programs by taking courses one day per week (either Friday evenings or Saturdays). Weekend College is quite prescriptive: students follow a sequence of online and face-to-face courses until their final six classes, which are typically electives. "They know what they will be taking," said Morales, which helps students plan and allows them to go back and forth between Weekend College and TCC Connect's eLearning programs as their schedules permit.

Weekend College started small, with seventy-eight students, but when nearly half of them graduated within two years, Morales knew his team was onto something. Since then, roughly four thousand students have completed a degree through Weekend College; average head-count enrollment in 2019 was roughly five hundred students. Morales credits his soft-launch approach for the rapid growth and popularity of the program. Originally conceived as a cohort model, in its first year the program ran into a few glitches with statewide requirements, forcing Connect Campus to allow students to enroll in each new seven-week term at their own pace. This ended up being a blessing in disguise, says Morales, as dissolving the cohort model allowed students to move freely between accelerated weekend courses and regular, sixteen-week programs. "It's either acute pain or chronic pain!" he said. "You choose the one that you like."

When Giovannini arrived at TCC in 2016, he encouraged Morales to create even shorter terms and adopt Rio Salado College's method of starting new classes as often as possible throughout the year so students don't have to wait for a new semester to start learning. Morales leaped at the opportunity, and because TCC Connect had already built a five-week summer program into its student information system, there were few administrative hurdles to creating additional short-term offerings. In December 2016, Connect Campus implemented the Wintermester—a five-week, fully online operation mirroring the summer program but run by staff and professors working remotely. Faculty, advisers, and support staff were handpicked for their responsiveness and ability to work on a tight timeline. The first Wintermester had only nineteen sections, "just to get it organized and see how complex it would be, what resources would be necessary." As Morales said, "It went well, with an 82 percent success rate." Morales immediately shared this information with the chancellor, whose response was "Double it." "I was not expecting that," laughed Morales, "but it was the green light for my next iteration. I didn't have to ask him" for permission again. TCC Connect doubled the number of sections offered in Wintermester 2017, achieving similar success rates, and enrolled thirteen hundred students in 2018. Wintermester alone now adds $150,000 to $180,000 to district coffers.

Looking to further capitalize on Giovannini's blessing to develop short-term programs, in fall 2017 Connect Campus deployed four-week accelerated programs with monthly starts, enrolling nearly three hundred students in the first several months. As Morales explained, the four-week program, which allows students to earn a degree in eighteen months, is "not for everybody, because you are going to be on a perennial-summer type of approach. But if you are up to that pace and that level of responsibility, you will excel." Following the same soft-launch strategy as he did with Weekend College and Wintermester, Morales had initially planned to "run a full cycle, a full year before we make any revisions or adjustments," but soon realized that the monthly starts allowed his team to iterate much more quickly, and "six months in, had already revised a few things." For example, after realizing that many students were enrolling in the monthly start classes without understanding that they followed an accelerated format, TCC Connect began designating them as "petition only" in the course catalogue to ensure that students knew what they were getting into. Connect advisers also started checking in with students early and often to prevent them from falling behind. After these two adjustments were put in place, success rates for monthly start courses increased to nearly 70 percent.

Building on this momentum, in spring 2018 TCC Connect deployed eight-week courses and—replicating the Weekend College model—created an eighteen-month online, accelerated degree program, allowing students to earn an applied associate of science in business administration in just six eight-week terms and three Summer- or Wintermesters. Now, Morales explained, you "have the sixteen-week lane, you have the Weekend College lane, you have the monthly start lane, and you have the eight-week lane." Students can pick and choose what is right for them at any given point, accelerating their progress toward a degree when they can, and slowing it down when they must. According to Morales, this flexibility doesn't just benefit students and TCC Connect, but is also a boon to the entire district, because once an accelerated or short-term course or program has been developed, it can immediately be implemented by any other TCC campus, in either an online or face-to-face setting. In this way, TCC Connect has revolutionized access for all TCC students, not just those utilizing its eLearning platform.

• • •

In early 2019 Connect Campus was not yet self-sufficient, nor was there yet a mandate that it provide a return on the district's investment, although Morales said he is prepared for that and has "instructed my team to find ways and to be attentive to that in case we are asked." Nonetheless, from a cost perspective, TCC Connect operates much more efficiently than its sister campuses. For example, it takes up only thirty thousand feet on one floor of a building in downtown Fort Worth. "Thirty thousand feet for twenty thousand students," said Morales. "Pick your formula, it's going to be a positive one." Furthermore, he added, the campus's rapid enrollment growth means that TCC Connect should soon reach an economy of scale that will allow it to subsidize other district functions.

Morales attributed the nascent success of TCC Connect to having "the opportunity to try out different things" and adjust on the go. Yet he is the first to acknowledge that his soft-launch strategy is only possible because nearly everything Connect Campus does is electronic. He explained, "It still requires people, but I don't have to ask for another wing to be built" in order to accommodate new classes. Furthermore, Connect Campus can quickly adopt new short-term and accelerated programs because instead of designing each one from scratch, the team borrows liberally from proven models. For example, Wintermesters were adapted from summer sessions, eight-week degree programs from Weekend College. Morales shared his favorite metaphor for this approach:

> In Texas we have these buildings that look like barns and they sell beer. So it's like a drive-through liquor store. You drive and there are coolers on both sides and then you swipe the card. So what I'm trying to say is that: Do you need a feasibility study to establish one of those in your town? I don't think so! You need some data, but you don't need tons of data, okay? You establish the need and then you start with the local beer. Maybe then you [add] the national one.

Like beer barns, TCC Connect was established to meet community needs in a more accessible, convenient manner, and like these establishments, the campus can quickly tailor its offerings based on what sells. This ability to take calculated risks and refine in real time, said Morales, is central to his campus's ability to act in an entrepreneurial manner.

ROLE OF COLLEGE LEADERS IN CREATING ENTREPRENEURIAL INSTITUTIONS

> *As a leader, if you're not willing to fail, others will not take a risk to succeed.*[4]

College leaders play an important role in creating entrepreneurial community colleges, although the specifics of the part may vary from institution to institution. At some, presidents, chancellors, provosts, and other senior leaders will introduce a focus on innovation and entrepreneurship to a campus that has not previously acted in such a manner. At others, perhaps those where an entrepreneurial mind-set has already been established, leaders will work primarily behind the scenes, ensuring that faculty and staff have the resources they need to pursue new ways of serving students and communities. At all colleges, leaders are responsible for creating and maintaining a culture that values an entrepreneurial mind-set and supports the risk taking and innovative thinking that can lead to new and improved ways to deliver on the college's mission.

Indeed, without entrepreneurial leaders—those who are willing to take measured risks to create something different that will have a positive impact on students or communities—colleges have little chance of becoming entrepreneurial themselves. Yet an entrepreneurial leader alone does not make for an entrepreneurial community college. As Maricopa's former chief strategy officer Sasan Poureetezadi reminded us, "innovation is a team sport." The most essential task of an entrepreneurial leader, then, is to create working environments where entrepreneurial activity can occur and where innovative thinking is rewarded. This entails—first and foremost—cultivating an entrepreneurial culture where faculty and staff are encouraged to explore what *is*, ask what *if*, seek what *wows*, and understand what *works*. It also involves managing the expectations of trustees; creating conditions that enable grassroots entrepreneurship and innovation from every office, division, or department; and establishing external partnerships that benefit all involved, including the surrounding community.

Cultivating an Entrepreneurial Culture

> *Colleges that embrace an entrepreneurial culture are positioned to lead in education innovation.*[5]

The hallmark of truly entrepreneurial community colleges—those exhibiting characteristics of third-wave entrepreneurship—is a pervasive culture that embraces innovation and rewards collaboration, enables risk taking and supports iterative problem solving.[6] Yet institutional cultures do not create themselves; they must be formed and reformed by those in leadership positions, especially those at the top of organizational hierarchies. Giovannini reminded us that it is the president's or chancellor's responsibility—perhaps their most important responsibility—to "imbue an entrepreneurial mind-set as part of the culture" and to "structure support systems to help such ideas flourish."[7] Jeff Goltz, executive dean of Valencia's School of Public Safety, agreed. Leadership is essential for building culture, he said. "It starts from the top. It's a very unique leadership culture at this college, and it trickles down to every level. It spreads. I'm telling you, there's not too many people that don't buy into this philosophy, this collaborative philosophy, this community philosophy."

So how do college leaders create entrepreneurial cultures? "How do we," Giovannini asked, "instill the principles of this practice in every individual, every faculty member, staff person, dean, vice president, and the president? How can we engage our college to think boldly, to challenge what has historically or politically persisted, and perhaps even dive deeper into models that have previously failed?"[8] The first step, design thinkers Thomas Lockwood and Edgar Papke write, is to understand what culture does. And "what culture does more than anything else is inform and reinforce [to] its members how to individually and collectively attain success. It's how to behave."[9] Creating an innovative and entrepreneurial culture, then, essentially boils down to setting expectations for faculty and staff; offering a framework and process for engaging in the work; leading by example; creating opportunities to collaborate and innovate; supporting taking risks and failing fast; transparently incenting the behavior you want to see; and prioritizing entrepreneurship and innovation in human resource decisions. The pages that follow explore each of these building blocks of culture creation in more detail, offering short vignettes from the colleges highlighted in this book along the way.

Set Expectations and Communicate Urgency

> *Explicit commitment from leadership to entrepreneurial thinking is important.*[10]

Culture creation begins by setting expectations: to paraphrase Lockwood and Papke, leaders must reinforce to faculty and staff alike that the way to attain success—individually and collectively—is to think creatively about how they might help the institution serve students or communities in new and fiscally sustainable ways. This is not a one-and-done task; expectations should be stated publicly and reinforced privately, must be repeated over and over again, and whenever possible should be tailored to target audiences. In particular, Kim Moss-Linnear, executive director of TCC's office of grants, development, and compliance, advises presidents to communicate to faculty that "no matter how you cut it, no matter where you sit, in any subject there are opportunities for entrepreneurship." Innovation is not limited to technical or business areas within the college; all professors can incorporate an entrepreneurial mind-set into their teaching, and as the NIACC example illustrates (see chapter 5), when given the opportunity to consider new ways of carrying out the college's mission, liberal arts faculty can be just as entrepreneurial as their colleagues in more applied disciplines.

Furthermore, former Maricopa chancellor Maria Harper-Marinick emphasized that leaders must "communicate a sense of urgency that . . . we are not waiting until 100 percent of the people are on board" to begin acting in an entrepreneurial manner. Culture creation takes time, she acknowledged, but time is not something colleges can afford to waste: "Every year that we wait, we lose an entire cohort of students." Giovannini concurred. In his mind, expectation setting comes down to clearly articulating *why* change is necessary. "So there are two messages, I think. One is that criticalness of the workforce need. And second is our value proposition. How we *are* the answer!" Get faculty and staff excited about how they can align existing programs and services with community needs, Giovannini advised. Talk about why it is necessary that they think entrepreneurially, focusing both on new opportunities and the costs of *not* innovating. That way, when leaders begin to codify their stated expectations in tenure and advancement processes, faculty understand the importance of the new requirements, as well as how they can be met.

In setting expectations, college leaders must be prepared to explicitly address the connection between acting in an innovative and entrepreneurial manner and generating new revenue for the institution. Must all new ideas consider financial sustainability or return on investment? What if meeting a community or workforce need—training more nurses, for example—would put further strain on college budgets? Should faculty and staff pursue mission-oriented innovations, even if they don't necessarily lend themselves to additional dollars? Specific answers to these questions will likely depend on each institution's unique circumstances—financial, historical, cultural—but it is clear that balancing what colleges need to do to ensure fiscal sustainability with what they must do to continue providing a public good is a core challenge for community college leaders. Presidents and chancellors interviewed for this book acknowledge the necessity of considering the financial impact of new ideas—nearly all have embedded a return on investment component into reviews of new and existing programs—but as described in chapter 4, each leader emphasized that business considerations must always be subservient to mission considerations. Some programs are important to offer even if they result in a financial loss for the college. Others are worth pursuing even if the fiscal impact is unclear. Steven Gonzales, interim chancellor for the Maricopa Community Colleges, instructs faculty and staff to focus on ideas, not costs or profits. "Good ideas attract money," he said. "Many colleges miss opportunities to develop worthwhile projects because they focus entirely too much on the money that would be required to implement them." Loren Bender, Valencia's vice president for business operations and finance, agreed: "Good mission makes good business."

Offer a Framework and Process for Entrepreneurship and Innovation

> *One of the greatest values to be gained from design thinking is the impact it can have on the culture of an organization and how it contributes to greater collaboration and innovation.*[11]

Echoing Bender, University of Alabama football coach Nick Saban is famous for saying that "a good process produces good results." Providing faculty and staff with a framework to guide innovative thinking and a process to iteratively test and refine new ideas is an essential component of establishing an entrepreneurial culture on campus. All four colleges highlighted in this book utilize aspects of the design thinking process, and some draw from other frameworks as well (entrepreneurial mind-set learning at NIACC and the four stages of design and creative problem solving at Valencia). While any of these approaches may be utilized to practice innovation and entrepreneurship in community colleges, I have argued throughout this book that design thinking is the most advantageous, as it ensures that all entrepreneurial activity is closely aligned with stakeholder needs and institutional mission. Lockwood and Papke remind us that there is another benefit to design thinking as well: its influence on culture. They write, "Design thinking cultures are not about just brainstorming or ideation, they are about developing a competency to identify and then focus on what is important, and to solve that."[12] When design thinking is embedded into the culture of an organization "with the goal of shifting mindset and making it part of the organization's DNA," faculty and staff are able to visualize and "commit to the idea of creating human-centered cultures and leveraging design thinking to inspire cultures of innovation."[13] In other words, entrepreneurial community colleges can utilize design thinking as a framework to innovate in mission-oriented ways and, in so doing, will continuously create and reinforce a culture that values the tenets of human-centered entrepreneurship.

Helping faculty and staff understand how they might approach educational innovation and entrepreneurship—giving them a framework for the work—is vitally important, but so is providing them with a road map for attaining approval and funding for their ideas. As described in chapter 5, NIACC does this through its annual strategic initiative process, Maricopa through college- and district-level innovation funds, and Valencia through its innovation funnel. Valencia's approach to supporting innovation on campus is the most comprehensive, as the funnel recognizes innovations in their infancy—President Shugart's "thousand flowers blooming"—all the way to those being institutionalized across the institution, scaling resources to each iterative refinement. Regardless of the process utilized for identifying and funding innovations, however, college leaders must ensure that it is open and available to all college constituents, that design criteria are consistently applied, and that financial support is reliable and transparent.

Lead by Example

> *The more successful leaders effectively role-model and reinforce the behaviors associated with design thinking, thereby gaining a reputation of being open and receptive to change, the greater their influence.*[14]

Sitting atop a bookcase in Sandy Shugart's office is the motto for his home state of North Carolina, the Latin phrase *esse quam videri*, which means "to be, rather than to seem." This phrase, Shugart said, lies at the heart of Valencia's student- and community-oriented culture, reminding faculty and administrators alike that "our focus is to do the work, do it well, do it right, and don't worry about who knows and who cares and all that stuff." It is also a subtle reminder for Shugart that he must do the same work he asks of his constituents, especially when it comes to educational innovation. Simply talking about Valencia's approach to entrepreneurship (or NIACC's, or Maricopa's, or TCC's) is not enough; college leaders must role-model the behaviors they ask of their colleagues: empathizing with stakeholders' needs, remaining fiercely committed to keeping those needs at the center of all new ideas, engaging in divergent thinking, iteratively prototyping and refining solutions, accepting failure as a necessary component of learning and organizational growth, and communicating and collaborating in ways that result in joint ownership of decisions.

Leading by example, Rio Salado interim president Kate Smith said, starts with listening: "Nothing happens when people aren't listening. No change happens if you don't have leaders that listen." No one person—not even the luminaries highlighted in this book—has all the answers; successfully meeting the challenges and opportunities of the next twenty years requires a diversity of thought, experience, and perspective. Steven Gonzales believes that leaders must also role-model a *yes, and* attitude, demonstrating to constituents that they, too, are willing to suspend disbelief in order to explore innovative—and sometimes off-the-wall—ideas. This can be uncomfortable, Gonzales allowed, but that discomfort is part of the process. "As simple as that sounds, it's tough for me at times to support something that I'm not 100 percent in-my-heart-sure that it's going to work. But I have to have confidence in my people to do it." Provide freedom and support for your employees to take calculated risks, he said. Don't let your discomfort be the barrier that precludes grassroots entrepreneurship.

Create Spaces and Opportunities to Communicate, Collaborate, and Ideate

> *If you've been in academia a long time, it's just there are so many silos and so many independent thinkers. You need to be able to get lots of different people to come together and have lots of different conversations.*[15]

Chapters 5 and 6 offer much information about how community colleges can create spaces for innovation to occur and provide opportunities for faculty and staff to collaborate and communicate about improving service to students and communities. We won't reinvent the wheel here, but it is worth emphasizing the importance of such activities to the development and maintenance of an entrepreneurial culture. However, simply providing opportunities to communicate, collaborate, and ideate is not sufficient; to be truly impactful, faculty and staff must understand how to utilize these skills to create change. Professional development that exposes employees to design thinking, an entrepreneurial mind-set, or other approaches to innovation—and also provides opportunities to practice new skills and apply them to existing challenges—is essential in creating an entrepreneurial culture. And, former Maricopa chancellor Rufus Glasper stated, professional development can also help faculty and staff "be better prepared to identify and connect with possible business, industry, and community partners and collaborators."[16]

Support Taking Risks and Failing Fast

> *In some settings the expectation is Don't Make a Mistake. And I don't think that is the expectation here. I think the expectation really is Take Risks to Help Students Do Better.*[17]

One of the most widely recognized aspects of an entrepreneurial culture is the freedom to take risks without fear of repercussions from failure. When "projects or ideas that do not prove to be of significant value to the college are considered the cost of creativity," when leaders repeatedly say, as Shugart has, that "it's okay to fail; a plan is only a plan," and when incentives and rewards are tied to innovative behaviors instead of outcomes, faculty and staff feel they have permission to experiment with new ideas, both in their classrooms and in the community.[18] Their fear of failure is lessened, first and foremost, because they understand that some failure is necessary in an iterative approach to innovation, and second, because they have confidence that they will not be punished for trying something that didn't work.

Presidents and chancellors can nurture a measured risk-taking culture in numerous ways. The most important thing, said Gonzales, is to "never hit anybody on the head for trying and making a mistake. Don't do it privately, don't do it publicly. You just acknowledge that it didn't work and that maybe there's a better way of doing it. That's it." Terry Allcorn, dean of business and hospitality at Valencia College, suggested periodically asking program chairs, "What risks are you taking in your program?" Most of the time what they tell him "are not roller-skating-on-the-roof risks," he said. "They are curricular risks: we are going to offer a Saturday night class or a Friday night class. And they know that if they offer the class and it doesn't get any new enrollment, I'm fine with that. And I'll say something insightful like 'Now we know!'" "It's a lot more fun," Allcorn shared, "when you feel freed up to free up people" to take risks in their work.

Being given explicit permission to take risks in your work is empowering, says Jeff Filko. He recalls his first day as Valencia's director of auxiliary services, when Loren Bender sat him down and said:

> Listen, I want you to be an innovator. I want you to be a risk taker. I'm gonna push you. You are going to learn things you don't know about. And I want you to fail often. Fail often and fail fast. But just keep trying new . . . ways to bring services to our students and new ways to generate revenue. Some of them we're going to tell you, "No, don't do that," and some we're gonna say, "Go ahead."

This happened on day one, Filko shared, and then Bender proved that he was serious: "Right away he had me make some calls immediately and then backed me up on those calls." Some of Filko's ideas—the cell towers and Smart Markets described in chapter 5, for example—have been "runaway successes." Others "didn't quite work as well as we hoped." For example, Filko once proposed a $5 fee for student parking permits to offset the costs of parking enforcement and security. He estimated that this small fee alone would raise around $200,000 per year, "but I didn't even get halfway through my pitch and [Bender] said, 'No. That is antithetical to what Dr. Shugart feels is necessary for our institution and how we don't want to fee our students to death.'" Ultimately, Filko realized, his idea failed because it did not meet the college's most important design criteria: to put students' and community needs first. But because he is rewarded for always trying instead of for sometimes succeeding, Filko feels supported in continuing to ask, "Well, what if we did this?" or "Why aren't we doing this?" Of course, he acknowledged, "I am still afraid to fail. I want everything to work. But it takes the risk of failure away. I'm not gonna lose my job or get a pay cut or demotion because I gambled a little bit and it didn't work."

Kate Smith believes that experiences like these are critical to helping faculty and staff internalize college leaders' support for taking risks and failing fast:

> If I were really starting somewhere small that really didn't have anything [entrepreneurial], I would probably make sure that we had something that failed. Nothing harmful, but something that failed that everyone could see you as the leader say, "Ah! Okay, so what can we learn from it? Okay, so now let's try [something else]." Because that to

> me would be the most powerful way to teach your culture. That it's okay to fail. And that will empower people to feel like, "Okay, I'll try, because I saw what my president did. They thought it was great that we tried and that we took that and did this." That message is so powerful when people see it. It's very different than just saying it. They need to see it.

Another key to giving faculty and staff permission to fail, said Lourdes Ramboa, chair of business, entrepreneurship, and small business management at TCC's Northwest Campus, is teaching them the difference between "little Fs" and "big Fs." Little Fs, little failures, "are okay. That's how we pivot. How we move this direction, move that direction, how we change. It doesn't mean that you have to start from scratch; it just means that you build on the thing that didn't work." By welcoming little Fs, Ramboa said, colleges can avoid the big Fs that occur when faculty and staff keep pushing an idea forward without iteratively checking their assumptions and refining what isn't working.

Similarly, Allcorn finds it useful to distinguish between calculated and mindless risks. "When I take a risk," he said, "I've looked at employment data and I've talked to employers and I've surveyed students. And so while I guess it is a risk in some senses, it's not like I did no homework at all and just [said] let's try this." He has the same expectations for his faculty. He tells them, "I'll promise you on tape that we'll try" whatever you want to do, but "I like risks to be a little more calculated than a lottery ticket."

Carlos Morales has a similar outlook. Along with doing extensive research to identify promising new ways to meet community needs, he always seeks to hedge his bets. As he described, "I'm not gonna bet $100, but I may bet $80 because I need my $20 to get back home if I fail." Succeeding is much more enjoyable than failing, he laughed, but failing can also yield important information: "Knowing that something will fail when you don't quite need it yet is much nicer than waiting to find out [it will fail] when you are bleeding students or whatever."

Of course, the idea of attempting something new and unproven is often daunting, despite leaders' assurances that there will be no repercussions for trying and failing. Even little Fs can be discouraging, and thus without explicit permission and encouragement to innovate, many faculty and staff will succumb to the comfortable predictability of the status quo. To help his colleagues push past this inertia, Steven Gonzales shared the concept of BATNA, or Best Alternative to a Negotiated Agreement (from Roger Fisher and William Ury's book *Getting to Yes: Negotiating Agreement Without Giving In*[19]). Your BATNA, Gonzales explained, "is essentially what you are arriving with and what you can live with if you are going to walk away" from an idea or a negotiation. Gonzales tells his staff that "anything we do here, or attempt to explore, our BATNA is always what we currently have. And after studying or trying, we can always go back." This "un-paralyzes people," he said, adding:

> It's a Version 1.0 mentality. Saying we know we're not going to get it perfect the first time, but this tremendous amount of learning will inform what Version 2.0 and Version 3.0 and 4.0 look like. And that—you can almost feel it in a room—when you remind people that "Oh yeah, you don't have to be perfect, let's just get to work!" And then, man, you see the ideas just start flowing. It's so cool to watch.

Incent the Behavior You Want to See (and Be Transparent About It)

> *In the simplest terms, what is measured and rewarded gets done.*[20]

Community colleges—like most institutions of higher education—are structured in ways that allow for independent, parallel work toward shared objectives; rewriting that code to support cross-campus collaboration, measured risk taking, and joint ownership of decisions will require college leaders to reexamine what is currently incentivized in their institutions and align rewards and accolades to these new priorities. Put more simply, allocating dollars to new ventures or innovation campaigns is not enough to override existing reward structures; these actions must be coupled with an understanding of the behaviors that are incented by existing organizational structures and funding models and a willingness to destroy in order to create anew.

Sandy Shugart understands this. When he arrived at Valencia in 1999, his primary goal was to make student learning the centerpiece of Valencia's culture. But in order to do that, he said:

> You have to dethrone the idols of community colleges, which [are] enrollment and money. So from the beginning, the agenda was to say, I understand why enrollment is king, why it has always been king. That's the way we were engineered in postwar America. But it's only a business outcome, and not a mission. So we've got to start doing things that improve outcomes, even if they put enrollment and revenue at risk.

Shugart knew it would be "hard for people to break the habit of . . . making their decisions around what would generate enrollment and what would generate revenue through that enrollment." But he also knew that ultimately, driving resource allocation off enrollment is "a losing proposition," as it ensures that innovative new approaches to serving students or communities are relegated to the margins of the institution where they are less likely to threaten the status quo.

Shugart's approach to cutting incentives tied to enrollment "out of the fabric of the organization" began by ensuring transparency in Valencia's budget. Shugart recalled the summer before he arrived at the college:

> Before I got here, I called the CFO and said, "Bob, we are going to be working together. And I need to know what is going on." He said, "Sure!" I said, "No, Bob. I need to *really* know what is *really* going on."
>
> "What do you mean?"
>
> "Well, I'm not accusing anybody of anything, but every college has pockets of money that only certain people know are there. I need to know where every penny is. I want to know where it is, and I want to know why it is there, even if it's a bad reason. I need to know. And Bob, you only have one shot at this. If I find later that there is something you forgot to tell me, I'll have to fire you because I won't be able to trust you, you understand?"
>
> So he prepared it as a PowerPoint presentation and sent it to me about a month before I officially arrived . . . And we spent a day going

> through it so I understood where the money was. There was a lot. Most of it was stranded. The old regime thought of it as a bank account that made them safe. I thought of it as nonperforming assets that were wasting away.
>
> So then I told Bob, "Good job. I get it. I'm on board. Now send it to every trustee. Send it to every senior manager. And send it to the faculty leadership." And he just about gagged. And I said, "This is how we are going to start. There will be nothing left to hide. You won't have to support any secrets ever again." And he did it. Scared him to death. There wasn't a huge revolution; it was more like, "Wow! We had always suspected that."

Thus began Valencia's 2001 strategic initiative to "Move the Money to Learning," which eventually became the college's innovation funnel. Now that everyone on campus knew how much money was stranded, each faculty and staff member was encouraged to identify ways to put those dollars to work to support student learning. "That," said Shugart, "earned confidence" that he meant what he said about realigning incentives to priorities. He continued:

> Then when we made some organizational, procedural decisions that had the potential to substantially interfere with enrollment, that earned some credibility as well. Like, let's have an application deadline. No college or community colleges did that. Let's eliminate drop/add. When we started doing those things, the old guys start saying, "These guys might actually be serious about this. We better tune it." So you had to uncouple at like a genetic level. You are really redesigning the chromosomes of the place so the natural response is "How does that impact learning, and how do we know it does," which are the two questions we kept asking. You can do the same for community.

Some aspects of this new incentive structure are harder than others to implement, particularly when it comes to the assignment of faculty. Shugart avoided being overly prescriptive in this arena, preferring instead to ask campus presidents to "figure this out so that it is manifestly a learning-centered decision, not an enrollment-centered decision." Similarly, TCC utilizes its Three Goals and Eight Principles framework to align campus decisions with institutional priorities. At both colleges, leaders have worked to replace an "I've got more numbers than you, so I get more resources" ethos with an incentive structure that rewards innovative thinking and collaborative problem solving around how to best serve students and communities. But as Shugart pointed out, this requires continuous effort:

> A Roman poet I like a lot used to say, "You can beat nature out with a stick, but she always comes back." And there's a sense in which this worship, reification of enrollment is in the nature of the beast. And so you are constantly beating it back. And again, it's not that enrollment is bad, it's just that it is only a business outcome. And none of us signed up just to run a business. There are more lucrative businesses. But it does come back. You have to push on it all the time.

Prioritize Entrepreneurship and Innovation in Human Resource Decisions

> *Hiring is job one, two, and three. You've got to have the right people.*[21]

The circular logic of human resources is that in order to cultivate an entrepreneurial culture on campus, you've got to hire and promote creative, collaborative risk takers, yet to attract and retain such talent, you must have a "culture that thrives on continuous learning and risk-taking."[22] As with the chicken and the egg, neither culture nor talent can come first; each begets the other, and investment in either will benefit both. Nonetheless, a few words about human resources is warranted.

In many ways, prioritizing entrepreneurship and innovation in hiring decisions is easier—or at least more straightforward—than incenting it in advancement or tenure processes, but it can and should be done in both. Along with other requirements, new position descriptions should clearly state the entrepreneurial skills, capabilities, and experience that college leaders seek in a candidate and illustrate how organizational structures and funding sources will support such work at the institution. In interviews, committees should ask candidates about their views of community college entrepreneurship (the necessity of it, any fears or reservations, how they would empower others to engage in such work) and outline the college's approach to mission-oriented innovation. With some tailoring, these factors can be incorporated into both faculty and administrative searches. In hiring people to run new ventures, however, especially those expected to generate a profit, Tom Schumann, executive director of Maricopa's Center for Entrepreneurial Innovation, stressed that colleges must prioritize entrepreneurial experience over subject-matter knowledge. Too often, he said, colleges and universities will "bring in a business professor" to run a new program, but "they are not a good match! They absolutely understand the subject matter, but they don't know how to" take the risks necessary to iteratively solve problems to better meet stakeholder needs.

When it comes to retaining and promoting existing employees, senior administrators must work closely with faculty leaders to incorporate collegewide expectations for innovative thinking, collaboration, and iterative problem solving into tenure and advancement procedures. The specifics of these requirements will vary from department to department—and certainly those for faculty will be different than those for staff and administrators—but the more consistent colleges can be in terms of describing entrepreneurial expectations and the reasons for them, the more likely they are to be incorporated into the institutional culture.

Managing Governing Boards

> *As it relates to the board, you always have to connect everything to the mission. And then: how does it serve the community?*[23]

As any leader understands, *managing up*—controlling bosses' expectations, anticipating their needs, communicating your priorities, bringing solutions instead of problems, and following through on your promises—is a critical skill for any professional. At community colleges, where the "bosses" are either elected or appointed and may or may not share the same vision for the future of the institution, managing up can be even more complicated, as college CEOs (presidents or chancellors) must navigate political dynamics as well as those directly related to institutional policy and administration. Indeed, as George Boggs and Christine Johnson McPhail write in *Practical Leadership in Community Colleges*, "assisting their boards in becoming as effective as they can be" is both the most important and most challenging aspect of a CEO's job.[24]

Much of what has been written about managing community college board relations in general takes on added significance as colleges implement the organizational, cultural, and financial changes necessary to act in more innovative and entrepreneurial ways.[25] For example, ensuring effective communication with board members and following the established chain of command—where the CEO's office is the main point of contact between the board and the college—become even more important as colleges seek improved ways to serve students and communities and generate alternative sources of revenue. As Kate Smith shared, board members who are supportive of such activities may be tempted to check in with those leading entrepreneurial ventures to assess progress and suggest strategies for moving faster. Yet keeping the board informed is the chancellor's job, she said. Therefore, "I really make sure that I always include the chancellor on any communications and really keep trying to direct everything to what I think is the established chain of command." William Coppola, president of TCC's Southeast Campus, concurred. Although Gene Giovannini encourages his campus presidents to have a relationship with board members, Coppola always keeps the chancellor in the loop: "I'll always let him know what we talked about. And I'll let the board members know, 'You need to know that there's nothing in confidence here. If there's something I think needs to go back to the chancellor, I'll take it to him.' I'll let them know that up front." College leaders must encourage board members to stay focused on long-range planning, Coppola said, so they don't interfere in the work happening on the ground: "Sometimes they push a little hard, they want this thing, and we'll say, 'Go back to the chancellor.' I can be up front with them too. The board knows their position. They value who they are and what role they play. They trust us."

Some of the keys to keeping trustees focused on overall policy direction and fiscal stewardship of the institution—rather than the specifics of any particular new venture—are being as transparent as possible, connecting all initiatives to the college's mission, and providing frequent updates about college or district progress toward agreed-upon goals. As Maria Harper-Marinick shared, Maricopa's board meets eleven times per year. At each meeting, Harper-Marinick would ask a faculty or staff member to present an update on a board-approved project "so that they know what the work is [and] they can ask the right questions." In prepping for these updates, she would specify: "When we're presenting, we are not repeating what we've said before, and we need to be outcomes-based. If you have data, show it. If you have a dashboard, show it." Focusing on mission-related outcomes rather than implementation specifics or (God forbid!) frustrations, said Chief of Staff Darcy Renfro—even when those outcomes are still works in progress—helps to separate "the operations of the place from the policy direction." Valencia's Loren Bender has a similar outlook:

> When we bring things forward to [the board], there's a general rule that it's pretty well baked. That we think this is a good idea, and that's where they come into play: to help us challenge some of the assumptions. They have unique backgrounds and can do such a thing. But we don't bring half-baked things to them. We have to feel very good about—when it is time to go to the board, we know we feel very, very good about [what we are proposing], which makes it much easier to sell.

In sum, by ensuring that proposals are fully developed before going for board approval—including specifying what investment is needed, how the idea connects to institutional mission, who will carry it out, and what the expected return to the college may be—and by insisting that updates focus on outcomes instead of processes, college leaders can keep their trustees focused on how new ventures support the college's long-term vision, allowing the experts on campus to determine how they will be implemented.

• • •

With roughly one-third of all community college trustees hailing from business and industry, governing boards are typically (though not always) supportive of entrepreneurial approaches to serving students and communities, especially those that may also generate a monetary return.[26] However, some trustees—particularly those with education or other social-sector backgrounds—may be more hesitant to move in this direction. This may also be true for newly elected or appointed board members who have little prior knowledge of the challenges and realities community colleges face. Educating reluctant board members about the need to act entrepreneurially, detailing how the institutions are uniquely positioned to play a lead role in economic and workforce development, and sharing the college's process for ensuring that the work remains mission-oriented will help to reassure trustees that innovation and entrepreneurship is in the institution's long-term best interests. Illustrating community support for new approaches can also help to educate board members, said Giovannini. "When you have community buy-in" for acting entrepreneurially, you show your board that "you are just leveraging your mission in a more direct way to the community. So the board can't ignore that."

More often than not, however, governing boards are eager for their colleges to act entrepreneurially, and CEOs must temper expectations about how quickly this can be accomplished. This is certainly the case at Maricopa, where Smith reported that entrepreneurship is "100 percent supported, across the board." In her words, the message from Maricopa's board is: "Come on people! Be Maricopa! Get it on! Let's go! Where are the big ideas? What are they? Where are we headed?" Harper-Marinick shared this perception:

> I think most of them are supportive. If anything, I think they are impatient that we haven't come up with some very creative partnerships. Some of them are big supporters of public-private enterprise. There may be a couple that are more traditional thinking, but I think that for the majority of the board members, they want to see innovation, they want to see more innovative ideas. They are—I know some of them are impatient with us because they feel we haven't moved fast enough.

Sandy Shugart has had a similar experience with Valencia's board. "They are all businesspeople," he says. "They ask great questions on the business plans, particularly when we are spending a lot of money at the start-up. But more often, they want to know why we aren't moving faster. If it works at twice the scale, why wouldn't it work at ten times the scale? . . . I'm holding them back a lot of the time." Clearly, a major challenge for community college leaders is balancing trustees' desire for "more, faster, sooner" with the time it takes to implement new initiatives in ways that honor the culture of the institution, the capabilities of faculty and staff, and the logistics of turning a large ship into the wind.[27]

Enabling Grassroots Entrepreneurship

> *My philosophy—besides saying that everybody is responsible for recruitment and retention of our students—is that everyone can lead from any place in the organization . . . A lot of great ideas come from our front line.*[28]

I have argued elsewhere that to be most impactful in improving student persistence and completion, community colleges should take a grassroots approach to student success efforts, enabling faculty to design and lead initiatives from the departmental level.[29] Doing so leverages the faculty's existing investment in student success and provides them with the necessary tools to improve upon what they already do. Similarly, community college faculty and staff have always tried to keep up with the changing needs of business and industry, and most have experimented with a multitude of initiatives aimed at improving student learning. In other words, community college personnel have long demonstrated that they *want* to innovate; they just haven't been given the tools necessary to do so at scale or been granted the leeway to propose and experiment with solutions that may disrupt long-standing traditions or organizational processes. Fortunately, the actions college leaders must take to cultivate an entrepreneurial culture will also help to enable entrepreneurship at a grassroots level.

College leaders interviewed for this book shared a few other keys to supporting grassroots innovation. Steven Gonzales, for example, advises presidents and chancellors to set firm expectations but provide faculty and staff with leeway to pursue entrepreneurial ideas in their own ways. "Giving them the flexibility to *do* is critical," he said. "People amaze you if you give them the space to do the work. They often come back with ideas that are far exceeding what I thought we could do." Joe Davis, NIACC's interim vice president of academic affairs, agreed. He is fond of saying, "You are the faculty, you lead the way," but cautioned that administrators must then follow through and support the ideas faculty generate instead of superimposing their own priorities.

Kate Smith believes it is also helpful to acknowledge how foreign this process is for many faculty and staff. Few discipline-based graduate programs teach an entrepreneurial approach to problem solving, and thus it can feel strange and perhaps even uncomfortable at first. Thus, she shared, leaders have to "help your team be comfortable with a little chaos, be comfortable with the unknown, be comfortable with the fact that it's going to change." Clearly stating that you expect even the best-laid plans to undergo iterative improvements is also critical, she said. "You just have to really build your team to understand that, yeah, we are going to be in some shifting sand while we build it! And yeah, we are going to make some decisions that we think are really good, and then later be like, 'Crud! Why did we do that? That was bad!' And now we need to undo it." College leaders can support faculty and staff in the innovation process by publicly supporting attempts—even if they fail—and by linking timelines to various stages of ideation and prototyping instead of to outcomes.

Finally, it may be useful to create cross-functional teams with specific areas of expertise to solve certain mission-related challenges. To arrive at solutions that hit the sweet spot between desirability, feasibility, and viability, design teams should include innovative thinkers, subject-matter experts, community liaisons, and staff with financial or budgeting expertise; don't expect faculty or others whose jobs do not regularly involve seeking revenue sources to solve such problems on their own. Nonetheless, asking faculty to take a leadership role in imagining how the college can better meet the needs of students and communities is key to cultivating a truly entrepreneurial culture. "In the end," Sasan Poureetezadi argued, "it's not going to work unless they're in on it. Besides the students, the greatest value that we offer is the instruction. That's what we do. That's the core value of our business." Listen to faculty, he advised. Be inclusive. And focus on building bridges between their experiences and any new ventures instead of "steamrolling" them into compliance. Shari Olson, president of South Mountain Community College, concurred. "If you want sustainable change and lasting change," she said:

> It's all through support at the grassroots for that change. Because as a leader, you come and go. But the faculty live in an organization for a very long period of time. And many staff do too. So if they are the impetus behind an idea, and you are just there to support them, when you come back and visit ten years from now, that idea is more likely to still be in place than anything you'd try to impose on them. Anything you try to impose on them will be gone. But if you have nurtured the process of grassroots involvement and faculty involvement in the creation of something, it's probably going to be there for a long time. That's where true culture change takes place.

Establishing Effective External Partnerships

> *Part of the strategy is really looking externally for partnerships and resources. This idea of going it alone anymore, especially at the community college level—or at the universities—is a difficult thing to do.*[30]

In creating entrepreneurial community colleges, much of the work for college leaders is internal to the institution: cultivating an entrepreneurial culture, managing governing boards, and enabling grassroots entrepreneurship among faculty and staff. Yet leaders must also be outward-facing, representing the college in the community and—crucially—identifying opportunities to collaborate with nearby businesses, municipalities, and other organizations in ways that benefit all involved. Establishing partnerships—especially those that can mitigate college costs or generate new revenue—has become especially necessary as states and localities disinvest in community colleges. Instead of thinking "we wish we could but we don't have the resources," Harper-Marinick said, the community college mindset has to be "we only have this many resources; how do we partner in a manner that brings in" more?

Giovannini concurred. "You've got to look at external partners right away," he said. "There's virtually nothing we can do—even as rich as we may be—or do right without external support." On the flip side, he laughed, there's very little that businesses or communities can do without the education or training provided by community colleges. "If there's an industry or there's a technology that's driving the workplace, how's that gonna happen without a workforce?" College leaders need to build a "coalition of understanding" with their counterparts in the private sector, he said. As soon as colleges and corporations recognize the intertwined nature of their business models, there are virtually no limits to the kinds of partnerships that can be created. NIACC president Steven Schulz echoed this point, noting that partnerships are especially important for small or rural institutions. For these colleges in particular, "what's going to be required is a larger private investment" if they are to grow and develop programs to meet new workforce needs.

Community college partnerships with external organizations vary tremendously in size and scope and, as such, benefit the institutions in multiple ways, including enabling colleges to stay informed of industry standards and changing workforce requirements; offering a window into how other industries are innovating service to customers or clients; mitigating college costs through the donation of equipment, software, tools, and so forth; sponsoring or providing scholarships to students; and through direct financial contributions. These types of arrangements are increasingly necessary as colleges offer more and more training programs geared toward technical or middle-skill occupations that require expertise with large, expensive machinery (autoclaves, supply chain robots, CNC machines, wind turbines, and the like). Clint Grant, dean of aviation, business, and logistics at TCC's Northwest Campus, joked, "I'm not above begging and whining when it comes to industry. I always point out to these guys that we are a poor, public community college. I give the puppy-dog eyes and it works to some degree. They understand a lot of these things, especially [that] a lot of these skills . . . take expensive equipment." He estimated that roughly half of everything his campus owns was donated. "We have access to equipment at cost or government auctions or things like that," he said, "and we're not above doing swippity-swaps: we need this airplane, you can have this one here. Things like that. I'll barter, trade, steal; whatever I've got to do."

Partnerships with area businesses can also improve employment outcomes for students upon graduation. Indeed, Carolyn McMorran and her colleagues at Valencia's Advanced Manufacturing Training Center have learned the hard way that short-term training programs are much more successful when employers and partners are lined up ahead of time. For example, she said, "with the clinical medical assisting [program], we went out the door without really solid partners. We have been able to recoup from that, but we shouldn't have done that. We should have done it right the first time." McMorran now asks corporate partners to provide students with tangible connections to the workforce while they are still enrolled. Some companies send guest speakers to students' classes. Others participate in mock interviews. Still others take students on tours of their facilities so they can visualize a future workplace. When students go on these tours, she shared, "they all now want to work there! So that's a really smart strategy." Sometimes this leads to little competitions among employers, she laughed, as they all want to woo the best students. All of these arrangements can improve program completion, provide jobs for graduates, and cut down on corporate on-boarding costs, said Liz Sisk, TCC's senior donor relations officer, leading to a "cyclical effect of win-win" for all involved.

Establishing mutually beneficial partnerships is the ultimate goal, Schulz said, and indeed is necessary "to really deliver on the new economy." At NIACC, staff are constantly asking, "What kind of partnerships can we create that are good for business, good for the college, good for the region?" We can't just ask for money, he said. There has to be "a direct benefit for them." Perhaps companies hire the students coming out of programs. Maybe their investment reduces the cost of recruiting and training new employees. Whatever it is, "the role we play now" is creating "those partnerships with employers so that we both benefit and [so] we serve our community."

Sisk agreed. "Acme Brick has just started an endowed scholarship for construction students. Why? They are relying on construction management students to help fill their jobs! Westwood Contractors: the same. They get to know—they see us, they know we're an economic engine from which they can hire. It's good for their business to have good students coming through." Similarly, she said, "Cisco did a hack-a-thon for our students where they could wear the black hat and try to hack in" to a Cisco system, and current Cisco employees had to defend against the attacks. Cisco "had teams of people afterward to interview these students," Sisk shared, as did some of their subsidiaries and sister companies. Everyone won: Cisco and other organizations identified potential new hires, students gained experience and—for some of them—a job, and TCC was able to showcase its cybersecurity program.

Michelle Terrell, director of work-based learning at Valencia College, shared another example of a mutually beneficial partnership: the college's Four Seasons Externship. Through this program, the luxury hotel chain hires at least three culinary students per semester as interns. Four Seasons representatives come to campus to recruit the students, sharing "information about the position and the opportunities, but also . . . to give them a realistic picture of what's expected. Because you can't work for the Four Seasons with a Holiday Inn mentality." Four Seasons pays the interns—a requirement of Valencia's culinary department—and covers tuition and fees for the course. If interns are still employed in six months, Four Seasons awards a bonus, with another paid after one year of employment. "It is a great opportunity for our students," shared Terrell, but it is also good for Four Seasons, as it allows it to "shape the minds and expectations of the students" about what it takes to succeed in high-end culinary establishments. Partnerships like Valencia's Four Seasons Externship, TCC's Cisco hack-a-thon, and others described here are exemplary of the kind of collaborations emerging in third-wave entrepreneurial institutions. Not only do they generate value for partner organizations, colleges, and students alike, but because they support economic and workforce development in high-growth industries (culinary arts, cybersecurity, health care, construction), they also contribute to the long-term stability of surrounding communities.

Yet collaborating in ways that benefit students, external partners, communities, and colleges themselves is much more easily said than done. Community colleges are not used to moving as fast as most private-sector institutions, and the committee work and sheer number of approvals required to green-light any new public-private collaboration can lead to missed opportunities and frustration all around. In addition, despite obvious financial and other benefits of bringing external partners to the table, many faculty are reluctant to engage in such collaborations, as doing so means relinquishing some control over curricular and other matters. These fears may be heightened when colleges approach potential partners asking, "What do you need from us and how can we get it to you as soon as possible? And how can we engage you in the design of the curriculum, in learner outcomes, in the selection of who is going to teach this class?"[31] While this is undoubtedly a productive approach to partnering, the sentiment can be quite scary for college faculty, who may rightly wonder what other aspects of their job description will be encroached upon next. But what faculty need to remember, said Valencia's Loren Bender, is that their jobs are also dependent upon students, who will enroll elsewhere if colleges don't adapt to changing workforce needs.

The key to developing effective partnerships, then, is understanding the expertise and talent that each stakeholder brings, empathizing with their needs, and working collaboratively to design a relationship that improves outcomes for all involved, including faculty, students, colleges, partners, and the surrounding community. "To get the best outcome," says Tim Putnam, director of NIACC's John Pappajohn Entrepreneurial Center, community colleges need to look at the entire ecosystem surrounding the college and assess where the gaps are and what each party can offer. "Really try to understand what the entrepreneurial ecosystem is, who is playing what role, who's doing things well and who's not," he said.

Partnerships should be approached with a win-win mind-set, advised Nassar Hedayat, assistant vice president for career and workforce education at Valencia College, but it is also important that each partner has some skin in the game. "Our students invest when they select a program," he said. "They make an investment, whether it is their time, or economically, they invest and get loans and what have you. And the college is committed as well. As the college we make an investment. So I believe it is important for our businesses to make an investment as well. And that means connect to students earlier. Don't wait for the student to graduate." Conversations about what each party will contribute should occur early in partnership discussions, Hedayat asserted, as this leads to open dialogues and better outcomes for all involved.

Community colleges must get better at asking partners to invest in their programs, agreed Fred Schmidt, assistant to the president of TCC's Northeast Campus, but contributions must be also sustainable over time. Lasting partnerships are those that are more relational than transactional. He explained: a transactional partnership is one where "you are the Quality Inn Express along the highway and you are getting the people who are traveling somewhere else." A relational partnership, on the other hand, is one where "you're Myrtle Beach, the resort, and you want the person who's going to come back every year." As community colleges, Schmidt said, "we want the relationship." As such, TCC has been actively trying to restructure partnerships with several long-term vendors so that they are not just involved in the business of the organization, but rather involved "in the mission of Tarrant County College." As Liz Sisk explained, the college is trying to help partners understand that an "investment in the local community college is an investment in individuals in your community"; when community members are living happier, healthier, more prosperous, fulfilling lives, everybody wins.

• • •

In the preface to *Practical Leadership in Community Colleges*, George Boggs and Christine Johnson McPhail write that "strong, stable, courageous, and effective leadership is essential" if institutions are to "realize their maximum impact."[32] Yet as I note at the top of this chapter, to create entrepreneurial community colleges, strong leadership must be coupled with a clear statement about *why* change is necessary; a culture that values and rewards an entrepreneurial mind-set and the innovation and risk taking that go with it; and a process or framework that enables all constituents—faculty and staff, full-time and contingent—to explore entrepreneurial ideas in an empathic manner, ensuring that new ventures amplify, rather than sacrifice, the institution's mission and the human needs of its stakeholders. This chapter focuses primarily on how college leaders can create the conditions necessary for entrepreneurial programs or initiatives to succeed; the final chapter of this book examines how underlying organizational and budgetary structures may also need to change in order to support the new paradigm, investigates the extent to which entrepreneurial actions have reduced the colleges' reliance on state or other sources of governmental funding, and offers ideas for how college leaders might design and sustain the next wave of entrepreneurship on their campuses and in their communities.

PART III

From Stories of Entrepreneurship Elsewhere to Innovation Everywhere

8 Designing the Next Wave of Community College Entrepreneurship

If you do not change direction, you may end up where you are headed.[1]

As I have argued throughout this book, community colleges are at an existential crossroads. Public disinvestment in institutions of higher education, coupled with heightened pressure for workforce credentials and greater educational attainment, mean that each year the institutions are asked to do more with less. Add opportunity to the mix—incredible opportunity, really, to play a central role in regional economic transformations and to reimagine training for jobs that do not yet exist—and it is clear that something beyond incremental changes to form and function must occur if the colleges are to continue carrying out their education, training, and community uplift missions. Indeed, if they are to survive today's challenges and be as influential in the twenty-first century as they were throughout the twentieth, our nation's colleges must act entrepreneurially, experiment with opportunities to serve students and communities in new and fiscally sustainable ways, and redesign outmoded organizational structures and financial processes that keep the colleges tethered to previous assumptions about the world.

This book offers numerous stories of how NIACC, Valencia College, TCC, and the Maricopa Community Colleges have utilized design thinking and similar processes for leading innovation to act in entrepreneurial ways. It illustrates how college leaders have worked to establish cultures that support and reward divergent thinking, risk taking, collaboration, and iterative problem solving. And it identifies how the colleges are exhibiting aspects of third-wave entrepreneurship, which is key to transcending a history of incremental change and ensuring the long-term sustainability of the institutions and the communities they serve. Yet several questions remain. How much have underlying organizational structures and budgetary processes within the colleges changed to support the new paradigm? What else must colleges modify to ensure that new or redesigned programs are not simply tacked on at the periphery but are instead central to the ways in which a college plans and budgets for the future? How does the size of an institution or its geographical location affect its ability to act entrepreneurially or innovate in ways that improve service to students and communities? And perhaps the stickiest question of all: how much has entrepreneurial activity helped to reduce the colleges' reliance on governmental allocations? This chapter examines these questions and then considers what the future may hold for community colleges seeking to ride the next wave of mission-oriented entrepreneurship.

MODIFYING ORGANIZATIONAL STRUCTURES AND FINANCIAL PRACTICES TO SUPPORT ENTREPRENEURSHIP

> *To ignore the forces that undermine long-term change in education is to repeat the futility that has characterized virtually thousands of well-intentioned attempts to alter education. These forces need to be taken seriously if there is any chance of overcoming them.*[2]

Community college organizational structures were, by and large, imported directly from the universities and K–12 districts and are typically characterized by central administrative structures that manage all back-end operations, combined with relatively autonomous academic departments or divisions, each responsible for oversight of the curriculum, teaching, and learning in their area. This traditional and highly standardized structure, write university leaders Clark Gilbert, Michael Crow, and Derrick Anderson, has "served higher education well until this point," as it allowed colleges and universities to replicate past successes and ensured consistency at a time when new institutions were being established in nearly every community. Yet because this structural conformity "arguably limits exploration, differentiation, and, in some cases, even system-wide quality," Gilbert et al. argue that existing org charts must be supplemented or displaced "by new models that embrace organizational innovation, responsivity, and adaptation."[3] These new models will look different at different institutions, but are likely to utilize what scholar Burton Clark termed a "strengthened steering core" that can work collaboratively across departments to support new entrepreneurial ventures and ensure their connection to existing programs and services.[4]

Similarly, if community colleges are to develop, support, and sustain innovative programs, they must also reexamine their financial practices, modifying or replacing those that perpetuate the status quo. In particular, college leaders should consider how they might shift from incremental and enrollment-based budgeting to a more flexible approach that ties internal allocations to outcomes, costs, or strategic objectives. Shedding the politically safe habit of absorbing funding declines without considering programmatic cuts or taking any other steps that might affect the colleges' *anyone, anywhere, anything, at any time* business model may also be required.[5] While these historic practices may have made sense when the colleges could depend on relatively consistent funding from the government and when they were more concerned with providing access then achieving particular outcomes, they limit the institutions' ability to adapt quickly and capitalize on opportunities to serve students and communities in new and fiscally sustainable ways.

The four colleges and districts highlighted in this book have begun experimenting with these and other internal changes to better support entrepreneurial efforts. TCC, for example, has reorganized its entire administrative structure to support the institution's Three Goals and Eight Principles.

As chapter 5 illustrates, campus presidents now act as champions of one or more principles, leading panels of faculty and staff from across the college to brainstorm, evaluate, experiment with, and implement new opportunities. This structure ensures that all new ideas support the institution's mission and prevents efforts from being duplicated at multiple campuses. As well, the TCC Foundation has become much more involved in how the college funds its mission priorities. Senior Donor Relations Officer Liz Sisk explained, "The change really has been from seeing the foundation as just scholarship support to being more impactful in some of these key program areas." The executive director of the foundation now sits on the chancellor's executive leadership team and is "in every meeting and every conversation." This allows the foundation to work closely with faculty and administrators developing new or expanding existing programs and approach corporate and philanthropic donors for investment early in the process. This reorientation, said Sisk, has been especially useful in funding programs focused on middle-skill jobs that are central to regional economic development efforts.

Valencia College is also experimenting with new organizational structures and financial processes. The School of Public Safety described in chapter 5, for example, utilizes a collaborative and distributed model that centralizes administrative functions for all public safety programs and acts as the master hub for credit and noncredit courses offered on each of Valencia's seven campuses. A public safety core team comprising faculty and administrators from across the college ensures collaboration and a seamless student experience across law enforcement, fire, and security programs. The success of this model has spurred Valencia to consider what other areas might benefit from a collaborative and distributed organizational structure and to think about how noncredit certificate programs can be similarly integrated into more traditional degree pathways. Indeed, the intentional integration of credit and noncredit programs may be key to ensuring a diversified income base and enabling revenue-generating units to offset the costs of infrastructure and instruction in other areas.

Taking a somewhat different tack, Maricopa is considering following in Arizona State University's footsteps and consolidating oversight of all entrepreneurial ventures under a separate structure connected to the district foundation, with an advisory board that can utilize its connections to business and community groups to support new initiatives. As Interim Chancellor Steven Gonzales said, "I think that's where we miss the ball at times at the community college level. We invite people to be a part of our groups and on foundations, and there's not always a lot of focus on how we are going to tap into their specific networks and their specific resources." This potential new structure would capitalize on these connections and allow entrepreneurial ventures to operate in a more flexible, outward-facing environment. In addition, Maricopa is creating an asset map of technology labs, manufacturing and maker spaces, equipment, incubation services, and other assets that could be leased to community groups or incorporated into partnerships to provide a win-win for all involved. We want to engage in a "collective conversation" about what the district can offer to strategic partners, said Kristen Gubser, director of external affairs at GateWay College, and "really get people more connected from an ecosystem perspective."

In addition to these organizational changes, Maricopa, Valencia, TCC, and NIACC have also started to modify financial practices to support their entrepreneurial efforts. Valencia has gone further than most in creating a transparent budget process and decoupling enrollment considerations and strategic decision making (see chapter 7). In doing so, the college has implemented a variant of formula budgeting which President Sandy Shugart called "purpose-based budgeting." This approach bases allocations on accurate projections of future costs (as opposed to former budgets) and directs supplemental funding toward strategic priorities. Purpose-based budgeting, said Valencia's Vice President of Business Operations and Finance Loren Bender, "helps maximize the use of funds" and ensures that the college has the flexibility to apply revenues generated in one area of the college to costs incurred elsewhere. This whole-college perspective is essential, Bender said, because "we don't have enough [money] to work with." The only way the institution can be successful is to figure out how cost and revenue centers can support one another.

Of course, any cost-based approach necessitates a fair amount of financial education for faculty, staff, and board members about "how the business works."[6] To that end, Bender's office widely shares a document that illustrates various sources of income to the college at the top of the page—including governmental allocations, tuition, grants, auxiliary services, revenue from noncredit ventures, and so forth—and at the bottom of the page outlines operating expenses needed to support the enterprise, including infrastructure, equipment, salaries, benefits, and wage increases. This document, said Bender, "clarifies for a lot of people how revenues and expenses combine and connect to each other." It also serves as a model for how faculty and staff can incorporate short business plans into proposals and program reviews in order to estimate the costs of new initiatives and align them with projected income. These business plans will not perfectly estimate the costs of maintaining new equipment or accurately project increases in wages and benefits, but this is okay, said Bender. The important thing is getting people to think about how to pay for programs on day one.

In addition to these changes, Richard Romano and James Palmer write in *Financing Community Colleges* that there may also be some logic behind adopting an activity-based costing model in which community colleges attempt to price out "the functions or activities that are part of a college's mission," including providing developmental coursework; registering, advising, teaching, and tutoring students; offering career or transfer counseling; and so on. As they note, "looking at costs in this way helps managers identify cost drivers and non-value adding activities, which in turn assists in the reallocation of resources to activities that provide the greatest value."[7] Greatest value, of course, can be defined in numerous ways including enhancing credential completion or job attainment; supporting the acquisition of basic skills; meeting community needs; or any other institutional goal defined in a college's strategic plan. Because activity-based costing looks at specific functions instead of programs or academic units, it may also help colleges separate enrollment considerations from planning and budgeting processes.

Activity-based costing thus holds promise, both for identifying the least costly approach to producing a particular outcome, and for purging expensive programs or activities that do not support institutional priorities. And indeed, community colleges may need to put processes in place to sunset programs that can no longer be justified by revenues or connection to mission, said Robert Muñoz, vice president for community and industry education at TCC. The colleges can't continue "trying to manufacture buggy whips when the automobile came in."

Purpose-based budgeting, activity-based costing, and other true-cost budgeting methods may be exceptionally useful in entrepreneurial organizations, as they enable colleges to rapidly assess the financial contributions of new ventures, as well as their projected impact on institutional goals, and compare both to those produced by the status quo. Coupled with reimagining how existing organizational structures can be modified to support innovation, adopting at least some elements of these financial practices will help community colleges respond more nimbly to future challenges and opportunities and sustain entrepreneurial efforts over time.

HOW SIZE AND LOCATION AFFECT OPPORTUNITIES FOR ENTREPRENEURSHIP

> *Give me the state and give me the regions with the biggest challenges and I'll give you the greatest opportunity.*[8]

Many of the community colleges that have received the most attention for their entrepreneurial efforts are large districts located in urban environments. For example, nine of the eleven institutions highlighted in John Roueche and Barbara Jones's 2005 book *The Entrepreneurial Community College* are large and/or urban.[9] Similarly, only one of the ten chapters in Rebecca Corbin and Ron Thomas's 2019 *Community Colleges as Incubators of Innovation* examines entrepreneurship in rural America.[10] This book also oversamples from large and urban institutions, and collectively this bias creates the perception that larger colleges have a greater ability to act entrepreneurially than their smaller or more rural counterparts. Whether or not this is true is an open question, but what is clear is that every type of institution faces inherent advantages and disadvantages in acting entrepreneurially and thus have somewhat different considerations for how to evaluate various opportunities and implement the organizational and financial shifts required to support and sustain them.

Large community colleges, for example, have the advantages of scale and scope, which allow them to experiment with a greater number of programs and services and risk substantially smaller percentages of their operating budgets on new and unproven approaches to meeting stakeholder needs. They also have more faculty and staff who can participate in entrepreneurial efforts, and those in metropolitan areas have access to a greater number of businesses and community organizations with which to partner. While this may translate to a greater number of possible alliances, colleges should carefully consider how they might structure collaborations so that they can be scaled to include multiple partners and still ensure that individual businesses gain enough from the partnership to help support it financially. This can be a tricky balancing act and likely requires careful mapping of entrepreneurial ecosystems and decisions about which corporations or community organizations to bring on as inaugural or anchor partners.

Large and urban (and to some extent, medium-sized and suburban) community colleges must also work hard to overcome factors that constrain entrepreneurial activity, including real or perceived competition from corporate, nonprofit, and other entities. In addition, in the past, policy makers and even some trustees have been skeptical of new ventures that would compete with private enterprise. This is famously the case at Maricopa, where one governing board member opposed an entrepreneurial exemption to the constitutionally mandated limit on how much community colleges can spend by arguing that in seeking new revenues, the colleges would be "taking away opportunities from other organizations."[11] Finally, large and multicampus districts are challenged by the sheer number of faculty and staff they employ, many of whom are highly specialized and thus more likely to orient toward disciplinary or departmental silos. Indeed, collaboration must be much more intentional at larger institutions, as there are fewer hallway encounters or watercooler conversations with colleagues outside one's immediate corner of the college. Well-designed organizational structures that incorporate Clark's "strengthened steering core" and encourage cross-campus collaboration may be even more imperative if large and medium-sized colleges are to embrace an entrepreneurial culture.[12]

The advantages and disadvantages faced by smaller and more rural community colleges are nearly inverse to those at large, metropolitan districts. For example, in many parts of the country, there is little or no competition among education providers; community colleges are often the only game in town. As such, said NIACC President Steven Schulz, "the opportunities are great, and the pressure is great. The pressure is great to deliver because they [the students] don't have anywhere else to go." As well, these institutions often have much more experience collaborating with business and community groups and sharing resources with external organizations. Rural areas, in particular, are often tightly knit, with the survival of one institution (a college, hospital, or business) inextricably linked to the survival of the community. In these regions, collaboration beyond campus borders has always been a way of life, and thus may not represent such a paradigm shift as it does in metropolitan environments. Furthermore, as NIACC Foundation Director Molly Knoll stated, "If you go into almost any business in Mason City or our area, you're going to find at least one graduate or two" that will do anything they can to help the college. "We've kind of been their hub, and they are willing to give back." This loyalty—combined with the fact that small, rural institutions have long had to be extremely responsive to economic and workforce shifts in order to preserve enrollments—may make it easier for these institutions to act quickly and in an entrepreneurial manner.

However, small rural colleges (and many midsized institutions) have fewer employees with enough extra bandwidth to experiment with innovative new approaches to serving students or communities and face far greater resource constraints than colleges located in more populous areas. In *The World Is Flat*, Thomas Friedman argues that technology and globalization have caused the global competitive playing field to flatten out, allowing a technologically savvy worker to live anywhere and still engage in meaningful and economically sustainable work that was once only available in large cities.[13] In theory, this means that remote communities should be just as desirable for companies and workers as metropolitan environments, providing a stable economic base to support community colleges and other social-sector institutions. But as Richard Florida points out in his rebuttal to Friedman's work, "globalization has changed the economic playing field, but it has not leveled it." As he explains, "the tallest peaks—the cities and regions that drive the world economy—are growing ever higher, while the valleys mostly languish."[14] As such, said Eli Mercer, dean of technology, health, and business at TCC's Southeast Campus, rural America is "really struggling to be significant," to attract and keep employers, and to preserve a middle-class standard of living. (Whether and by how much this changes as a result of the COVID-19 pandemic forcing more and more employees to work from home is an open question.)

Regardless, for community colleges in many parts of the United States, continued existence—with or without innovative thinking about how to mitigate expenses and tap new revenue streams—is not guaranteed, and these institutions will need to do far more than tinker around the edges if they are to survive. Careful evaluation of how every subject, instructional approach, or student service contributes to a college's mission priorities and/or bottom line will need to be incorporated into all proposals and program reviews. Back-end operations such as human resources, instructional technology, and so forth might need to be outsourced to colleges or universities with more resources. And small colleges may need to constrain their offerings to a narrower band of courses and programs that are directly connected to workforce and economic development needs, finding ways to partner with other education providers to allow students to enroll in more traditional academic and transfer programs. In other words, while there are incredible opportunities for small and rural community colleges to participate in economic revitalization efforts and develop entrepreneurial ecosystems that can sustain communities, they—far more than their larger urban and suburban counterparts—will need to structure partnerships and internal operations in a way that preserves their ability to keep the doors open and the lights on.

THE FINANCIAL IMPACT OF ENTREPRENEURSHIP, WITH A VIEW TO THE FUTURE

> *We're not necessarily contributing yet to helping the budget situation. But we're not hurting it . . . We're not using anybody else's money, because all the money coming in, we are using it to pay for everything.*[15]

The question of whether and by how much community college entrepreneurship has shored up the institutions' bottom lines and reduced their reliance on governmental allocations is a tricky one. It first presumes a one-to-one relationship between state and local subsidies and entrepreneurial revenues that in truth is far more complicated. For example, what counts as a state subsidy: Only operating revenues? Or other grants and contracts as well? What about nonrecurring apportionments? And as for local support, do we count bond measures passed by localities to fund infrastructure and other capital improvements or only tax dollars? Federal grants and contracts further muddy the waters, as do state allocations earmarked for areas that policy makers deem important for economic development. (Arizona, for example, recently provided Maricopa and Pima Community Colleges with $6.8 and $20 million, respectively, for their allied health and avionics programs—the first state money to go to these institutions since they were written out of the state constitution in 2015—but these dollars cannot support any other operations.)

State workforce development funds add another layer of complexity to the question, as these dollars are often critical to the success of entrepreneurial ventures such TCC's Opportunity Center and Maricopa Corporate College (MCOR), but could not be utilized to the same extent without these structures in place. Receivables spreadsheets for colleges with robust corporate training programs—including those that bring in enough revenue to offset other college expenses—may thus show *increased* state support for community colleges, as the more the institutions build their capacity to train workers and serve local businesses, the more they can access state dollars set aside for that purpose. Thus, while entities such as MCOR and the TCC Opportunity Center have found a way to utilize funds available under Arizona's Proposition 301 and Texas's Workforce Innovation and Opportunity Act for their intended purpose and turn profits from the work into undesignated cash for their institutions, the financial impact of such ventures is rarely straightforward at the institutional level, let alone in aggregate.

Furthermore, national averages mask incredible variation across colleges. Some institutions earn substantial sums from their entrepreneurial ventures—Valencia College, for example, brings in between $16 and $18 million annually from international students, the intensive English program, and auxiliary revenues alone—but few colleges make this kind of money, even on a per-FTE basis. Thus, although we know that over time and on average, governmental support has diminished while income from tuition, fees, and other private sources has increased, stating definitively that entrepreneurship has reduced community colleges' reliance on state or local allocations is next to impossible.

Perhaps a better question is, has an increased focus on entrepreneurship and innovation improved the colleges' ability to serve students and play a pivotal role in the economic sustainability of their communities? As the stories and vignettes offered throughout this book illustrate, the answer to this question is unequivocally *yes*. It has helped. And to the extent that many of these efforts are (or will soon be) able to cover their own costs, there is cause for optimism that an entrepreneurial approach will enable the colleges to continue growing and innovating. However, as the entertainment industry has long known, a diverse slate of films and television shows developed to appeal to multiple potential audiences is a surer bet than a single, tentpole movie that might or might not be a box office smash. Applied to community colleges and other institutions of higher education, a broad, diverse portfolio of entrepreneurial ventures—the majority of which are self-sustaining or produce a small return and all of which are closely tied to community needs—is more likely to be successful than any single undertaking, no matter how profitable.

However, a slate of stand-alone entrepreneurial activities, even if they can each cover their own costs, may not be enough to overcome future financial challenges. If community colleges hope to sever the Gordian knot that has tethered them to the ebbs and flows of enrollments and public largesse for nearly a century, entrepreneurial efforts must be integrated into larger organizational, financial, and cultural shifts that position the colleges for success in a wildly uncertain future. Indeed, the events of 2020—the year in which much of this book was written—will likely exacerbate the need to innovate and adapt quickly. The global COVID-19 pandemic and ensuing economic fallout resulted in substantially reduced allocations for the colleges, and if previous patterns hold, public support will not return to 2019 levels even after the crisis abates. Furthermore, although community colleges have always been in competition with other agencies "lined up at the state trough (e.g., healthcare, K–12 education, and corrections)," the contest for funds may become even more fierce as each sector bases its financial pleas on the essential nature of the services it provides.[16] Community college leaders will have to get much better at illustrating the institution's value proposition to policy makers, municipalities, and partners in industry. They will also need to maintain a meticulous commitment to pursuing entrepreneurial strategies in an empathic, mission-oriented manner and identify new ways to share ideas across state and institutional boundaries so that the sector itself becomes more responsive and financially secure. For without an entrepreneurial mind-set and the ability to collectively implement new, financially sustainable ways of meeting student and community needs, many colleges will fail, and with them higher education's built-in mechanism for social mobility and the improvement of individual and regional circumstances.

THE COMMUNITY COLLEGE SECTOR AS ONE GIANT LEARNING LABORATORY (AND OTHER IDEAS FOR EXTENDING THE WORK)

> *What are the needs of your community? What are the needs of the businesses in the community that you serve? You need to be even more future, forward-looking than we are. Because the*

> *sustainability of your community depends on you being able to see two steps ahead of where the trends are.*[17]

There are more than a thousand community colleges in the United States. While they are an incredibly diverse set of institutions, they share many organizational characteristics, face similar challenges—particularly those related to funding—and are equally committed to improving the lives and livelihoods of community members, principally those from marginalized and economically or educationally disadvantaged populations. As such, the institutions are well positioned to function as one giant (or several regional) learning laboratory(ies) in which the creation, testing, and refining of new entrepreneurial approaches can be shared across institutional boundaries and tailored to fit each organization's historic, demographic, political, and cultural contexts.

Much of this work is already occurring through existing consortia in which colleges, government agencies, and corporate partners collaborate to improve training and preparation for various industries. The Viticulture Enology Science and Technology Alliance, a partnership between the National Science Foundation, Missouri colleges and universities, and vineyards and wineries across America, is one such example. The Multi-State Advanced Manufacturing Consortium, with forty industry partners and thirteen colleges in ten states is another. Learning laboratories may also be organized and supported by national community college associations, provided they work intentionally to create centers of practice focused on specific topics and regions, share processes and frameworks for the work, and stress the importance of designing new programs and services around local needs rather than national trends. NACCE has become a particularly effective platform for sharing entrepreneurial strategies across the sector. Steven Schulz, for example, believes that the annual NACCE conference "is probably the best thing I do professionally every year" as it allows him to learn about how other colleges are implementing innovative practices and to think about how NIACC might engage in the work more deeply.

NACCE also provides organizational and financial support for regional centers of practice. One such group was formed after trustees from a handful of Iowa community colleges met at NACCE's fall 2018 conference to discuss how they might connect entrepreneurial initiatives occurring across the state. This center of practice is helmed by Tim Putnam, director of NIACC's John Pappajohn Entrepreneurial Center, and includes colleagues from five other Iowa community colleges. The group speaks regularly to share lessons learned and best practices for incorporating an entrepreneurial mind-set across the curriculum, and in fall 2019 came together to share its challenges and successes with the broader NACCE community. One of the most important things they have learned, Putnam shared, is that specific approaches to instilling an entrepreneurial mind-set among students, faculty, and staff cannot be exported from one institution to another. Rather, colleges must *import* the strategies or components that are most likely to meet local needs and fit the culture of their organization.

In addition to the Iowa consortium, NACCE also provides seed funding and organizational support for centers of practice focused on design thinking, equity and diversity, global entrepreneurship, maker spaces, student engagement, women in entrepreneurship, and workforce development. These collaborations are prototypes of what Gene Giovannini hopes will eventually become a NACCE-driven hub-and-spokes model for sharing industry-specific entrepreneurial resources and ideas. As he explained, because certain industries are clustered in regions across the United States—Texas, for example, is a leader in transportation, aviation, aerospace, and energy—one college with "access to training facilities, current models for effective coworking, and . . . strong industry partnerships" will act as the hub, with connecting spokes including community colleges in the surrounding area, as well as those in other regions where that industry exists. "All of these would benefit from the resources the hub provides, and in turn offer their own geographic areas with centralized resources, support, and programmatic offerings."[18] Giovannini envisions multiple, overlapping sets of hubs and spokes across the country, each dedicated to a particular industry such as agriculture, telecommunications, health care, or advanced manufacturing, and each working to ensure that community colleges are at the center of sustainable entrepreneurial ecosystems.

Indeed, a regional ecosystem approach may well be necessary if community colleges are to survive, said Eli Mercer. He believes that institutional transformation alone will not be sufficient to meet future challenges and opportunities; change must extend beyond campus borders and involve municipalities, business groups, and community organizations. Only when "public resources, private resources, and political clout" are aligned, Mercer said, will external forces that once constrained entrepreneurial activity work in tandem with internal changes to allow for true innovation to occur.

A first step in this process may be engaging business, community, and governmental partners in conversations about the future of work. However, planning for the future when you don't have enough resources for today can be challenging. As well, while community colleges are very good at "producing what we have the money, the mandate, and a clear challenge" to do, operating in situations where the lines are not as clearly drawn is more difficult.[19] For example, Clint Grant shared, TCC trains technicians to manufacture and operate drones and other unmanned aircraft systems. Yet despite numerous conversations with the Federal Aviation Administration about future regulatory actions and other issues that might affect the way the college trains workers in this area, he doesn't receive much guidance. "We are trying to work with government agencies . . . to look into the future and get a handle on what we need to be thinking about. They are not always forthcoming, and a lot of times they don't know. They are behind the eight ball. There's a million of these things in the country now, and they still have no practical regulations for how we operate them in airspace." Yet despite these challenges, Grant believes that community colleges must engage in more of these conversations and think proactively about how to meet future needs if they are to be effective players in regional economic transformations.

Similarly, Kristen Bollini, chief lobbyist for Arizona's community colleges, advises community college leaders to engage *legislators* in future of work conversations, arguing that doing so may be necessary to preserve funding for critical college functions. "Let them hear from our business partners, our industry partners, where they think the industry is going in fifteen years," she said, "and *then* let them hear from our community colleges about how we are going to be the solution and how we are growing with them." This, she believes, will get policy makers invested early in entrepreneurial ecosystems and remind them that the colleges are critical partners in ensuring the economic health and vitality of communities. Because at the end of the day, said Idaho State University professor Sue Kater, "it's a niche that only community colleges can fill."

A LAST WORD ABOUT DESIGN THINKING AND MISSION-ORIENTED ENTREPRENEURSHIP

> *Society . . . is moving faster than we can keep up with, so we just have to focus on doing the right thing . . . An entrepreneurial mind-set and practical tools like design thinking and so forth can be very helpful in terms of solving problems.*[20]

As I wrote at the start of this book, there has never been a more exciting or a more frustrating and frightening time to work in community colleges. The difficulty of the trials ahead is matched only by the opportunities that exist to radically rethink how colleges educate and train students, participate in the economic transformations of their communities, and experiment with the internal changes necessary to sustain innovative ideas. The challenge, of course, is achieving all this in a way that prioritizes the needs of college stakeholders and ensures that new ventures, initiatives, programs, and processes amplify—rather than sacrifice—the institution's mission and values.

There are numerous approaches to entrepreneurship and innovation, and many overlap substantially in terms of their emphases on curiosity, creativity, risk taking, and iterative problem solving. All of these processes can guide community colleges toward greater economic sustainability, but because design thinking forces us to relentlessly empathize with students, faculty, community members, and other stakeholders—keeping their needs at the center of all new ideas—it holds particular promise for ensuring that change occurs in a mission-oriented manner. Design thinking can also help overcome challenges unique to community colleges and other social-sector organizations, including communication and collaboration across institutional silos and resistance from faculty and others who fear that entrepreneurship is antithetical to serving the public good. And because at its core, design thinking is a framework for improving the ways in which humans interact with and benefit from systems and environments, it can be applied to many other community college endeavors, including the development of guided pathways to improve student persistence and completion; recruiting the next generation of college leaders; updating enrollment management, budgetary, advising, and other internal processes; redesigning curricula to best meet societal needs and workforce demands; and shifting from a *students must be college-ready* philosophy to a *student-ready* culture that is prepared to meet learners where they are, regardless of the assets and advantages they bring and the challenges and barriers they face.[21]

In short, design thinking is a powerful approach to mission-oriented change in community colleges. Colleges that embrace this framework, provide training and opportunities for faculty and staff to practice it, and work collaboratively to develop a culture that values and rewards an entrepreneurial mind-set will be well positioned to design a future that is not confined to the realm of what has always been done but is instead grounded in local needs and limitless in possibility. Think of this book as one data point in your process of asking What *Is*, in better understanding what your institution needs if it is to survive, and in learning what your students, faculty, staff, and community members need to improve their lives and livelihoods. What happens next—the beautiful and exciting process by which your college comes up with and iteratively implements new ideas for serving students and communities—is up to you. Bon Voyage!

NOTES

INTRODUCTION

1. Sandy Baum and Charles Kurose, "Community Colleges in Context: Exploring Financing of Two- and Four-Year Institutions," in *Bridging the Higher Education Divide: Strengthening Community Colleges and Restoring the American Dream* (New York: Century Foundation, 2013), 73–108; Donald J. Phelan, "The Clear and Present Funding Crisis in Community Colleges," in *Budget and Finance in the American Community College. New Directions for Community Colleges*, no. 168, ed. Trudy Bers, Ronald B. Head, and James C. Palmer (San Francisco: Jossey-Bass, 2014), 5–16; Billy Roessler, Stephen G. Katsinas, and David E. Hardy, *The Downward Spiral of State Funding for Community Colleges, and Its Impact on Rural Community Colleges* (Meridian, MS: University of Alabama Education Policy Center for the Mid-South Partnership for Rural Community Colleges, 2006); Douglas A. Webber, "State Disinvestment and Tuition at Public Institutions," *Economics of Education Review* 60 (2017): 1–4; William Zumeta, *Higher Education Enters a New Era. The 2013 Almanac of Higher Education* (Washington, DC: National Education Association, 2013).
2. Donna Desrochers and Steven Hurlbert, *Trends in College Spending: 2001–2011,* A Delta Data Update (Washington, DC: American Institutes for Research, 2014); Richard M. Romano and James C. Palmer, *Financing Community Colleges. Where We Are, Where We're Going* (Lanham, MD: Rowman & Littlefield, 2016); *State Higher Education Finance: FY 2017* (Boulder, CO: State Higher Education Executive Officers Association [SHEEO], 2017).
3. Matthew M. Mars and Amy S. Metcalfe, "The Entrepreneurial Domains of American Higher Education," *ASHE Higher Education Report* 34, no. 5 (2009).
4. Tim Brown, *Change by Design* (New York: Harper Collins, 2009); Thomas Lockwood and Edgar Papke, *Innovation by Design: How Any Organization Can Leverage Design Thinking to Produce Change, Drive New Ideas, and Deliver Meaningful Solutions* (Wayne, NJ: Career Press, 2018).
5. Paul Axelrod, *Values in Conflict: The University, the Marketplace, and the Trials of Liberal Education* (Montreal: McGill-Queens University Press, 2002); Derek Bok, *Universities in the Marketplace: The Commercialization of Higher Education* (Princeton, NJ: Princeton University Press, 2003); Rosemary Deem, "Globalisation, New Managerialism, Academic Capitalism, and Entrepreneurialism in Universities: Is the Local Dimension Still Important?," *Comparative Education* 37 (2001): 7–20; Adrianna Kezar, "Obtaining Integrity? Reviewing and Examining the Charter between Higher Education and Society," *Review of*

Higher Education 27, no. 4 (2004): 429–59; Adrianna Kezar et al., *Higher Education for the Public Good: Emerging Voices from a National Movement* (San Francisco: Jossey-Bass, 2005).

6. All non-cited quotations appearing in this book are from interviews conducted at Valencia College, October 22–23, 2018; at TCC, February 27–March 1, 2019; at the Maricopa Community Colleges, January 24–25, 2019; and at NIACC, May 28–29, 2019. Exceptions to these dates and locations are as follows: Loren Bender, Shari Olson, and Rebecca Corbin were interviewed via telephone on December 7, 2018, February 5, 2019, and April 5, 2019, respectively. Carlos Morales participated in a follow-up telephone interview on May 8, 2020.
7. Throughout the book I employ the term *historically underserved* to denote students from those races and ethnicities traditionally underserved in institutions of higher education, specifically Blacks/African Americans, Latinx, Native Americans, Native Hawaiians, and Other Pacific Islanders.
8. *Statistical History Fact Book, 2017/2018* (Orlando, FL: Valencia College, 2019).
9. From 1918 to 1966, NIACC was known as Mason City Junior College.
10. *About NIACC* (Mason City: North Iowa Area Community College, 2019).
11. *Fast Facts 2017/18* (Tempe, AZ: Maricopa County Community College District, 2019).
12. Angela Gonzales, "Bill Introduced to Help Community Colleges Become More Entrepreneurial," *Phoenix Business Journal*, February 3, 2016, https://www.bizjournals.com/phoenix/news/2016/02/03/bill-introduced-to-help-community-colleges-become.html.
13. *Statistical Handbook, 2018FL* (Fort Worth, TX: Tarrant County College, Office of Institutional Research, 2019).

CHAPTER 1

1. Shari Olson, president, South Mountain College.
2. Matthew M. Mars and Amy S. Metcalfe, "The Entrepreneurial Domains of American Higher Education," *ASHE Higher Education Report* 34, no. 5 (2009).
3. Jeanne Liedtka, Randy Salzman, and Daisy Azer, *Design Thinking for the Greater Good: Innovation in the Social Sector* (New York: Columbia University Press, 2017).
4. Tim Brown, *Change by Design* (New York: Harper Collins, 2009); Thomas Lockwood and Edgar Papke, *Innovation by Design: How Any Organization Can Leverage Design Thinking to Produce Change, Drive New Ideas, and Deliver Meaningful Solutions* (Wayne, NJ: Career Press, 2018).
5. Paul Axelrod, *Values in Conflict: The University, the Marketplace, and the Trials of Liberal Education* (Montreal: McGill-Queens University Press, 2002); Derek Bok, *Universities in the Marketplace: The Commercialization of Higher Education* (Princeton, NJ: Princeton University Press, 2003); Rosemary Deem, "Globalisation, New Managerialism, Academic Capitalism, and Entrepreneurialism in Universities: Is the Local Dimension Still Important?," *Comparative Education* 37 (2001): 7–20; Adrianna Kezar, "Obtaining Integrity? Reviewing and Examining the Charter between Higher Education and Society," *Review of Higher Education* 27, no. 4 (2004): 429–59; Adrianna Kezar et al., *Higher*

Education for the Public Good: Emerging Voices from a National Movement (San Francisco: Jossey-Bass, 2005).

6. Sasan Poureetezadi, former chief strategy operator, Maricopa Community Colleges.
7. William Coppola, president, Tarrant County College, Southeast Campus.
8. Donna Desrochers and Steven Hurlbert, *Trends in College Spending: 2001–2011,* A Delta Data Update (Washington, DC: American Institutes for Research, 2014); Donna Desrochers and Steven Hurlbert, *Trends in College Spending: 2003–2013. Where Does the Money Come From? Where Does it Go? What Does it Buy?* (Washington, DC: American Institutes for Research, 2016); Richard M. Romano and James C. Palmer, *Financing Community Colleges. Where we are, where we're going* (Lanham, MD: Rowman & Littlefield, 2016); *State Higher Education Finance: FY 2017* (Boulder, CO: State Higher Education Executive Officers Association [SHEEO], 2017).
9. *State Higher Education Finance: FY 2018* (Boulder, CO: State Higher Education Executive Officers Association [SHEEO], 2018).
10. Romano and Palmer, *Financing Community Colleges,* 22.
11. Sara Goldrick-Rab, *Paying the Price: College Costs, Financial Aid, and the Betrayal of the American Dream* (Chicago: University of Chicago Press, 2016), 4.
12. Andrew Gold and Mary Beth Kerly, "An Entrepreneurial Approach to Entrepreneurial Education," in *Community Colleges as Incubators of Innovation. Unleashing Entrepreneurial Opportunities for Communities and Students,* ed. Rebecca A. Corbin and Ron Thomas (Sterling, VA: Stylus, 2019), 23.
13. Laura Wood, agriculture, business, and industrial division chair, North Iowa Area Community College.
14. The Century Foundation Task Force on Preventing Community Colleges from Become Separate and Unequal, *Bridging the Higher Education Divide: Strengthening Community Colleges and Restoring the American Dream* (New York: Century Foundation, 2013), 4.
15. *New Vision for Education: Fostering Social and Emotional Learning through Technology* (Geneva: World Economic Forum, 2016); Patrick Gillespie, "Intuit: Gig economy is 34% of US workforce," *CNN Business,* May 5, 2017, https://money.cnn.com/2017/05/24/news/economy/gig-economy-intuit/index.html; Amber Ravenscroft, "EdVenture and the Future of Work," (address to the National Association for Community College Entrepreneurship annual conference, Newport Beach, CA, October 14, 2019).
16. David J. Demming, *The Growing Importance of Social Skills in the Labor Market* (Cambridge, MA: Harvard University and NBER, 2015).
17. Bree Langemo, "Leading with an Entrepreneurial Mindset," in *Community Colleges as Incubators of Innovation. Unleashing Entrepreneurial Opportunities for Communities and Students,* ed. Rebecca A. Corbin and Ron Thomas (Sterling, VA: Stylus, 2019), 7.
18. Gold and Kerly, "An Entrepreneurial Approach to Entrepreneurial Education," 26.
19. Lourdes Ramboa, chair of business, entrepreneurship, and small business management, Tarrant County College, Northwest Campus.
20. John E. Roueche and Barbara R. Jones, *The Entrepreneurial Community College* (Washington, DC: American Association of Community Colleges, 2005), vii.

21. Ted Dintersmith, "Entrepreneurship," (address to the National Association for Community College Entrepreneurship annual conference, Newport Beach, CA, October 14, 2019).
22. Mars and Metcalfe, "The Entrepreneurial Domains of American Higher Education," 3.
23. Suzanne L. Flannigan, Thomas G. Greene, and Barbara R. Jones, "Setting the Stage for Action: Entrepreneurship at Work," in *The Entrepreneurial Community College,* ed. John E. Roueche and Barbara R. Jones (Washington, DC: Community College Press, 2005), 3.
24. Gregory Dees, "The Meaning of 'Social Entrepreneurship'" (working paper, Graduate School of Business, Stanford University, Palo Alto, CA, 1998).
25. George R. Boggs, foreword to Roueche and Jones, eds., *The Entrepreneurial Community College,* v.
26. Joi Ito and Jeff Howe, *Whiplash: How to Survive our Faster Future* (New York: Hachette Book Group, 2016), 116.
27. Steven R. Wallace, "A Wave of Innovation at Florida Community College," in *The Entrepreneurial Community College,* ed. John E. Roueche and Barbara R. Jones (Washington, DC: Community College Press, 2005), 13.
28. Scott D. Anthony, *The Little Black Book of Innovation: How it Works, How to Do It* (Boston: Harvard Business Review Press, 2012).
29. Anthony, *The Little Black Book of Innovation,* 17–18.
30. Kate Smith, interim president, Rio Salado College.
31. Rebecca Corbin, president and CEO, National Association for Community College Entrepreneurship.
32. Constance Carrol, "Entrepreneurship," (address to the National Association for Community College Entrepreneurship annual conference, Newport Beach, CA, October 14, 2019).
33. Ramboa.
34. Ramboa.
35. US Army General Eric Shinseki, quoted in Langemo, "Leading with an Entrepreneurial Mindset," 20.
36. Paul Axelrod, *Values in Conflict: The University, the Marketplace, and the Trials of Liberal Education* (Montreal: McGill-Queens University Press, 2002), 3.
37. Mars and Metcalfe, "The Entrepreneurial Domains of American Higher Education," 22.
38. John S. Levin, "The Business Culture of the Community College: Students as Consumers; Students as Commodities," in *Arenas of Entrepreneurship: Where Nonprofit and For-Profit Institutions Compete. New Directions for Higher Education,* no. 129, ed. Brian Pusser (San Francisco: Jossey-Bass, 2005), 12.
39. Sheila Slaughter and Larry L. Leslie, *Academic Capitalism: Politics, Policies, and the Entrepreneurial University* (Baltimore, MD: Johns Hopkins University Press, 1997).
40. Sheila Slaughter and Gary Rhoades, *Academic Capitalism and the New Economy: Markets, State, and Higher Education* (Baltimore, MD: Johns Hopkins University Press, 2004).
41. Amy S. Metcalfe, "Examining the Trilateral Networks of the Triple Helix:

Intermediating Organizations and Academy-Industry-Government Relations," *Critical Sociology* 36, no. 4 (2010): 503–19.

42. John S. Levin, *Globalizing the Community College: Strategies for Change in the Twenty-First Century* (New York: Palgrave, 2001); Levin, "The Business Culture of the Community College."
43. Giroux, "Neoliberalism, Corporate Culture, and the Promise of Higher Education."
44. Deem, "Globalisation, New Managerialism, Academic Capitalism, and Entrepreneurialism in Universities"; Stanley Aronowitz, *The Knowledge Factory: Dismantling the Corporate University and Creating True Higher Learning* (Boston: Beacon Press, 2001).
45. Levin, *Globalizing the Community College,* xviii.
46. Derek Bok, *Universities in the Marketplace: The Commercialization of Higher Education* (Princeton, NJ: Princeton University Press, 2003), viii.
47. Bok, *Universities in the Marketplace,* x.
48. Bok, *Universities in the Marketplace*; Kezar, "Obtaining Integrity? Reviewing and Examining the Charter between Higher Education and Society"; Kezar et al., *Higher Education for the Public Good*; Brian Pusser and Dudley J. Doane, "Public Purpose and Private Enterprise: The Contemporary Organization of Postsecondary Education," *Change: The Magazine of Higher Learning* 35, no. 5 (2001): 18–22.
49. Levin, "The Business Culture of the Community College"; Wesley Shumar, *College for Sale: A Critique of the Commodification of Higher Education* (Philadelphia: Routledge, 1997).
50. Clint Grant, executive dean of aviation, business, and logistics, Tarrant County College, Northwest Campus.

CHAPTER 2

1. James D. Tschechtelin, "Increased Enrollment + Student Success – Funding = ?," in *Presidents and Analysts Discuss Contemporary Challenges. New Directions for Community Colleges,* no. 156, ed. John J. Prihoda (San Francisco: Jossey-Bass, 2011), 49.
2. Arthur M. Cohen, Florence B. Brawer, and Carrie B. Kisker, *The American Community College,* 6th ed. (San Francisco: Jossey-Bass, 2014), 3.
3. Cohen, Brawer, and Kisker, *The American Community College*; Bernie Ronan and Carrie B. Kisker, eds., *Civic Learning and Democratic Engagement. New Directions for Community Colleges,* no. 173 (San Francisco: Jossey-Bass, 2016).
4. A Texas college's slogan that it would teach "anyone, anywhere, anything, at any time whenever there are enough people interested in the program to justify its offering" was lauded in Jesse P. Bogue, *The Community College* (New York: McGraw Hill, 1950).
5. Charles R. Dassance, "The Next Community College Movement?," in *Presidents and Analysts Discuss Contemporary Challenges. New Directions for Community Colleges,* no. 156, ed. John J. Prihoda (San Francisco: Jossey-Bass, 2011), 33.
6. George B. Vaughan, "The Community College Mission," *AACJC Journal,* February/March 1988, 25–27.

7. Dassance, "The Next Community College Movement?," 33.
8. Tschechtelin, "Increased Enrollment + Student Success – Funding = ?," 52.
9. Tschechtelin, "Increased Enrollment + Student Success – Funding = ?," 52.
10. Patricia J. Gumport, "The Demand-Response Scenario: Perspectives of Community College Presidents," *Annals of the American Academy of Political and Social Science* 586 (2003): 39.
11. Dassance, "The Next Community College Movement?"; Cary A. Israel, and Brenda Kihl, "Using Strategic Planning to Transform a Budgeting Process," in *Sustaining Financial Support for Community Colleges. New Directions for Community Colleges,* no. 132, ed. Stephen G. Katsinas and James C. Palmer (San Francisco: Jossey-Bass, 2005), 77–86; James C. Palmer, "Budgeting Approaches in Community Colleges," in *Budget and Finance in the American Community College. New Directions for Community Colleges,* no. 168, ed. Trudy Bers, Ronald B. Head, and James C. Palmer (San Francisco: Jossey-Bass, 2014), 29–40; David S. Murphy and Stephen G. Katsinas, "Community College Budgeting and Financing Demystified," in *Budget and Finance in the American Community College. New Directions for Community Colleges,* no. 168, ed. Bers et al., 17–27 et al.; Laura Saunders, "Linking Resource Decisions to Planning," in *Budget and Finance in the American Community College. New Directions for Community Colleges,* no. 168, ed. Bers et al., 65–75.
12. Saunders, "Linking Resource Decisions to Planning," 71.
13. Palmer, "Budgeting Approaches in Community Colleges."
14. Ellen E. Chaffee, *The Link between Planning and Budgeting,* NCHEMS monograph 1 (Boulder, CO: National Center for Higher Education Management Systems, 1981).
15. Margaret J. Barr and George S. McClellan, *Budgets and Financial Management in Higher Education* (San Francisco: Jossey-Bass, 2011). Cited in Palmer, "Budgeting Approaches in Community Colleges," 31; Israel and Kihl, "Using Strategic Planning to Transform a Budgeting Process," 82.
16. Palmer, "Budgeting Approaches in Community Colleges."
17. Saunders, "Linking Resource Decisions to Planning," 71.
18. Palmer, "Budgeting Approaches in Community Colleges," 38.
19. Murphy and Katsinas, "Community College Budgeting and Financing Demystified," 26.
20. Palmer, "Budgeting Approaches in Community Colleges," 30.
21. Murphy and Katsinas, "Community College Budgeting and Financing Demystified."
22. James C. Palmer, "Literature on Fiscal Support for Community Colleges," in *Sustaining Financial Support for Community Colleges. New Directions for Community Colleges, no. 132,* ed. Stephen G. Katsinas and James C. Palmer (San Francisco: Jossey-Bass, 2005), 99–106.
23. Stephen G. Katsinas and Janice N. Friedel, *Uncertain Recovery: Access and Funding Issues in Public Higher Education* (Tuscaloosa: University of Alabama, Education Policy Center, 2010).
24. *Competencies for Community College Leaders* (Washington, DC: American Association of Community Colleges, 2006), 82.

25. Suzanne L. Flannigan, Thomas G. Greene, and Barbara R. Jones, "Setting the Stage for Action: Entrepreneurship at Work," in *The Entrepreneurial Community College,* ed. John E. Roueche and Barbara R. Jones (Washington, DC: Community College Press, 2005), 1–2.
26. Alvin Toffler, *The Third Wave* (New York: Bantam Books, 1989).
27. Mark D. Milliron, Gerardo E. de los Santos, and Boo Browning, "Feels Like the Third Wave. The Rise of Fundraising in the Community College," in *Successful Approaches to Fundraising and Development. New Directions for Community Colleges,* no. 124, ed. Mark D. Milliron, Gerardo E. de los Santos, and Boo Browning (San Francisco: Jossey-Bass, 2003), 81–93.
28. Brent D. Cejda and Michael R. Jolley, "Entrepreneurship: The College as a Business Enterprise," in *Budget and Finance in the American Community College. New Directions for Community Colleges,* no. 168, eds. Bers, Head, and Palmer, 92.
29. Cejda and Jolley, "Entrepreneurship: The College as a Business Enterprise," 99.
30. Rebecca A. Corbin and Ron Thomas, eds., *Community Colleges as Incubators of Innovation: Unleashing Entrepreneurial Opportunities for Communities and Students* (Sterling, VA: Stylus, 2019), 1.
31. Corbin and Thomas, *Community Colleges as Incubators of Innovation,* 8.

CHAPTER 3

1. Tim Brown, *Change by Design* (New York: Harper Collins, 2009), 40.
2. Joi Ito and Jeff Howe, *Whiplash: How to Survive our Faster Future* (New York: Hachette Book Group, 2016), 25, 19.
3. Ito and Howe, *Whiplash,* 25, italics in the original.
4. Brown, *Change by Design,* 3.
5. Brown, *Change by Design,* 7.
6. Thomas Lockwood and Edgar Papke, *Innovation by Design: How any Organization can Leverage Design Thinking to Produce Change, Drive New Ideas, and Deliver Meaningful Solutions,* (Wayne, NJ: Career Press, 2018), 221.
7. Jeanne Liedtka, Randy Salzman, and Daisy Azer, *Design Thinking for the Greater Good: Innovation in the Social Sector* (New York: Columbia University Press, 2017).
8. Amy Collier, "Surprising Insights, Outliers, and Privilege in Design Thinking," *Middlebury Digital Learning Blog,* April 17, 2017, http://digitallearning.middcreate.net/reflections/surprising-insights-outliers-and-privilege-in-design-thinking/.
9. Liedtka et al., *Design Thinking for the Greater Good,* 8.
10. Liedtka et al., *Design Thinking for the Greater Good,* 248.
11. Liedtka et al., *Design Thinking for the Greater Good,* 251.
12. Lockwood and Papke, *Innovation by Design,* 113.
13. Lockwood and Papke, *Innovation by Design,* 143.
14. Lockwood and Papke, *Innovation by Design,* 126–127.
15. Brown, *Change by Design.*
16. Michael Lewrick, Patrick Link, and Larry Leifer, *The Design Thinking Playbook: Mindful Digital Transformation of Teams, Products, Services, Businesses and*

Ecosystems, (Hoboken, NJ: Wiley, 2018); *Design for Delight: Student Playbook. A Guide to Everyday Innovation,* (Mountain View, CA: Intuit Education, 2019).

17. Jennifer Hawkins, director of corporate solutions and economic development, Tarrant County College Opportunity Center
18. Liedtka et al., *Design Thinking for the Greater Good,* 262–263.
19. Liedtka et al., *Design Thinking for the Greater Good,* 262.
20. Lewrick et al., *The Design Thinking Playbook,* 53.
21. Brown, *Change by Design,* 217-218.
22. Liedtka et al., *Design Thinking for the Greater Good,* 273.
23. *Design for Delight,* 9.
24. Brown, *Change by Design,* 68.
25. Brown, *Change by Design,* 78.
26. This is a fictional account of a real situation at NIACC. In response to the nursing shortage in northern Iowa, NIACC entered into a partnership with Mercy Medical Center to build new simulation nursing bays on campus–modeled after those at Mercy–and jointly employ instructors and staff to supervise clinical work. Roughly 90 percent of all nurses trained at NIACC go on to work at Mercy Medical Center after graduating.
27. Liedtka et al., *Design Thinking for the Greater Good,* 276.
28. Liedtka et al., *Design Thinking for the Greater Good,* 275.
29. Brown, *Change by Design.*
30. Liedtka et al., *Design Thinking for the Greater Good,* 277.
31. Lockwood and Papke, *Innovation by Design,* 23.
32. Brown, *Change by Design,* 27; Lewrick et al., *The Design Thinking Playbook.*
33. Brown, *Change by Design,* 29.
34. Lewrick et al., *The Design Thinking Playbook.*
35. Lockwood and Papke, *Innovation by Design,* 164.
36. Brown, *Change by Design,* 32.
37. Brown, *Change by Design,* 105.
38. Brown, *Change by Design,* 231.
39. Liedtka et al., *Design Thinking for the Greater Good,* 283.
40. Brown, *Change by Design,* 16–17.
41. Brown, *Change by Design,* 105.
42. Liedtka et al., *Design Thinking for the Greater Good,* 280.
43. Lewrick et al., *The Design Thinking Playbook,* 108.
44. Liedtka et al., *Design Thinking for the Greater Good,* 285–286.
45. Liedtka et al., *Design Thinking for the Greater Good,* 295.
46. Kevin Lee, quoted in Lockwood and Papke, *Innovation by Design,* 102.
47. Liedtka et al., *Design Thinking for the Greater Good,* 281.
48. Liedtka et al., *Design Thinking for the Greater Good,* 286.
49. Liedtka et al., *Design Thinking for the Greater Good,* 287.
50. Brown, *Change by Design,* 75.
51. Lockwood and Papke, *Innovation by Design,* 186, italics in the original.
52. Brown, *Change by Design,* 175.
53. Lockwood and Papke, *Innovation by Design,* 29.
54. Eli MacLaren, quoted in Liedtka et al., *Design Thinking for the Greater Good,* 301.

55. Liedtka et al., *Design Thinking for the Greater Good*, 298.
56. Lockwood and Papke, *Innovation by Design*, 141–143.
57. Lockwood and Papke, *Innovation by Design*, 209.

CHAPTER 4

1. Tom Schumann, executive director, Center for Entrepreneurial Innovation, Maricopa Community Colleges.
2. Jeanne Liedtka, Randy Salzman, and Daisy Azer, *Design Thinking for the Greater Good: Innovation in the Social Sector* (New York: Columbia University Press, 2017).
3. Sanford (Sandy) Shugart, president, Valencia College.
4. Shugart.
5. *BLS Reports: A Profile of the Working Poor, 2016* (Washington, DC: US Department of Labor, Bureau of Labor Statistics, 2018).
6. *Centers for Accelerated Training* (Orlando, FL: Valencia College, 2019), 1.
7. *Centers for Accelerated Training*, 1.
8. Carolyn McMorran, assistant vice president for professional and continuing education, Valencia College.
9. Kathleen Plinske, executive vice president and provost, Valencia College.
10. *Centers for Accelerated Training*, 2.
11. Kate Smith, interim president, Rio Salado College.
12. Allison Bailey et al., *Making Digital Learning Work: Success Strategies from Six Leading Universities and Community Colleges* (Boston: The Boston Consulting Group and Arizona State University, 2018), 47.
13. "Arizona SARA," last modified March 12, 2020, https://azsara.arizona.edu/.
14. Smith.
15. Jennifer Hawkins, director of corporate solutions and economic development, TCC Opportunity Center.
16. Hawkins.
17. Hawkins.
18. Hawkins.
19. Schumann.
20. Eugene Giovannini, "Building an Entrepreneurial Ecosystem: Innovate and Flourish," in *Community Colleges as Incubators of Innovation: Unleashing Entrepreneurial Opportunities for Communities and Students*, ed. Rebecca A. Corbin and Ron Thomas (Sterling, VA: Stylus, 2019), 39.
21. *About CEI* (Phoenix, AZ: Center for Entrepreneurial Innovation, 2020), https://www.ceigateway.com/about.
22. Schumann.
23. Schumann.
24. Nick Esquer, "CEI LabForce Sets Foundation for New Workforce Development Center," *Chamber Business News*, August 23, 2019, https://chamberbusinessnews.com/2019/08/23/cei-labforce-sets-foundation-for-new-workforce-development-center/.
25. Maria Harper-Marinick, former chancellor, Maricopa Community Colleges.
26. Steven Schulz, president, North Iowa Area Community College.

27. Shugart.
28. Schulz.
29. Steven Gonzales, former president, GateWay College and interim chancellor, Maricopa Community Colleges.
30. Edmund J. Gleazer Jr., *The Community College: Values, Vision, and Vitality* (Washington, DC: American Association of Community and Junior Colleges, 1980), 10.
31. American Association for Community and Junior Colleges (AACJC). *Building Communities: A Vision for a New Century. A Report of the Commission on the Future of Community Colleges* (Washington, DC: AACJC, 1988), 3; AACJC, 35.
32. Arthur M. Cohen, Florence B. Brawer, and Carrie B. Kisker, *The American Community College,* 6th ed. (San Francisco: Jossey-Bass, 2014).
33. *The Power to Serve: Valencia's Five-Year Impact Plan Study. Building Community by Serving Community, 2016–2021* (Orlando, FL: Valencia College, 2017), 1.
34. Shugart.

CHAPTER 5

1. Terry Allcorn, dean of business and hospitality, Valencia College
2. Heather Rissler, biology instructor, North Iowa Area Community College.
3. Clifton Taulbert and Gary Schoeniger, *Who Owns the Ice House? Eight Life Lessons from an Unlikely Entrepreneur* (Cleveland: ELI Press, 2010), xvii.
4. Lindsey Dalrymple, auditorium leadership series director, North Iowa Area Community College.
5. Trevor Noah, *Born a Crime: Stories from a South African Childhood* (New York: Random House, 2019), 182.
6. Allcorn.
7. Allcorn.
8. As recounted by Allcorn.
9. Allcorn.
10. William Coppola, president, Tarrant County College, Southeast Campus.
11. "College Goals and Principles," last modified March 5, 2020, https://www.tccd.edu/about/mission-and-vision/college-goals-and-principles/.
12. Jeff Filko, director of auxiliary services, Valencia College.
13. National Center for Education Statistics, *Digest of Education Statistics, 2018* (Washington, DC: US Department of Education, 2019).
14. Jeffrey W. Goltz, "The School of Public Safety at Valencia College: Visioning and Implementation of a College-Wide Distributive and Collaborative Program Model for the Central Florida Community," *Community College Journal of Research and Practice* 40, no. 5 (2015): 422.
15. Goltz, "The School of Public Safety," 420.
16. Jeffrey Goltz, director, Valencia College School of Public Safety.
17. Goltz, "The School of Public Safety," 420.
18. *School of Public Safety: A "School of Excellence"* (Orlando, FL: Valencia College, 2014), 8.
19. Joe Battista, executive vice president, global, professional, and continuing education, Valencia College.
20. Goltz, "The School of Public Safety," 421.

21. *Public Safety Leadership Development Certification Program,* (Orlando, FL: Valencia College, 2018), 1.
22. Kathleen Plinske, executive vice president and provost, Valencia College.
23. As recalled by Rufus Glasper, former chancellor, Maricopa County Community College District.
24. Shari Olson, president, South Mountain Community College.
25. Katie Tagye, director, Collaborative Design Center, Valencia College.

CHAPTER 6

1. Lisa Eli, assistant vice president for global and continuing education, Valencia College.
2. Jeanne Liedtka, Randy Salzman, and Daisy Azer, *Design Thinking for the Greater Good: Innovation in the Social Sector* (New York: Columbia University Press, 2017), 37.
3. Patti O'Brien, director, Maricopa Corporate College.
4. Eugene Giovannini, "Building an Entrepreneurial Ecosystem: Innovate and Flourish," in *Community Colleges as Incubators of Innovation*, ed. Rebecca A. Corbin and Ron Thomas (Sterling, VA: Stylus, 2019), 45.
5. Rufus Glasper, former chancellor, Maricopa Community Colleges.
6. O'Brien.
7. Eli.
8. Steven Schulz, president, North Iowa Area Community College.
9. Sasan Poureetezadi, former chief strategy officer, Maricopa Community Colleges.
10. Poureetezadi.
11. Darcy Renfro, chief of staff, Maricopa Community Colleges.
12. Poureetezadi.
13. Eugene (Gene) Giovannini, chancellor, Tarrant County College.
14. Sanford (Sandy) Shugart, president, Valencia College.
15. Brent D. Cejda and Michael R. Jolley, "Entrepreneurship: The College as a Business Enterprise," in *Budget and Finance in the American Community College. New Directions for Community Colleges*, no. 168, ed. Trudy H. Bers, Ronald B. Head, and James C. Palmer (San Francisco: Jossey-Bass, 2014), 98.
16. Kathleen Plinske, executive vice president and provost, Valencia College.
17. Plinske.
18. Michael Lewrick, Patrick Link, and Larry Leifer, *The Design Thinking Playbook: Modern Digital Transformation of Teams, Products, Services, Businesses and Ecosystems* (Hoboken, NJ: John Wiley & Sons, 2018).
19. Maria Harper-Marinick, former chancellor, Maricopa Community Colleges.
20. Giovannini; Harper-Marinick.
21. Matthew Reed, *Confessions of a Community College Administrator* (San Francisco: Jossey-Bass, 2013), 25.
22. Carrie B. Kisker and Susan T. Kater, "Deconstructing Governance and Expectations for the Community College, in *Understanding Community Colleges,* ed. John S. Levin and Susan T. Kater (New York: Routledge, 2013), 161.
23. Faculty fear shared by Lourdes Ramboa, chair of business, entrepreneurship, and small business management, Tarrant County College, Northwest Campus.

24. Schulz.

CHAPTER 7

1. Thomas Lockwood and Edgar Papke, *Innovation by Design: How Any Organization Can Leverage Design Thinking to Produce Change, Drive New Ideas, and Deliver Meaningful Solutions* (Wayne, NJ: Career Press, 2018), 192.
2. Carlos Morales, president, Tarrant County College, Connect Campus.
3. Jeanne Liedtka, Randy Salzman, and Daisy Azer, *Design Thinking for the Greater Good: Innovation in the Social Sector* (New York: Columbia University Press, 2017).
4. Lockwood and Papke, *Innovation by Design*, 14.
5. Andrew Gold and Mary Beth Kerly, "An Entrepreneurial Approach to Entrepreneurial Education," in *Community Colleges as Incubators of Innovation: Unleashing Entrepreneurial Opportunities for Communities and Students* ed. Rebecca A. Corbin and Ron Thomas (Sterling, VA: Stylus, 2019), 27.
6. Mark D. Milliron, Gerardo E. de los Santos, and Boo Browning, "Feels Like the Third Wave. The Rise of Fundraising in the Community College," in *Successful Approaches to Fundraising and Development: New Directions for Community Colleges,* no. 124, ed. Mark D. Milliron, Gerardo E. de los Santos, and Boo Browning (San Francisco: Jossey-Bass, 2003), 81–93; Brent D. Cejda and Michael R. Jolley, "Entrepreneurship: The College as a Business Enterprise," in *Budget and Finance in the American Community College. New Directions for Community Colleges,* no. 168, ed. Trudy Bers, Ronald B. Head, and James C. Palmer (San Francisco: Jossey-Bass, 2014), 91–101.
7. Eugene Giovannni, "Building an Entrepreneurial Ecosystem: Innovate and Flourish," in *Community Colleges as Incubators of Innovation: Unleashing Entrepreneurial Opportunities for Communities and Students*, eds. Corbin and Thomas, 38.
8. Giovannini, "Building an Entrepreneurial Ecosystem," 38.
9. Lockwood and Papke, *Innovation by Design*, 47.
10. Maria Harper-Marinick, former chancellor, Maricopa Community Colleges.
11. Edgar Papke, "Designing Culture," *Edgar Papke Blog*, August 9, 2018, http://edgarpapke.com/2018/08/09/designing-culture/.
12. Lockwood and Papke, *Innovation by Design,* 118.
13. Lockwood and Papke, *Innovation by Design,* 84.
14. Lockwood and Papke, *Innovation by Design,* 186.
15. Shari Olson, president, South Mountain Community College.
16. Rufus Glasper, "Conclusion: Entrepreneurial Community Colleges–Sustainability and Lessons from the League," in *Community Colleges as Incubators of Innovation: Unleashing Entrepreneurial Opportunities for Communities and Students,* ed. Corbin and Thomas, 155.
17. Terry Allcorn, dean of business and hospitality, Valencia College.
18. Michael D. Summers and David H. McGilvray, "Entrepreneurial Leaders," in *The Entrepreneurial Community College,* ed. John E. Roueche and Barbara R. Jones (Washington, DC: Community College Press, 2005), 120.
19. Roger Fisher and William L. Ury, *Getting to Yes: Negotiating Agreement without*

Giving In (New York: Random House, 1981).
20. Lockwood and Papke, *Innovation by Design,* 52.
21. Steven Gonzales, former president, GateWay College, and interim chancellor, Maricopa Community Colleges.
22. Papke, "Designing Culture."
23. Eugene (Gene) Giovannini, chancellor, Tarrant County College
24. George R. Boggs and Christine J. McPhail, *Practical Leadership in Community Colleges: Navigating Today's Top Challenges* (San Francisco: Jossey-Bass, 2016), 111.
25. For example, Boggs and McPhail, *Practical Leadership in Community Colleges*; George E. Potter and Daniel J. Phelan, "Governance Over the Years, A Trustee's Perspective," in *Governance in the Community College. New Directions for Community Colleges,* no. 141, eds. Robert C. Cloud and Susan T. Kater (San Francisco: Jossey-Bass, 2008), 15-24; George R. Boggs, *Handbook on CEO-Board Relations and Responsibilities* (Lanham, MD: Rowman and Littlefield, 2006); John S. Levin, "The Importance of the Board-President Relationship in Three Community Colleges," *The Canadian Journal of Higher Education* XXI, no. 1 (1991); Terry O'Banion, *The Rogue Trustee: The Elephant in the Room* (Phoenix, AZ: League for Innovation in the Community College, 2009); William E. Piland, "The Governing Board," in *Managing Community Colleges: A Handbook for Effective Practice,* ed. Arthur M. Cohen and Florence B. Brawer (San Francisco: Jossey-Bass, 1994), 79–100.
26. David Moltz, "Who are Community College Trustees?," *Inside Higher Ed,* April 6, 2009.
27. Harper-Marinick.
28. Gonzales.
29. Carrie B. Kisker, *Enabling Faculty-Led Student Success Efforts at Community Colleges*, Key Topics for Community College Leaders Series (Washington, DC: American Council on Education, 2019), https://www.acenet.edu/Documents/Enabling-Faculty-Led-Student-Success-Efforts.pdf.
30. Sasan Poureetezadi, former chief strategy officer, Maricopa Community Colleges.
31. Olson.
32. Boggs and McPhail, *Practical Leadership in Community Colleges*, xix.

CHAPTER 8

1. Lao Tzu, Chinese philosopher.
2. Henry M. Levin, "Why is This so Difficult?" in *Educational Entrepreneurship: Realities, Challenges, Possibilities*, ed. Frederick M. Hess (Cambridge, MA: Harvard Education Press, 2006), 182.
3. Clark G. Gilbert, Michael M. Crow, and Derrick Anderson, "Design Thinking for Higher Education," *Stanford Social Innovation Review*, Winter 2018, 2.
4. Burton R. Clark, *Creating Entrepreneurial Universities: Organizational Pathways of Transformation* (Guilford, Surrey, UK: Biddles, 1998). Cited in Brent D. Cejda and Michael R. Jolley, "Entrepreneurship: The College as a Business Enterprise," in *Budget and Finance in the American Community College. New*

Directions for Community Colleges, no. 168, ed. Trudy Bers, Ronald B. Head, and James C. Palmer (San Francisco: Jossey, Bass, 2014), 96.

5. A Texas college's slogan that it would teach "anyone, anywhere, anything, at any time whenever there are enough people interested in the program to justify its offering" was lauded in Jesse P. Bogue, *The Community College* (New York: McGraw Hill, 1950).
6. Loren Bender, vice president of business operations and finance, Valencia College.
7. Richard M. Romano and James C. Palmer, *Financing Community Colleges. Where We Are, Where We're Going* (Lanham, MD: Rowman & Littlefield, 2016), 148.
8. Eli Mercer, dean of technology, health, and business, Tarrant County College, Southeast Campus.
9. John E. Roueche and Barbara R. Jones, *The Entrepreneurial Community College* (Washington, DC: Community College Press, 2005).
10. Rebecca A. Corbin and Ron Thomas, *Community Colleges as Incubators of Innovation: Unleashing Entrepreneurial Opportunities for Communities and Students* (Sterling, VA: Stylus, 2019).
11. As recalled by Rufus Glasper, former chancellor, Maricopa Community Colleges.
12. Clark, cited in Cejda and Jolley, "Entrepreneurship," 96.
13. Thomas L. Friedman, *The World Is Flat. A Brief History of the Twenty-First Century* (New York: Farrar, Straus, and Giroux, 2005).
14. Richard Florida, "The World Is Spiky," *Atlantic Monthly,* October 2005, 48.
15. Joe Battista, executive vice president for global, professional, and continuing education, Valencia College
16. Romano and Palmer, *Financing Community Colleges*, 19.
17. Lourdes Ramboa, chair, business, entrepreneurship, and small business management, Tarrant County College, Northwest Campus.
18. Eugene Giovannini, "Building an Entrepreneurial Ecosystem," in *Community Colleges as Incubators of Innovation: Unleashing Entrepreneurial Opportunities for Communities and Students,* ed. Rebecca A. Corbin and Ron Thomas (Sterling, VA: Stylus, 2019), 50.
19. Mercer.
20. Rebecca Corbin, president and CEO, National Association for Community College Entrepreneurship.
21. Thomas Lockwood and Edgar Papke, *Innovation by Design: How Any Organization Can Leverage Design Thinking to Produce Change, Drive New Ideas, and Delivery Meaningful Solutions* (Wayne, NJ: Career Press, 2018).

ACKNOWLEDGMENTS

When Jayne Fargnoli first contacted me in January 2018 about the possibility of writing a book about community colleges for Harvard Education Press, I nearly laughed out loud. It was a mere four years after Art Cohen, Florence Brawer, and I had published the sixth edition of *The American Community College*, and like many writers coming off texts of that size, I had sworn off any more books: they take too much time, pay next to nothing, and force one to live for years with a deeply unsettling sense of insecurity, wondering if you are doing your topic justice, if your ideas have any merit, if anyone will ever read—let alone benefit from—this *thing* that consumes your waking hours and detracts from other personal and professional priorities. Nonetheless, Jayne performed a spectacularly impressive Jedi mind trick in our early conversations, getting me to think deeply about the pressing issues community colleges face, the steps that will need to be taken to ensure their viability in the next decades, and somehow leading me to believe that I was the best person to tackle a book about creating entrepreneurial community colleges. Two and a half years later, with a finished manuscript sitting in front of me, I can only thank Jayne for her prescience, her insights in helping me develop and present my argument, and her unwavering support for this project. You are truly an editor extraordinaire, Jayne, and I thank you from the bottom of my heart.

I would like to think that all of the ideas presented in this book are mine and mine alone, but in truth I merely gathered a handful of different puzzles, learned as much as I could from them, and put all the pieces together in a way that made sense to me and (I hope) will be useful to others who are concerned with how community colleges must evolve in order to continue educating and training our most marginalized and vulnerable populations and contributing to the economic vitality of communities across our nation. In particular, I drew heavily from design thinkers and writers Tim Brown, Thomas Lockwood, Edgar Papke, Joi Ito, Jeff Howe, Michael Lewrick, Patrick Link, Larry Leifer, and especially Jeanne Liedtka, Randy Salzman, and Daisy Azer, whose *Design Thinking for the Greater Good* provided a conceptual and structural frame for my thinking and writing. Special thanks also to educator Peter Boylan, whose enthusiasm for the advantages of utilizing design thinking to improve K–12 education inspired much of my own.

From my own field, I thank the numerous community college leaders and scholars who have strengthened my understanding of institutional budgeting, finance, and entrepreneurship, especially colleagues Jim Palmer, Steven Katsinas, Dick Romano, Brent Cejda, and Michael Jolley. John Roueche and Barbara Jones's 2005 book *The Entrepreneurial Community College* and Rebecca Corbin and Ron Thomas's 2019 *Community Colleges as Incubators of Innovation* provided much useful information about entrepreneurial practices at colleges other than those I visited. An additional thank-you to Rebecca Corbin, who not only spent time on the phone but also invited me to attend the National Association for Community College Entrepreneurship's fall 2019 conference. John Levin, one of the two community college scholars and mentors to whom I owe my professional career, sat like an angel of academic judiciousness on my shoulder throughout the writing of this book, metaphorically reminding me to check and recheck my assumptions as well as the theoretical bases for my arguments and counterarguments.

These scholars and writers helped me formulate the central premise of this book—that community colleges can pursue entrepreneurial opportunities in ways that amplify rather than sacrifice their mission and the needs of their stakeholders, and that design thinking can assist college leaders in accomplishing this objective—but the literature alone could never have provided the education I received from the luminaries highlighted in this book. To Sandy Shugart, Gene Giovannini, Steven Schulz, Maria Harper-Marinick, Rufus Glasper, Steven Gonzales, and all of the other presidents, administrators, faculty, and staff who generously lent their time and expertise to teach me about entrepreneurship on your campuses: you have my deepest gratitude. I hope I have done your stories and your actions justice and that they inspire the readers of this book as much as they inspired me. Any errors in describing your programs, practices, or ideas are my own. My heartfelt appreciation also goes to Barbara Halstead at Valencia, Wendy Hammond at TCC, Jennifer Demoney at Maricopa, and Mary Spitz at NIACC for arranging my visits, scheduling interviews, and hosting me on their campuses. Faculty and administrators typically get all the credit in books and articles about community colleges, but we all know who really keeps the machine running.

I owe a profound thanks to my friend and colleague Sue Kater, who read every word of this book prior to publication and whose experience as both a community college educator and scholar put her in the unenviable position of being peppered with texts and emails from me, asking her to read or reread certain sections to make sure I got everything right. Thank you, Sue, for your wisdom and reassurance throughout the last months of writing! Of course my deepest respect, admiration, and everlasting gratitude goes to my colleague, mentor, and dear friend Art Cohen, in whose office I first understood the importance of community colleges to a democratic society, and under whose guidance, encouragement, and love I became the scholar and writer that I am today. Thank you for providing unflinching feedback on this and every other project, and for over fifteen years of partnership and friendship. I am fortunate beyond words to have you in my life.

This book—and indeed my entire career as an independent researcher and consultant—would not be possible without the support of my husband, Sean, who daily inspires me to be a kinder, more thoughtful human being. Thank you for being my partner and best friend for nearly half of our lives, for giving me our two incredible children, and for always making me laugh. Your one fault, of course, is not truly appreciating the cleverness of my puns, but luckily my father, Rick, and a long line of Bourdons are more than adequate in this regard, having also taught me to see the beauty in a well-constructed sentence. To Lucie (whose love and support I can only hope to emulate with my own children), Rick, Sean, Meredith, Grayson, Hansell, Leland, Allen, Megan, and Mac: thank you for loving me, for sharing your lives with me, and for allowing me to plan every family vacation. And finally to my LA clan—Jackie, Clint, Alex, and Juliet, of course, but also Eri, Auggie, Dusty, Marie, Brian, Love, Laura, Arik, Ari, Dolly, and Esmie—I am exceedingly grateful for your friendship and lucky as hell to share this journey with you.

ABOUT THE AUTHOR

DR. CARRIE B. KISKER is an education research and policy specialist with Kisker Education Consulting in Los Angeles and a director of the Center for the Study of Community Colleges. Drawing from her own and others' research, she regularly consults with college leaders on issues related to entrepreneurship and innovation, program and policy development, strategic planning and accountability, civic learning and democratic engagement. Kisker holds a BA in psychology and education from Dartmouth College and an MA and PhD in higher education from the University of California, Los Angeles. She cowrote *The American Community College* (Jossey-Bass, 2014) with Arthur M. Cohen and Florence B. Brawer and *The Shaping of American Higher Education: Emergence and Growth of the Contemporary System* (Jossey-Bass, 2010) with Arthur M. Cohen.

INDEX